THE TOMB OF CHRIST

MARTIN BIDDLE

SUTTON PUBLISHING

First published in 1999 by
Sutton Publishing Limited · Phoenix Mill
Thrupp · Stroud · Gloucestershire · GL5 2BU

Paperback edition first published in 2000

British Library Cataloguing in Publication Data
A catalogue record for this book is available from the British Library.

ISBN 0 7509 2525 6

Front endpaper: The Tomb Chamber with the normal arrangement of candlesticks, vases, and pictures on the red marble shelf above the burial slab. For further details, see the caption to Fig. 101 (Photograph John Crook)

Back endpaper: Robert Willis's plan of the Church of the Holy Sepulchre published in 1849, based on a survey by J.J. Scoles in 1825. For further details, see the caption to Fig. 14.

Typeset in 10/14pt Sabon.
Typesetting and origination by
Sutton Publishing Limited.
Printed in Hong Kong by
Midas Printing Limited.

CONTENTS

Birthe
optimae conjugi
adjutrici carissimae

LIST OF
ILLUSTRATIONS

Front end-paper
  The Tomb Chamber with the normal arrangement of decorations and
  pictures

Fig. 1   The Tomb Chamber, looking down onto the burial slab, with the
  decorations and pictures removed

Fig. 2   The walled city of Jerusalem from the air, looking north-east

Fig. 3   The Church of the Holy Sepulchre from the air, looking north

Fig. 4   The Church of the Holy Sepulchre from the air, looking south-west

Fig. 5   The parvis of the Church of the Holy Sepulchre

Fig. 6   The south side of the Edicule seen through the columns of the
  Rotunda of the Anastasis

Fig. 7   The east face of the Edicule

Fig. 8   The north side of the Edicule, looking down south-west from the
  gallery of the Rotunda

Fig. 9   Plans of the Edicule, as reconstructed in 1809–10 and in 1555

Fig. 10   The restored dome of the Rotunda of the Anastasis, inaugurated on
  2 January 1997

Fig. 11   The south side of the Edicule, looking down north-west from the
  gallery of the Rotunda: photogrammetric pair

Fig. 12   The floor of the Rotunda of the Anastasis, 1990–2

Fig. 13   Stone record 'card' derived from the computerised relational database
  of the photogrammetric survey

Fig. 14   Willis's engraved plan of the Holy Sepulchre with plans of the Edicule,
  1849

Fig. 15   Russian engraving of the plan of the Edicule as rebuilt in 1809–10

Fig. 16   The Narbonne marble model, showing the curved niche and shell
  hood at the back of the portico, ?5th century

Fig. 17   Painted wooden lid, detail showing the Edicule below the Rotunda,
  late 6th to early 7th century

Fig. 18   Ampulla showing the Edicule below the Rotunda, c. 600

Fig. 19   Medallion showing the Edicule, late 6th to early 7th century

Fig. 20   Ampulla showing the Cross on the Rock of Golgotha and the Edicule,
  6th century

Fig. 21   Gold finger-ring with a structure representing the Edicule or the
  Rotunda, ?6th century

PREFACE

What can we really know of the Tomb of Christ? This book tries to answer that question, using written documents, the visual materials available in an extraordinary range of media, and the evidence of the present structure of 1809–10 and what it can tell us about its predecessors.

One of the difficulties has been the need to cut away at the thickets of confusion which have grown up over the centuries in the study of the tomb and Edicule, the little house that has covered the tomb since the early fourth century. If the first principle of the work has been the critical evaluation of as wide as possible a range of the relevant materials, the second has been to simplify rather than complicate the sequence: *Ediculae non sunt multiplicandae praeter necessitatem*, 'no more Edicules than necessary', to paraphrase William of Occam. Thus the idea that the ivory carvings suggest that the Edicule was several times rebuilt in the fourth century (p. 21), that Willibald's description as reported by Hugeburc requires a rebuilding after the Persian sack of 614 (p. 71), and that the Crusaders rebuilt the Edicule in 1119 (p. 89) have all been rejected.

In the course of doing this it became clear that the conventional dating of the reconstruction of the Church of the Holy Sepulchre by the Byzantines needed to be revised: it was not the Emperor Constantine IX Monomachos (1042–55) who carried out the work, as has been believed in the West since William of Tyre wrote his *Chronicon* in the late twelfth century, but Constantine's predecessor, Michael IV Paphlagon (1034–41)(pp. 77–81). The date of the Crusaders' rebuilding required a comparable revision. The Crusader church was not consecrated on 15 July 1149, the fiftieth anniversary of their taking of Jerusalem, but fifteen or so years later between the accession of Amalric in 1163 and the years 1167/9 (pp. 92–8).

The materials are so rich, and exist in so many languages, and as representations in so many countries and museums, that no one can hope for completeness. Indeed this study does not aim at it, and in dealing with the visual evidence deliberately sets out to define the *types* of evidence available rather than to provide a critical list of every representation in each medium, a task that would in any case be virtually impossible. What is more, new discoveries are being made all the time – mosaics in the churches of Jordan, texts and drawings in libraries, objects from excavations or in museums or on the market, early photographs, records in state archives – which add to our understanding of the Edicule and its setting at each of its successive stages.

A word may be said about the title, *The Tomb of Christ*. As explained below, it is not known why the rock-cut tomb now covered by the Edicule was

(Opposite)
Fig. 1. The Tomb Chamber, looking down northwards on to the marble slab covering the burial couch, with the lesser pictures and other decorations removed. The ikon of the Resurrection and the surrounding decorations are work of 1809–10; the marble slab with the false crack cut across it was there by 1345; the red marble shelf, and the wall panels may be work of 1555, except for the right-hand arm of the shelf which is a recent replacement. (Photograph Palphot Ltd, Jerusalem)

identified in 325/6 as the tomb in which the body of Jesus was laid in the early evening of the day of crucifixion (pp. 19, 66). To have called the book *The Tomb of Jesus* would have prejudged this issue, and would have qualified my intention to write a rigorously detached and independent account based strictly on verifiable evidence.

The origin of the present study is described elsewhere. Its fundamental premise is that there is much to be discovered when the now urgent restoration of the Edicule takes place and during the relaying of the floor of the Rotunda. Without the good will, trust and kindly interest of the Religious Communities in the Church of the Holy Sepulchre – Greek Orthodox, Latin, Armenian and Coptic – this study could not have been undertaken. It is very much to be hoped that they will extend their support to permitting investigations and records to be made to the standards of modern archaeological and structural scholarship when the floor is eventually relaid and the Edicule restored.

One sometimes reads in the press about the problems which divide the religious communities in the Church of the Holy Sepulchre. What has happened to the actual building in recent years shows that the reality is somewhat different. In the 1960s and 1970s, the church was brilliantly restored by a Common Technical Bureau working for the three Great Communities. The columns, walls, and dome of the Rotunda surrounding the Edicule were all restored as a part of this programme. In 1996 the decoration of the dome was completed, the scaffold removed, and on 2 January 1997 the works dedicated in a ceremony intended to mark the beginning of a Triennium of Preparation for the Great Jubilee of AD 2000 (Fig. 10). Plans are now being made to restore the floor of the Rotunda, hopefully before the Millennium. In due course the decisions will be taken which will lead to the restoration of the Edicule. This extensive and successful programme, now well on its way to completion, is not a catalogue of dissent and delay but a record of agreement and achievement.

Martin Biddle
Hertford College, Oxford
25.v.1998

PILGRIMS, THE CITY AND THE TOMB

Jesus was executed outside Jerusalem in 30 or perhaps 33. Ten years later the places of his crucifixion and burial were incorporated within the walls by the expansion of the city. Decades later these places were buried beneath immense dumps of rubble brought in by the Romans to level the area. Even so, Golgotha, the place of crucifixion, was still pointed out inside the city three centuries later. It served as a landmark for excavations which discovered several rock-cut tombs under the rubble. For reasons never stated, one of these tombs was immediately hailed as the Tomb of Christ. The emperor Constantine ordered that Golgotha and the tomb should be preserved and embellished, and that a great church should be erected beside them. This basilica, known as the Martyrion, 'The Testimony' or 'The Witness', was dedicated on 17 September 335 inside the walls of the Roman veteran colony of Aelia Capitolina, soon again to be known by the ancient name of Jerusalem.

For the last seventeen centuries this great complex of buildings, now called the Church of the Holy Sepulchre (or to use its Greek name, the Church of the Anastasis, the Resurrection), has stood within the walls of Jerusalem. Added to after Constantine, often damaged, once virtually demolished, but always restored, the church and the holy places within it, Golgotha and above all the tomb, have been throughout these centuries the goal of countless thousands of pilgrims from all over the world. Then, as now, these pilgrims did not find a hill outside a city wall and a tomb in a garden nearby. They found instead a walled city and hidden in the heart of the city, reached by narrow and crowded streets, a vast church which came into view only at the last moment, at the last turn in the street.

These pilgrims journeyed to Jerusalem because it contained so many places associated with the life and last days of Jesus, but above all because it contained the Tomb of Christ, the place of his resurrection, the place of their salvation, the Saving, the Life-Giving Tomb. Their first view of Jerusalem, after a long and perilous journey, was a moment of high emotion. Whether coming from the south along the road from Egypt through Bethlehem, or from the north from Acre or from Jaffa through Ramla, pilgrims would fall to their knees and weep,

Fig. 2. The walled city of
Jerusalem from the air,
looking north-east.
(Photograph Gideon Avni,
Israel Antiquities Authority)

as many recorded in accounts of their pilgrimage. For many, Jerusalem came first
into sight from the distant hill which is the traditional site of the tomb of the
Prophet Samuel, Nabi Samwil today. It was from this hill that the Crusaders first
saw Jerusalem on the morning of 7 June 1099, and here that they later built the
Church of *Mons Gaudii*, Montjoie. From here in 1192 Richard the Lionheart
looked down on the city he had come to liberate but was never to enter. Seven
centuries later a British post on this hill, controlling the road from Jaffa, played a
key role in Allenby's capture of Jerusalem on 9 December 1917.

When the pilgrims went home, they took with them remembrances of the
Tomb of Christ: oil from the lamps burning above it, strips of cloth or paper
showing its exact length, scraps of the rock, if they could get some. Others made
notes, took careful measurements, made drawings, even bringing artists with
them to do so. They purchased models of stone or wood. And after their return
some wrote accounts of what they had seen and some built replicas of the
interior of the tomb, as in the Jeruzalemkerk in Bruges or in the crypt of the
chapel of La Hougue Bie on Jersey. Others erected full-scale copies of the whole
tomb, complete with the Edicule, the little house that enclosed it, as at Eichstätt
in Bavaria or in the Tuscan hills at San Vivaldo in Valdesa. And in eastern lands a
few even constructed replicas of the whole Church of the Holy Sepulchre, most
remarkably at the Novoierusalimsky Monastyr, near Istra, east of Moscow. They

did these things for remembrance and to provide a setting in which the events of Christ's death and resurrection could be celebrated each year in the Easter liturgy.

Pilgrims did not show much interest in the original rock-cut tomb. Some, like Felix Faber in 1483, searched hard for traces of the rock itself, but on the whole they were content with the Edicule that covered whatever remained of the rock and with a sight of the marble slab which concealed the burial couch where Christ, they believed, had lain. Artists, by contrast, few of whom ever went to Jerusalem, when faced with the task of painting the Deposition or the Resurrection, did not hesitate to draw a rock-cut tomb as the gospels described it. And for the burial place itself, a Piero della Francesca or a Mantegna might provide a magnificent classical sarcophagus out of which the Risen Christ strode triumphant over death.

For pilgrims who had undertaken the harsh journey precisely to see the place, it was what they saw when they arrived that mattered. It was there they had remembered the death and resurrection of Christ, and had celebrated or partaken in the mass. Thus, it was of *their* Edicule, as they saw it in their time, that they wrote descriptions, took measurements, made sketches and purchased models to take back home, and of which some built replicas small or grand.

Fig. 3. The Church of the Holy Sepulchre from the air, looking north. (Photograph Gideon Avni, Israel Antiquities Authority)

Thus each in their generation recorded or copied the Edicule in the form they saw it. In the fifth or sixth century a pilgrim from Narbonne made drawings or purchased a model of the Edicule as erected by Constantine in the fourth century, from which a mason back home cut the great replica in Pyrenean marble which still survives. In the twelfth century another pilgrim recorded the Edicule as rebuilt by the Byzantines in the eleventh century and modified by the Crusaders in the twelfth, and from his records masons at Eichstätt in Bavaria about 1160 built the large-scale copy which stands today, albeit rebuilt in a new position, in the Kapuzinerkirche. In the seventeenth century the Edicule as rebuilt by the Franciscans in 1555 was copied in the same way at Oberglogau in Oberschlesien in 1634.

These pilgrim words, drawings, models and actual buildings provide a record, over a period of more than a thousand years, of the changes made to the Edicule that surrounds and protects whatever still remains of the rock-cut Tomb of Christ. It is an archive beyond compare in quantity, variety and duration, and it has been quarried by generations of scholars. But it brings with it immense problems of interpretation. The medieval mind was not interested in architectural history, nor necessarily in the kind of accuracy today's scholars find important. The necessary skills of measurement and drawing were not always available. Modern historians may not understand the contemporary meaning of words used in descriptions. The actual date of some of the evidence may be uncertain and its significance disputed.

The structure of the Edicule as it survives today, combined with the records in all their variety made by generations of pilgrims, allows us to recover something of the original form of the rock-cut tomb discovered by Constantine in 325/6 and the changes through which it passed, first at the hands of the emperor's agents, and then through the centuries of embellishment, destruction, restoration, decay, rebuilding, fire and reconstruction. The comparison and analysis of these two very different kinds of record, the one structural, the other essentially devotional, are the underlying themes of this book.

CHAPTER 1

THE TOMB AND THE EDICULE

THE NEED FOR INVESTIGATION

The Tomb of Christ has been little studied. Standing within a building which has been the subject of many investigations over a century and a half, the Edicule (*aedicula*, 'little house') containing the tomb has often been ignored or dismissed. In part this attitude stems from a belief that the present Edicule dates entirely from the nineteenth century and must necessarily have destroyed what went before. But in great part it is the result of not looking closely at the visible structure and its component parts – in other words from a failure to apply to this

Fig. 4. The Church of the Holy Sepulchre from the air, looking south-west. The photograph covers the whole site of Constantine's church from the diagonal line of the cardo, lower left, to the large dome over the Rotunda of the Anastasis, above the tomb, middle right. The minarets of the Mosques of Omar and al-Khanqah rise to left and right of the Holy Sepulchre, and the Church of the Redeemer (Erlöserkirche) and its bell-tower are seen to the left of the photograph. (Photograph Pantomap Israel Ltd)

Fig. 5. The parvis of the Church of the Holy Sepulchre, looking north towards the double portals of the entrance in the facade of the south transept of the Crusader church. (Photograph John Crook)

most important of the shrines of Christianity the approaches and methods of systematic archaeological enquiry. The structural history of the tomb and the Edicule has usually been studied from the earliest (beginning with the Gospel narratives) to the latest, with increasingly less attention paid to the more recent stages. The present work reverses this approach, proceeding from the known (what is there now) to the earlier stages, the proper archaeological procedure,[1] and does so in the anticipation that the now urgently necessary restoration of the Edicule will in due course produce entirely new evidence for the earlier stages.

The question may perhaps be asked, what is there to be gained from detailed investigation of an early nineteenth-century monument (Figs 6–8, 11)? Is not the fact that the present Edicule has been more or less ignored by most previous students of the Church of the Holy Sepulchre a sure sign that there is nothing to be learnt from it? And in any case what can or could be learnt from such an investigation that might throw light on the death and burial, let alone upon the resurrection, of Jesus?

The answer to the last question is the simplest, for the answer is 'nothing'. It is almost inconceivable that archaeology could throw any direct light on the life and death of a specific individual who would have seemed of relative insignificance in first-century Palestine. But it is the question which is at fault. The right questions may elicit more helpful replies. Among the many which might be asked three stand out. What is the original form and date of the rock-cut tomb at the heart of the present Edicule? What, if anything, can be learnt of the treatment of this tomb between the time of its first use and its rediscovery in 325/6? What have been the forms of the successive structures (*aediculae*) which have enclosed this tomb since 325/6? These questions are worth serious attention, for few buildings have exerted in their form and setting so profound an influence over the development of architecture across the centuries.

An archaeologist approaching a place of cult, especially that at the heart of one of the world's major religions, in a building (Figs 3–5) occupied by three greater and three lesser communities of religious, must be aware, whatever his or her beliefs, of the privilege which surrounds the central fact of being permitted to undertake any form of investigation, and of the responsibility for scrupulous and impartial observation and record which rests upon the work. The circumstances within the Church of the Holy Sepulchre are such, in the variety of its occupation and in the pressure of pilgrimage and tourism to which it is subject, that the fact of our being permitted to undertake our survey without restrictions of any kind being placed upon us is little short of miraculous. Every kindness and courtesy has been shown to us by all involved, and extraordinary privileges have been awarded in terms of access and trust. The extent of our indebtedness is set out in the acknowledgements at the end of this book.

In 1927 the Church of the Holy Sepulchre was shaken by an earthquake. The building was already in a parlous state from years of structural neglect and inadequate maintenance,[2] but the three great Religious Communities – Greek, Latin and Armenian – could agree only on the most urgent works, notably the reconstruction of the dome over the crossing of the Crusader church. This was

Fig. 6. The south side of the Edicule seen through the restored columns of the Rotunda of the Anastasis, looking north-west. (Photograph John Crook)

completed in 1935 to the design of the British architect William Harvey. In despair, the Mandate Government of Palestine resorted to the only possible option and in 1934–5 and subsequent years propped up the building with steel and timber shores.[3] For most of us these were to form the principal visual impact of the Holy Sepulchre for the next thirty years.

In the improved ecumenical climate of the 1960s restoration became possible. A Common Technical Bureau, working on behalf of the three Religious Communities, achieved a brilliant recovering of the ancient fabric, Constantinian, Byzantine and Crusader (Figs 5–6). Above the Tomb of Christ a new dome crowning the Rotunda of the Anastasis – the Resurrection – was the work of two firms of British engineers (Figs 3–4).

For many years the interior of the dome remained scaffolded and undecorated (Figs 6, 8, 11), but on 2 January 1997 the restored dome was at last inaugurated in an ecumenical ceremony marking the beginning of the triennium of preparation for the Great Jubilee in the Year 2000 (Fig. 10).

Beneath the dome, at the focus of the Rotunda, the Tomb of Christ alone stands unrestored (Figs 6–8, 11). The present Edicule encloses two compartments (Fig. 9), the Tomb Chamber to the west and the Chapel of the Angel, the latter entered by a relatively small doorway in the elaborate eastern façade (Fig. 7). This doorway is reached by a low step from a raised platform (the Entry: Fig. 9.1) and is flanked by stone benches fronted by stone candelabra (Fig. 90). A separate chapel constructed in a similar but not identical style and attached to the rear (west end) of the Edicule belongs to the Copts (Figs 9.4 and 67, 82, 84–5).

To outward appearance the present Edicule dates only from 1809–10 (pp. 103–8). It was badly shaken in the earthquake of 1927, and had to be strapped together by the Mandate Government in March 1947 to stop it collapsing.[4] Their cradle of timber and steel still remains (Figs 6, 8, 11, 74), the girders marked BURN STEEL INDIA S.C.O.B., emblematic of a vanished world.[5]

In the last few years Professor George Lavas, architect to the Greek Orthodox Community, has successfully completed the restoration of the Rock of Calvary.[6] The restoration of the Tomb of Christ cannot long remain neglected, especially now that the dome above has been so splendidly decorated (Fig. 10). Its present tottering condition is such that the Edicule will have to be taken down to the floor, stone by stone, and rebuilt. In the process earlier structures, or what remains of them, will inevitably come to light. The question is whether anyone will be on hand to record what becomes visible.

There are those who say: 'We know what happened here. There is no need for archaeology.' Many may find the first statement common ground, but even these may feel that what happened to the Tomb of Christ in later years, after the events of the Resurrection, is of absorbing interest and importance. In terms of the architectural expression of cult, there can be no more significant or influential structural sequence in the western world.

Fig. 7. The east face of the Edicule. (Photograph John Crook)

The prime mover behind the recent investigations is Dr G.S.P. Freeman-Grenville, who has long been urging the need for recording before and during any restoration of the Tomb.[7] At his suggestion my wife, Birthe Kølbye-Biddle, and I put forward to the Religious Communities in the Holy Sepulchre a scheme for a comprehensive investigation and record of the present state of the Edicule. Nothing was to be disturbed – there is no question of excavation or of any investigation requiring disturbance of the structure until the actual work of restoration begins – but the Edicule would be recorded inside and out using both the traditional methods of architectural archaeology and the most recent techniques of photogrammetry. To undertake the photogrammetric investigation and record we were joined by Professor M.A.R. Cooper, Director of the Engineering Surveying Research Centre at City University, London. We had already worked together on recording the shrine of St Alban in St Alban's Abbey in Hertfordshire, a project which has proved in several ways to be a model for the investigation of the Tomb of Christ.

Fig. 8. The north side of the Edicule with the steel shoring erected in March 1947, looking down south-west from the gallery of the Rotunda. (Photograph John Crook)

PRINCIPLES AND PROCEDURES

Structures which have been many times restored and even completely rebuilt around an enduring core usually preserve indications of their structural development in anomalies detectable in their final form. The tomb of St Peter under the papal high altar of St Peter's in Rome is a case in point: an anomalous alignment in the present marble pavement of the Niche of the Pallia in front of the altar is now known to reflect the alignment of the memorial structure of the second century AD, itself invisible for more than a thousand years.[8]

This was the rationale behind the survey of the Tomb of Christ. Although the present structure appeared to be essentially a work of 1809–10, it seemed probable that evidence – hitherto unobserved – for its earlier history might be detectable by analytical description and accurate survey. The kinds of evidence sought included minor anomalies of alignment in walls or floors, unexplained changes in plan, elevation and section, and variations in stone jointing, surface dressing, condition, wear and geological type. The task facing the project was to

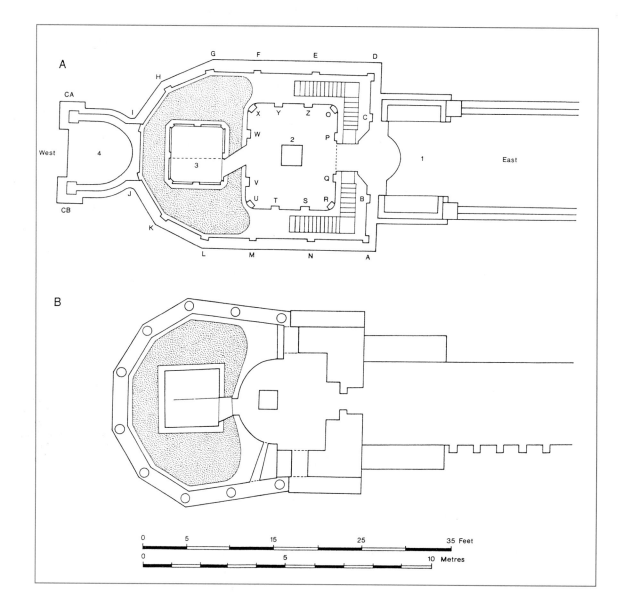

discover and define such variations. With a structure as complex as the Edicule the necessary precision of survey could be obtained only by the use of photogrammetry.[9]

Photogrammetry is a technique mainly developed for aerial mapping, but it can equally well be used at ground level to record in three dimensions the form of structures both natural and man-made. It relies on the taking of photographic stereo images (e.g. Fig. 11) which include an array of independently surveyed markers. These images are viewed in an analytical photogrammetric plotter in such a way that any individual point within the area of the image can be registered and its XYZ co-ordinates automatically stored. From these data, elevations, sections, plans and three-dimensional views can be produced on a computer screen and printed to any required scale, the level of detail depending only on the amount of time devoted to logging the detail in the images (Figs 81–2, 84–8, 97, 102).

An additional advantage of photogrammetry is that the photographic negatives form a permanent record, which can be archived in multiple copies and reinterrogated in the future to recreate any desired representation of the object recorded. Digitizing techniques can also be used to record early views, models and dimensions, in this case of the Edicule, thus allowing us to test hypotheses about its development by visualization and analysis of these records (e.g. Figs 48–9).

During the 1990 and 1992 seasons the photogrammetric record was augmented by complete photographic cover in colour of both the interior and the exterior of the Edicule using a Nikon FM 35mm camera with an 85mm lens. This colour record has been digitally scanned and incorporated in the database, colour images from which can be called up on a split screen for direct comparison with the relevant portion of the wire-frame and/or surfaced photogrammetric model.

The methods of architectural archaeology employed were simple and traditional, involving description by drawing, photograph and word. The surfaces were all described and drawn to scale stone by stone, recording visible characteristics and thus defining variations. The individual parts of the structure, for example the Entry and its flanking benches (Figs 74, 89–90), or the doorway between the Chapel of the Angel and the Tomb Chamber (Figs 93–5, 100), were described in continuous prose. When systematically carried through, this procedure compels the writer to observe closely, to define problems and to attempt an explanation. The drawn and written record is complemented by descriptive photography (as distinct from photography for photogrammetry) designed to record the evidence noted in the course of the drawn and written description (e.g. Figs 67, 74, 89–96, 100–1). Most of the drawing undertaken in the course of this work is measured sketching, a process which again compels the observer to a critical description of structure. This drawing does not seek to duplicate the dimensionally more accurate photogrammetric survey, but rather to supplement it with a range of evidence – such as stone joints in angles, stone type, thickness (where measurable) and surface treatment – which may not be observable in the photogrammetric record and may thus be obtainable only by 'ground correction'. An archaeological survey of the floor of the Rotunda was made at a scale of 1:20 using gridded planning frames in the XY co-ordinate system used for the photogrammetry (Fig. 12). This survey has now been digitally scanned and incorporated in the database.

During the plotting of the photogrammetric data, information derived from the archaeological architectural description – such as the stone reference number, bay letters (Fig. 9), inscription number (if any), stone type, surface treatment, thickness (if known) and decoration (if any) – is added to a computerized relational database stone by stone, together with an assignment of each stone to structural period and a tentative date (Fig. 13). Additional information can be

(Opposite)
Fig. 9. Plans of the Edicule: A, as reconstructed in 1809–10; B, as reconstructed in 1555. Drawn by Nicholas Griffiths. 1: the Entry; 2: the Chapel of the Angel; 3: the Tomb Chamber; 4: the Coptic Chapel (added between 1809–10 and 1818). The letters applied to the pilasters were used to identify the bays in the 1989–92 survey (omitted in the Tomb Chamber for clarity). The stipple indicates the extent of the surviving rock as supposed by Willis. Although A was the best plan of the Edicule of 1809–10 available until the plotting of the present photogrammetric survey (cf. Fig. 85), it is inaccurate in detail, exaggerates the angle of the passage between the Chapel of the Angel (2) and the Tomb Chamber (3), and has straightened up the alignment of the Tomb Chamber. Enlarged from Willis 1849, Pl. 2, Figs 7 (after Amico) and 8 (after a plan of 1825 by J.J. Scoles). See here below, Fig. 14.

Fig. 10. The restored dome of the Rotunda of the Anastasis, inaugurated on 2 January 1997 in an ecumenical ceremony marking the beginning of the triennium of preparation for the Great Jubilee. The decoration of twelve indirectly lit rays represents the Twelve Apostles and the spreading out of the Church in the World. The restoration marks the first stage in a programme which will continue with the re-laying of the floor of the Rotunda, and will culminate in the restoration of the Edicule. (Photograph KNA)

Fig. 11. The south side of the Edicule with the steel shoring erected in March 1947, looking down north-west from the gallery of the Rotunda. Photogrammetric (stereo) pair. (Photographs Stuart Robson)

added as free text to the record of each stone. The system is designed for expansion as further information becomes available, particularly when the restoration of the Edicule reveals remains of earlier structures. This stone-by-stone record, reproducible at any required scale, is ideally suited for the work of dismantling and reconstruction, and is able to produce images, including sections, of the surface of any stone at a scale of 1:1 to guide the masons at the bench.

Within days of the start of the work in 1989 it was clear that the Tomb of Christ was no exception to the usual rules of structural archaeology. The points which emerged then and from observations made in 1990 and 1992 are described below (pp. 120–37). Much of the information required for analysis of the structure of the tomb will only become available when the plotting of the photogrammetric survey is complete, but the results of the archaeological survey are already posing new questions of the photogrammetric data, and the process will certainly be reciprocal.

THE STUDY OF THE EDICULE

A clear distinction must be drawn between the attempts which have been made to establish the original form of the tomb as described in passing in the Gospels and the study of the Edicule itself. From a logical point of view, evidence derived

Fig. 12. The floor of the
Rotunda of the Anastasis,
1990–2. (Drawn by Steven
Ashley)

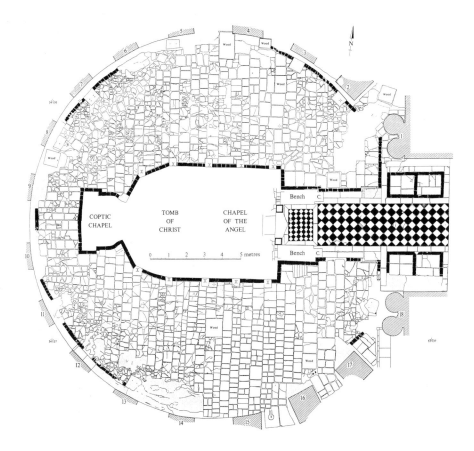

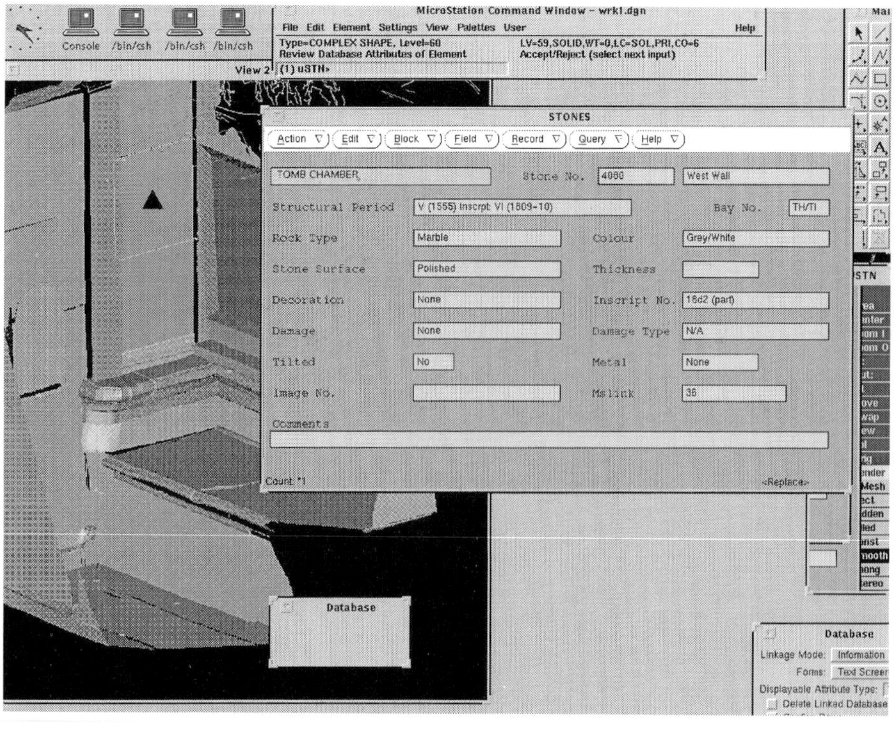

Fig. 13. Display in the
Microstation Command
Window of a stone record
'card' derived from the
computerized relational
database of the
photogrammetric survey,
showing the attributes of
Stone 4080 in the west
wall of the Tomb Chamber
recorded in the course of
the archaeological
architectural description.
The 'card' is shown
superimposed on a
surfaced photogrammetric
wire-frame 3D computer
graphics perspective model
of the north-west angle of
the Tomb Chamber,
showing part of the marble
slab covering the burial
shelf. Stone 4080 is marked
with a black triangle for
this illustration only.
(Engineering Surveying
Research Centre, City
University, London)

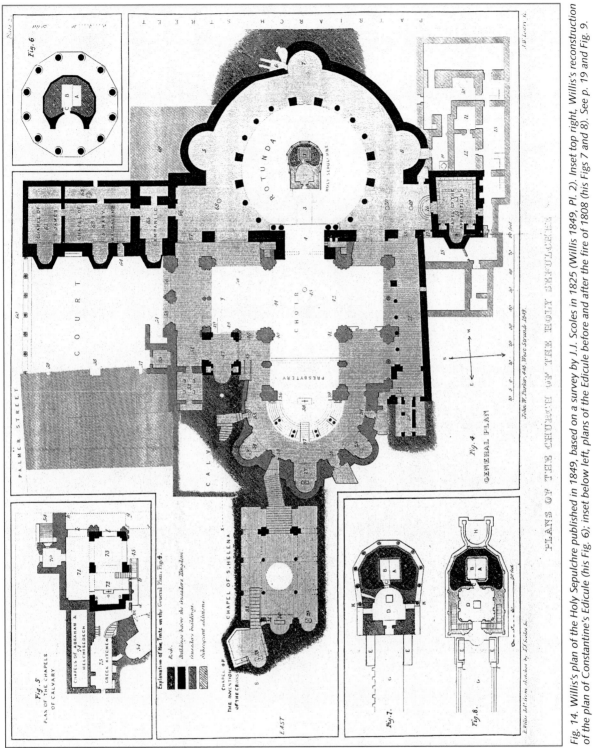

Fig. 14. Willis's plan of the Holy Sepulchre published in 1849, based on a survey by J.J. Scoles in 1825 (Willis 1849, Pl. 2). Inset top right, Willis's reconstruction of the plan of Constantine's Edicule (his Fig. 6); inset below left, plans of the Edicule before and after the fire of 1808 (his Figs 7 and 8). See p. 19 and Fig. 9.

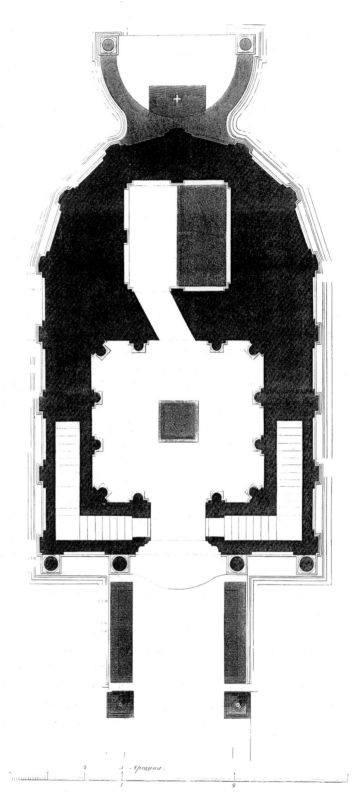

*Fig. 15. Russian engraving
of the plan of the Edicule
as rebuilt in 1809–10,
preserved among Willis's
papers in the library of the
Palestine Exploration Fund.
Pre-1849, but date and
place of publication not yet
traced. See here p. 19 and
n. 18. (Palestine
Exploration Fund)*

from the latter should not be applied to the former, for we have to rely on the statement of Eusebius that the rock-cut tomb found in 325/6 was in reality the Tomb of Christ, and neither he nor any other contemporary witness tells us the evidence on which this claim was based (see below, p. 66). The only acceptable procedure is to establish the possible form of the tomb described in the Gospels on the one hand, and the form of the rock-cut tomb within the Edicule on the other, and to compare the results. This is exactly the approach adopted by Robert Willis in his pioneering analytical account of 1849, still essential reading and all the more remarkable for the virtually undetectable fact that Willis had not himself been to Jerusalem.[10]

Attempts have often been made to define the form of the tomb described in the Gospels, but it is only with the discovery and archaeological description of early rock-cut tombs in the Jerusalem area that the study was put on a reasonably firm basis. Willis[11] was able to do this by reliance on the studies of W.R. Wilde, E.G. Schulz, and G.N. Grenville,[12] and on a series of drawings of tombs in the Jerusalem area and elsewhere prepared by J.J. Scoles and now preserved in the library of the Palestine Exploration Fund. The start of serious archaeological work in the second half of the nineteenth century allowed Vincent and Abel to undertake a detailed analysis (Fig. 78),[13] and this was followed by Dalman.[14] Information about rock-cut tombs in the Jerusalem area has increased enormously in the last eighty years, particularly in recent decades,[15] and some of this has passed into the manuals,[16] but this approach to understanding the tomb of the Gospels is limited by the inadequacy of the details they provide (see below, pp. 54–5).

Analytical study of the Edicule in its present form can also be said to have begun with Willis,[17] an attempt which relied in part on earlier Russian scholarship.[18] Willis included three plans showing the form of the Edicule 'as originally fitted up by Constantine', 'from the Crusaders' Conquest to the Fire of 1808', and in its 'present' state (Fig. 14).[19] A large-scale engraved plan of its present state had already appeared in Russia (Fig. 15)[20] and a longitudinal section was published by Pierotti.[21] The Edicule was surveyed as part of the Ordnance Survey of Jerusalem in 1864–5,[22] and a detailed description followed in the work of Benjamin Ioannides.[23] The major work is again that of Vincent and Abel,[24] which remains of permanent value, but they were openly hostile to the present structure[25] and this certainly coloured their perception of what might be learnt from it, as the brevity of their account of its more recent history and present form shows.[26]

In recent times the key studies are those by John Wilkinson.[27] Set out with clarity and incorporating a series of plans and models showing the probable appearance of the Edicule at successive periods, Wilkinson has drawn upon a wide range of evidence of many kinds. His work, although now to be revised in some aspects, particularly in its treatment of the period since 1555 (see below, pp. 100–1), is the foundation of modern study of the structural history of the Edicule.

CHAPTER 2

VISUAL SOURCES FOR THE STUDY OF THE EDICULE

One of the most fruitful and methodologically challenging approaches to the study of the Edicule is provided by the extraordinary variety of visual sources available to supplement the wide range of written accounts[1] and whatever may survive of the structure itself. For the 'pre-Edicule' phases the evidence as a whole is slight, being limited to the accounts in the Gospels (pp. 54–6) and to the two or three later references in the period down to 325/6 (pp. 60–4). But from then onwards the materials multiply in bewildering variety and include an immense quantity of pilgrim literature. Some of the principal written sources will be mentioned below in the historical survey (Chapters 3 to 6). For the period down to the fall of Jerusalem in 1187 the most important pilgrim texts have been made readily available in translation in two volumes edited with detailed commentaries by John Wilkinson.[2] Travel texts of the Crusader period, twelfth and thirteenth centuries, have been brought together by de Sandoli.[3] For the subsequent period there is no such easy guide, although some of the more important texts are given by Baldi.[4] In common with Edicule studies as a whole, the later the texts, the less the attention paid to them.[5] These later texts still have much to teach us.

The visual evidence for the Tomb of Christ presents many problems of interpretation at every period in its history. In the period from 1555 to 1808, and from 1809–10 to the present, the visual evidence can be checked by the physical evidence of the structure itself. For the earlier periods, from 325/6 to 1009, and from 1009 to 1555, the visual evidence cannot be controlled by the physical evidence which, so far as it survives, is almost all hidden within the present structure. The problem is complicated by the existence side by side of both representational and non-representational depictions of the tomb. This difficulty is at its greatest in the earlier period, from 325/6 to 1009.

THE EDICULE FROM THE 4TH CENTURY TO 1009

For the seven centuries between construction of Constantine's buildings in 325/35 and their destruction by the Fatimid Caliph al-Hakim in 1009 there are at least thirteen kinds of visual evidence for the appearance of the Edicule. Each is subject to complex and difficult problems of interpretation, and it is not always certain that it is indeed the Edicule which is shown. Grabar reviewed and illustrated some of this evidence in *Martyrium* in 1946[6] and Wilkinson has used it to produce reconstruction drawings and models of the Edicule constructed by Constantine.[7] This is as close as we are likely to get to the original form of the structure unless new representations are found or until evidence for its precise plan and dimensions are recovered in the restoration of the present structure.

Both during this early period and later the tomb appears in a wide range of media: painting on wood and vellum, ivory carving, stone sculpture, mosaic, metal, pottery and glass. The depictions fall into four categories:

1. a rock-cut tomb in a rock face
2. an empty sarcophagus with the Risen Christ above[8]
3. an elaborately architectural tomb structure, usually of two stories[9]
4. a single-storied structure with a conical roof and lattice grilles (examples in nos 1–12 below).

It is evident that the first two categories are non-representational: they are ideas of the tomb derived from either the topographical or the theological content of the Gospels. Problems have arisen in the evaluation of the third and fourth categories. Some writers have taken the elaborate architectural compositions of the third category as representations of reality,[10] but they are in fact ideal tombs of the most elaborate kind and their detail finds no reflection in contemporary written descriptions of Constantine's Edicule. This third category is therefore also non-representational. Only the fourth category appears to represent the Edicule as built by Constantine.

Representations of the third category appear principally on ivories of the highest quality, some perhaps of Alexandrian origin and others possibly from Rome or Milan. By contrast, representations of the fourth type appear in a wide variety of materials and are of very varied quality. Where an origin can be suggested, they seem to derive from Syro-Palestine, and the elements they depict appear to correspond to those described in the contemporary written accounts. Because of their region of origin and because they were, in many cases, pilgrim eulogia or mementoes designed to recall the places depicted, objects in this

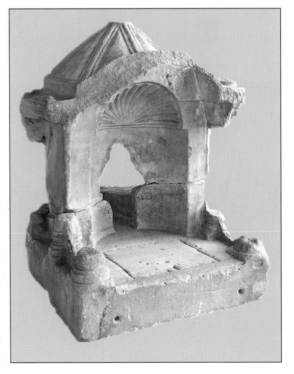

Fig. 16. The Narbonne model: the curved niche and shell hood at the back of the portico, the columns of which have been broken away. Height 1.24 m. Pyrenean marble. ?5th century. See p. 22, no. 2, and cf. Figs 64C and 76, and pp. 69, 100. (Photograph John Crook)

fourth category have a special value as evidence for the original form of Constantine's Edicule.

Examples of the various kinds of visual evidence in this fourth category are listed here in approximate chronological order (with recent references which refer back to older publications):

1. the carving on the right side of the ivory casket from Samagher, near Pola in Istria, ?c. 440, now in the Museo Archeologico, Venice.[11]

2. the Narbonne marble model, pre-tenth century (probably fifth century) (Figs 16 and 76), now in the Musée d'Art et d'Histoire, Narbonne.[12]

3. the painted wooden lid of a casket of pilgrimage relics ('eulogiai') from the treasure of the chapel of the Sancta Sanctorum in the Lateran in Rome, late sixth to early seventh century (Fig. 17), now in the Museo Sacro, Biblioteca Apostolica in the Vatican.[13]

4. the cast representations on pewter pilgrim-flasks, late sixth to early

Fig. 17. Painted wooden lid of the casket from the treasure of the Sancta Sanctorum in the Lateran, Rome, detail of the upper left section showing the Edicule and the Rotunda. Approx. 70 x 80 mm. Late 6th to early 7th century. See this page, no. 3. (Biblioteca Apostolica Vaticana, Museo Sacro, Inv. nr. 1883 A–B)

Fig. 18. Ampulla showing the Edicule below the Rotunda. Diam. 47 mm. Tin-lead. c. 600. See p. 24, no. 4. (Byzantine Collection, Dumbarton Oaks, Washington, DC, Acc. no. 48.18)

Fig. 19. Medallion showing the Edicule. Diam. 44 mm. Pewter. Late 6th to early 7th century. See p. 24, no. 5. (Württembergisches Landesmuseum, Stuttgart, Inv. nr. 1981–165)

Fig. 20. Ampulla with representations of (left) the Cross on the Rock of Golgotha and (right) the Edicule. Height 66 mm. Pottery. 6th century. See p. 24, no. 7. (Studium Biblicum Franciscanum)

(Above)
Fig. 21. Gold finger-ring with a four-sided domed structure representing the Edicule or the Rotunda of the Anastasis and its dome. ?6th century. Found in Jerusalem in 1974 in a Byzantine house south of the Temple Mount. See this page, no. 8. (Courtesy of Eilat Mazar, Temple Mount Excavations; photograph Zev Radovan)

(Above right)
Fig. 22. The Holy City (Η ΑΓΙΑ ΠΩΛΙΣ) of Jerusalem, detail from a mosaic in the Church of St Stephen at Kastron Meffaa (Umm al-Rasas), Jordan. The conical roof and columns of the Edicule are seen at the centre. Height of panel 1.34 m. ?785. See this page, no. 9. (Studium Biblicum Franciscanum)

seventh century, now in the treasures of the cathedrals of Monza and Bobbio in Lombardy and elsewhere (Fig. 18).[14]

5. a pewter medallion in the same lead-tin alloy as the ampullae and bearing a closely related image of the Edicule, now in Stuttgart (Fig. 19).[15]

6. the cast representations on glass pilgrim-flasks: one may specifically represent the Edicule and the hexagonal shape of others may reflect its form, late sixth to early seventh century.[16]

7. the stamped representations of the Edicule (and of Golgotha) on pottery pilgrim-flasks, e.g that purchased in Jerusalem in 1988 (Fig. 20), ?sixth to early seventh century, now in the Museum of the Studium Biblicum Franciscanum, Jerusalem.[17]

8. a series of gold rings having on the bezel a four-sided structure with a cone- or dome-shaped roof topped by a knob, ?sixth century (Fig. 21 is an example from Jerusalem) and sixth to seventh or possibly eighth century (e.g. from the Frankish Grave III.73 at the Church of St Severin in Cologne).[18]

9. the mosaic in the church of St Stephen at Kastron Mefaa (Umm al-Rasas), Jordan, dated ?785,[19] which has an image identified in Greek as 'The Holy City' with a representation of what may be the Edicule at the centre of the city (Fig. 22). This should be compared with the mosaic of

Fig. 23. The Edicule as the Fountain of Life, fragment of a mosaic of unknown but possibly Syrian origin. Height of fragment 2.15 m. ?5th to 6th century. See p. 26, no. 9. (Copenhagen, National Museum, Antiksamling, Inv. Nr. 15.137)

Fig. 24. Stone plaque with a representation of the Edicule, cut down to the shape of the Edicule from a larger slab, probably a chancel barrier, and said to have come from Syria. Height 685 mm; width 570 mm. Late 6th to early 7th century. See this page, no. 10. (Byzantine Collection, Dumbarton Oaks, Washington, DC, Acc. no. 38.56)

unknown, but possibly Syrian, origin now at Copenhagen (National Museum, Antiksamling, Inv. Nr. 15.137), ?fifth to sixth century, which shows the Edicule as the Fountain of Life (Fig. 23).[20] A third representation in mosaic of about the same date is found in the Passion sequence above the windows on the right (south) wall of the nave of S Apollinare Nuovo, Ravenna. This forms part of Theodoric's original decorative scheme of 493/526. It shows the conical roof over the Tomb Chamber but conflates this with the columns of the vestibule.[21]

10. the marble plaque, a fragment of a chancel barrier, later sixth to seventh century (Fig. 24), said to be from Syria, now at Dumbarton Oaks, Washington, DC.[21A]

11. the series of drawn plans which occur in four or more manuscripts of Adomnán's version of Arculf's account of the Holy Places, ninth century, but ultimately derived from a drawing made by Arculf for Adomnán on a wax tablet sometime in the years between 680 and the end of the seventh century.[22]

12. miniatures in manuscripts, e.g. the three views of the rotunda and/or the Edicule in a Greek manuscript, ninth century, but based on much earlier ?Palestinian source(s).[23]

13. the cast representations on bronze censers of Syrian or Palestinian origin, e.g. the example now in the Coptic Museum in Old Cairo, said to be thirteenth century, but clearly showing the Edicule before the destruction of 1009 (Fig. 26).[24] A second group of bronze censers, more than thirty or even forty of which are now known, carries cruder, heavily moulded New Testament scenes in relief, including the Women at the Tomb. Although of uncertain origin and date, Hamilton concluded from a detailed study of the group as a whole that they should be assigned to 'North Syria [possibly, but I think less probably, Egypt] in the early centuries of Islam, spanning the controversy on images'.[25]

THE EDICULE FROM THE ELEVENTH CENTURY TO 1555

Fig. 27. Imitator of Andrea Mantegna, The Resurrection, ?1460–1550. An outstanding example of the non-representational type of the depiction of the Tomb of Christ. 42.5 x 31.1 cm. Oil on wood. See this page. (London, National Gallery, Acc. no. NG 1106)

The structure of the Edicule saw several changes during its 'medieval' phase, in the twelfth century at the hands of the Crusaders and probably again in the thirteenth century following the sack of Jerusalem by the Khwarazmian Turks in 1244. The sources available for the study of this phase are as varied as those for the earlier Edicule and much greater in quantity, but they have not yet been used systematically to recover the form and details of the structure and the changes it may have undergone. This should certainly be done, for the 'medieval' Edicule was essentially the reconstruction created after the wholesale destruction of 1009 and the form then created has influenced the appearance and arrangement of the Edicule ever since, surviving through the major rebuildings of 1555 and 1809–10.

The same four categories of depiction are seen in images of the tomb produced during this period. The first, the rock-cut tomb in a rock face, occurs frequently. The second, the Risen Christ over an empty sarcophagus, is seen in some of the finest works of medieval art: Aldous Huxley memorably described Piero della Francesca's *Resurrection* of 1463 at Sansepolcro as the 'best picture in the world';[26] the National Gallery *Resurrection* by an imitator of Mantegna gives as vivid an idea of this kind of depiction (Fig. 27). As in the earlier period, however, these images are non-representational.

The same is true of the third category of depiction, showing an elaborate tomb structure of two stories. This kind of tomb, seen in the ivories of the early fifth century was perpetuated by images in manuscripts of the ninth, tenth, and even eleventh centuries.[27] These images have, however, no more value for the actual

Fig. 28. Large-scale copy of the Edicule, Eichstätt, Bavaria. c. 1160, rebuilt in its present position in the Kapuzinerkloster, 1623–5. The cupola and balustrade were renewed in 1877. The structure is a contemporary copy of the Edicule in the state it had reached by c. 1160. See p. 31, no. 1, and cf. pp. 84, 97, 113. (Foto-Nitsche, Eichstätt)

appearance of the tomb than did those at an earlier period. The addition of a cupola in the rebuilding of the Edicule in the eleventh century confuses the position with regard to the images of this third category, but a sharp distinction must be drawn between the non-representational images of ultimately Late Antique origin and those of the fourth category which, from the twelfth century onwards, begin to depict the form of the rebuilt Edicule as it actually then stood.

The various kinds of visual evidence of this fourth category for the form of the Edicule in the period from the mid-eleventh century to the rebuilding of 1555 are also listed, but in order of scale rather than date:

Figs 29 and 30. Large-scale copy of the Edicule, San Vivaldo in Valdesa, Montaione, Florence: Fig. 29, the exterior (the cupola survives only in detached fragments), restored 1971–6, and Fig. 30, the Tomb Chamber. Before 1516 (?before 1509). See p. 31, no. 1. (Photographs John Crook)

Fig. 31. The Edicule in the Church of St Anna, Augsburg, Bavaria, built 1507–8 by Georg Regel and his wife Barbara Lauginger. Due to lack of space, the Edicule was built approximately half-size and the Chapel of the Angel omitted. The cupola appears to be the only surviving built copy of the medieval cupola over the Edicule in Jerusalem. Restoration in 1590 seems not to have altered the form of the cupola as comparison with Figs 32, 34, 36–9, and 42 shows. (Photograph Paolo Liverani)

1. full-size copies or large-scale versions in or beside churches in western Europe.[28] The ?full-size copy built at Eichstätt in Bavaria *c.* 1160 appears in plan and internal arrangements (including the three 'portholes', see below nos 5, 7 and 8, and pp. 85–8) to be a remarkably close representation of the original as it was in the earlier part of this period (Fig. 28).[29] Of perhaps equal importance, from the very end of the period and thus reflecting changes which had taken place in the intervening centuries (the least known in the history of the Edicule), is the edicule built before 1516 (?1509) at San Vivaldo in Valdesa, Montaione, Florence, by Fra Tommaso da Firenze (d. 1534) as one of originally twenty-two or twenty-four structures in a *Nuova*

Fig. 32. Melchior von
Seydlitz, woodcut of the
Edicule from his
Gründtliche Beschreibung
der Wallfart . . . (Görlitz,
1591). The date above the
woodcut is that of
Melchior's visit to the
tomb, restored the year
before by Boniface of
Ragusa. The woodcut
appears to show not the
restored Edicule of 1555
but, despite its title, the
large-scale copy built at
Görlitz (the place of
publication) between 1481
and 1504. See pp. 34, 41.
(Studienbibliothek
Dillingen)

Fig. 33. Jan van Scorel, The
Knightly Brotherhood of the
Holy Land in Haarlem,
1527–30. 144.5 x 276 cm.
Oil on wood. See p. 37,
no. 3. (Haarlem, Frans
Halsmuseum, Cat. nr. 263)

Dit es de figuer van tgraf ons heren
dat ic Thijs tomasz opelic toone.
menigen tijt diende ic dees broeders in eeren
bid dat ic mach crigen goods rijc ten loone

ic luchs om hair

× lever ×

Fig. 34. Jan van Scorel, The Knightly Brotherhood of the Holy Land in Haarlem, *1527–30, detail of Fig. 33 showing the Edicule, presumably based on a drawing made during Scorel's visit to the Holy Land in 1520 and possibly related to Fig. 38. See p. 37, no. 3. (Haarlem, Frans Halsmuseum, Cat. nr. 263)*

Fig. 35. Santo Brasca, woodcut of a sketch plan of the Edicule in 1480, from his Viaggio in Terrasanta (Milan, 1481), f. 58v. See p. 37, no. 4.

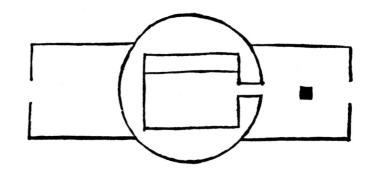

Gerusalemme (Figs 29–30).[30] The San Vivaldo copy is too early to be based upon any of the well-known representations such as those by Amico (see below, p. 46, no. 4; Figs 46–7)[31] and probably derives from records made or acquired by Fra Tommaso. Although the San Vivaldo edicule must share all the problems inherent in early architectural drawings and descriptions, it presents an important record of the medieval Edicule on the eve of the 1555 reconstruction, and should be compared with the plan by Santo Brasca (p. 37, no. 4; Fig. 35) and the pilgrim accounts by Capodilista, Wey and Faber. The half-scale copy in the Church of St Anna at Augsburg, Bavaria (Fig. 31), provides the only surviving built copy of the cupola over the medieval Edicule (cf. pp. 84–5). The Edicule at Görlitz consecrated in 1504 provides another

Fig. 36. Erhard Reuwich, woodcut of the Edicule apparently from the north-east but actually from the south-east (reversed), presumably based on a drawing made during his visit to the Holy Land in 1483, from Bernhard von Breydenbach, Peregrinatio (Mainz, 1486), on the back of the large folding view of Jerusalem following f. 142. See p. 37, no. 4.

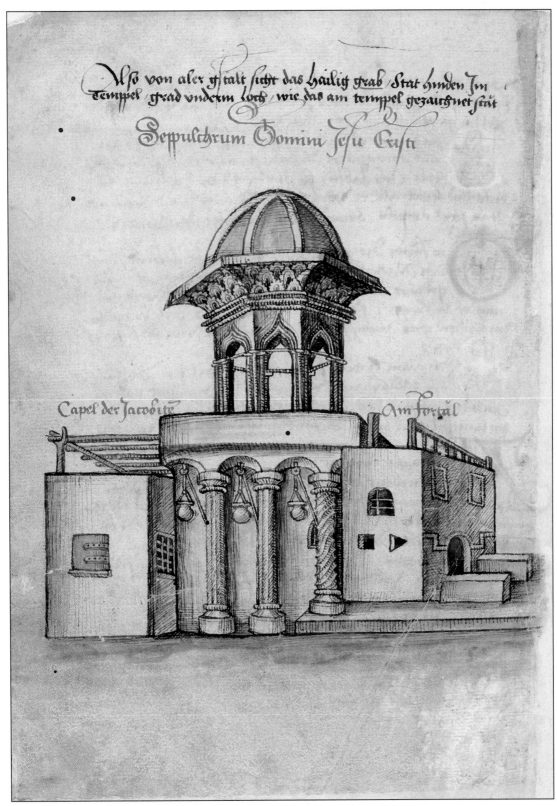

Fig. 37. Konrad von Grünenberg, coloured ink drawing of the Edicule from the south made in 1487 presumably from sketches taken during his visit in 1486. See p. 37, no. 4. (Photograph Badische Landesbibliothek, Karlsruhe, St. Peter pap. 32, f. 45v)

Fig. 38. Herman von Borculo, woodcut of the Edicule from the northeast. Inset in his view of Jerusalem, published at Utrecht, 1538, but possibly derived from a drawing made by Jan van Scorel in 1520 and related to Fig. 34. See p. 37, no. 4. After Nijhoff 1933–6, Pls 114–15. (Centraal Museum der Gemeente Utrecht)

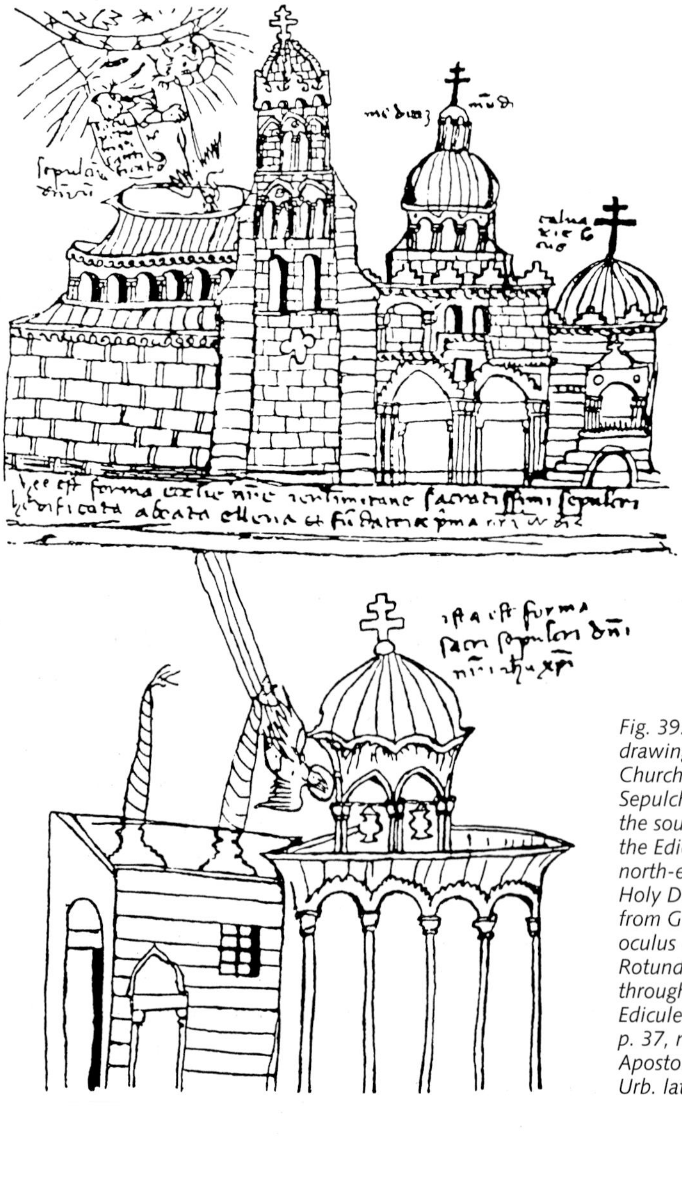

large-scale copy of about the same date (Fig. 32).[32]

2. small-scale models. None is known to survive from this period, but references in pilgrim accounts and elsewhere show that they were produced,[33] and it seems probable that they remain to be identified in museums and church treasures. They are presumably the forerunners of those made in Bethlehem in the seventeenth and eighteenth centuries (see below, p. 44, no. 3 and cf. p. 43, no. 2).

Fig. 39. Anonymous ink drawing of (above) the Church of the Holy Sepulchre seen from the south and (below) the Edicule seen from the north-east, showing the Holy Dove descending from God through the oculus of the dome of the Rotunda and thence through the cupola of the Edicule, 14th century. See p. 37, no. 4. (Biblioteca Apostolica Vaticana, Cod. Urb. lat. 1362, f. 1ᵛ)

3. a painting of the Edicule from the north, in the upper left-hand corner of *The Knightly Brotherhood of the Holy Land in Haarlem*, oil on panel, by Jan van Scorel, 1527–30, but presumably based on a drawing made by him during his visit to the Holy Land in 1520 (Figs 33–4).[34] A woodcut of the Edicule possibly related to a drawing by van Scorel is noted in the next paragraph (Fig. 38).

4. drawings of the Edicule, such as the sketch plan made in 1480 and published as a woodcut in Santo Brasca, *Viaggio in Terrasanta* (Milan, 1481), f. 58v (Fig. 35);[35] the woodcut by Erhard Reuwich showing the Edicule apparently (see below) from the north-east first published in Mainz in 1486 in Bernhard von Breydenbach's *Peregrinatio* but presumably based on a sketch made by Reuwich during their visit in 1483 (Fig. 36);[36] the precise and coloured ink drawing from the south made by Konrad von Grünenberg in 1487 presumably from sketches taken during his visit in 1486 (Fig. 37);[37] the ink view from the south-east by Stefan Baumgartner dated 1498;[38] the woodcut showing the Edicule from the north published by Herman van Borculo in 1538 in Utrecht (Fig. 38), which may be derived from a drawing made by van Scorel in 1520 and related to no. 3 above (Fig. 34);[39] and the ink view from the north showing the Holy Spirit flying down as a dove with the Holy Fire into the cupola of the Edicule (Fig. 39).[40]

Fig. 40. Reverse of a lead seal of the Canons of the Augustinian Priory of the Holy Sepulchre, showing in section the Edicule below the dome of the Rotunda. Diam. c. 36 mm. Attached to a document of 1175 in the Archives of the Knights of St John at Malta. (After de Vogüé 1860, 184)

These drawings are of varying value as evidence. Those which exist only in printed form present an additional problem, for if cut directly on to the block, they will appear reversed when printed. This is almost certainly the case with Reuwich's famous and often reproduced woodcut (Fig. 36). Reuwich's view appears to have been taken from the north-east, but comparison with von Grünenberg's drawing (Fig. 37) suggests that it is a reversed view taken from the south-east. The key is the column shaft with twisted flutes. We know from other sources such as Shaw's drawings of 1722 (see below, p. 50), Horn's views of 1724–44 (see below, p. 49, Figs 53–4), the full-size replica at Oberglogau of 1634[41] and the Amsterdam and Ashmolean models (Figs 43, 46–7), that the fluted shaft stood on the south side of the Edicule and was not matched by a similar fluted shaft on the north, where the shafts were all plain, either round or angular (?hexagonal). Reuwich must therefore have failed to reverse his drawing when cutting the block, with the result that his view appears to be from the north-east when in reality it was taken from the south-east.

5. small pictures of the Edicule showing three 'port-holes' in the face of the burial shelf, e.g. on the Plan of Jerusalem of *c.* 1170[42] or in manuscript pictures (cf. below, pp. 85–8).[43]

6. Crusader coins with stylized representations of the Edicule, or more precisely the Tomb Chamber, with the abbreviated legend SEPVLCHRVM DOMINI, or similar, base silver, possibly an emergency issue struck during the siege of Jerusalem in 1187 from metal taken from the cladding of the Edicule.[44]

Fig. 41. Nicholas of Verdun, engraved gilt and enamelled copper-alloy plaque, SEPVLCRVM DOMINI, showing Joseph of Arimathea and Nicodemus laying the dead Jesus in a sarcophagus in the front of which are three large roundels representing the 'port-holes' which were a key feature of the burial couch in the Edicule from c. 1100 or before until the 14th century. From the Klosterneuburg pulpit, completed 1181. Height (including inner inscription), 205 mm; width, 165 mm. See pp. 39–40, no. 8. (Chorherrenstift Klosterneuburg, Stiftsmuseum; photograph AV Medienstelle der Erzdiözese Wien)

7. Crusader seals with representations of the Edicule: e.g. reverses of the seals of the Patriarchs of Jerusalem, Guermond (1118–28) and Guillaume (1130–45), showing the Three Marys and the Angel beside the tomb which has three 'port-holes' in the face of the burial shelf;[45] reverses of seals of the Canons of the Holy Sepulchre attached to documents dated *c.* 1155, 1172, 1175 (Fig. 40), and 1180/9 showing the Edicule in section below the dome of the Rotunda, and some showing the three 'port-holes' in the face of the burial shelf;[46] the reverse of the seal of Peter, prior of the Holy Sepulchre (1225–7), showing the Edicule in section below the dome and with the three 'port-holes';[47] and the reverse of the seal of the Almonry of the Confraternity of St Andrew at Acre, showing the exterior of the Edicule below the dome.[48]

8. engraved gilt copper-alloy plaques with champlevé enamel, part of a set originally of forty-five, formerly arranged across the three projecting sides of the Klosterneuburg pulpit, made by and under the direction of Nicholas of Verdun, completed in 1181. Plaque II/11, titled SEPVLCRVM DOMINI, shows Joseph of Arimathea and Nicodemus laying the dead Jesus in a sarcophagus, the front of which has three large roundels ('port-holes') filled with flecked dark blue enamel (Fig. 41). Plaque II/13, originally titled RESVRRECTIO DOMINI, shows the three soldiers asleep 'as dead' in front of a similar three-holed sarcophagus, from which Christ arises.[49] Plaque II/11 is the defining representation of the three openings ('port-holes') in the vertical face of

Fig. 42. The Women at the Tomb, detail showing the Edicule, on the west face of the square stone font from the Cluniac Priory of The Holy Trinity, Lenton, Nottingham, later 12th century. See p. 40, no. 11. (Photograph John Crook)

the medieval tomb shelf (see below, pp. 85–8). Similar features appear on nos 1, 5 and 7, above.

9. lead or pewter *ampullae* showing the Edicule beneath the rotunda and dome of the Anastasis, twelfth to thirteenth century.[50]

10. lead or pewter openwork models of the Edicule possibly designed to hold a light (cf. the Holy Fire: below, p. 138 and Fig. 103): examples are known from the Seine at Paris and a date of *c.* 1500 has been suggested, although the Edicule represented seems to be of ?Crusader date and to be covered with lozenges, lilies, and ?palms in a diaper pattern.[51] While this pattern may be simply decorative, the possibility that it represents either the Crusader marble covering of the Edicule or the silver cladding stripped off in 1187 for minting into coins should perhaps be considered (cf. above, no. 6). A schematic representation of what seems to be the Edicule on a map of 1151–4 now in Copenhagen[52] shows what appear to be crosses (?fleurs de lys) in a pattern comparable to that on the Paris models. These two apparently quite independent sources suggest that the exterior of the Edicule may have been decorated in some such manner in the Crusader period, but the possibility that the patterns represent decorative hangings rather than integral structural elements should not be ignored (cf. the hangings used in the eighteenth century, below, p. 102).

11. Romanesque stone sculptures, such as the Tomba dei Rotari at Monte Sant' Angelo and a fragment from Modena, both of which show the 'port-holes' in the vertical face of the burial shelf.[53] More remarkable is the square stone font of the mid-twelfth century now preserved in the church of The Holy Trinity, New Lenton, Nottingham, but probably from the Cluniac Priory of the same dedication founded at Lenton between 1102 and 1108 (Fig. 42).[54] This sculpture, on the west face of the font as currently set, may be the earliest large-scale detailed representation of the Edicule as rebuilt following the destruction of 1009.

THE EDICULE FROM 1555 TO 1808

The Edicule rebuilt by Boniface of Ragusa in 1555 vanished in the rebuilding of 1809–10. The visual sources for this period are almost as varied as those for the earlier Edicules and exist in greater quantity. Some of them are well known in their own right, but they have been even less used for study of the structure. They also present new problems. The advent of printing meant that woodcuts and engravings were now widely disseminated, reworked, reprinted and copied in different media. Without detailed comparison (which has rarely been undertaken) it is sometimes impossible to decide whether a particular representation has any independent evidential value.

It is of course also possible that representations created after 1555 made use of pre-1555 sources and thus reflect the form and detail of the medieval rather than the Renaissance Edicule. The most striking instance of this is perhaps the

Fig. 43. Stone model of the Edicule as rebuilt in 1555, seen from the 'south-east'. Restored from fragments found in Amsterdam in 1977 in a 17th-century cess-pit at Egelantiersstraat 162–168. 13.2 cm high by 17 cm long, composed of nine dismountable sections. Streaky pink limstone, probably from the Jerusalem/Bethlehem area (?Gilo). Late 16th to early 17th century. See pp. 43–4, no. 2. (Collection Archeologie Depot, Amsterdam; photographs W. Krook, afdeling Archeologie, dienst Amsterdam Beheer)

woodcut which seems first to have appeared in 1580 illustrating the printed version of Melchior von Seydlitz's account of his pilgrimage of 1556–9 (Fig. 32, from the edition of 1591). Although apparently dated July 1556 (the date of Melchior's visit to the tomb), and titled (in German) 'Picture of the Holy Sepulchre as can be seen now in Jerusalem', it is in fact a view of the large-scale replica of the Edicule built at Görlitz between 1481 and 1504.[55] The woodcut is thus derived from a copy of the 'medieval' Edicule as it stood until August 1555. It is not a representation of the Edicule rebuilt that month and seen by Melchior the following summer.

With these warning examples in mind the types of visual evidence can be listed as before:

1. full-size or large-scale versions continued to be made in Europe after 1555.[56] Oberglogau, dating from 1634,[57] has details of the decoration of the columns not yet known to have been available by this date from published engravings (see above, p. 37). This information was perhaps therefore derived from drawings now lost or unidentified. If so, this indicates the possible independent value of these late large-scale built copies for study of the Edicule of 1555–1808, and possibly of its predecessor. By the seventeenth century full-size or large-scale built

Figs 44 and 45. Model of the Church of the Holy Sepulchre: Fig. 44, with the roofs in position and Fig. 45, with the roofs removed. Olive wood, ivory and/or bone, and mother-of-pearl. Bethlehem work, 17th or early 18th century. (Musée de la Société des Antiquaires de l'Ouest, Poitiers. Photographs Martin Biddle)

versions were beginning to appear in Orthodox lands, for example at Novoierusalimsky (New Jerusalem) on the River Istra east of Moscow (cf. San Vivaldo, above, p. 31) built by the Patriarch Nikon (1605–81), badly damaged in 1944 but under restoration in 1991.[58] The source or sources of such eastern versions is a matter of current investigation, and their significance (if any) for the form of the Jerusalem Edicule remains to be established, but it must be relevant that an olive-wood model (of the darker, less decorated, type) of the Church of the Holy Sepulchre is preserved today at New Jerusalem (see below, no. 3).

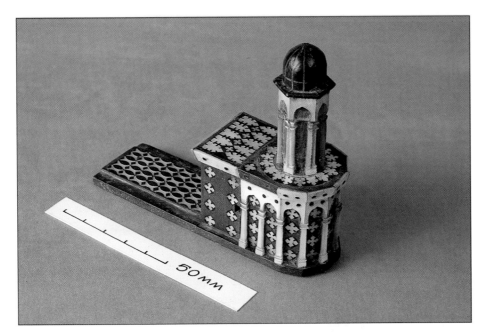

Figs 46 and 47. Model of the Edicule: Fig. 46, with the cupola and roof in position and Fig. 47, with the roof removed, showing the Chapel of the Angel with the relic of the rolling stone (white square) and the Tomb Chamber with the marble-covered burial shelf. Olive wood, ivory and/or bone, and mother-of-pearl. Bethlehem work, perhaps 17th century. (Ashmolean Museum, Oxford, Acc. no. 3089.1887. Photographs John Crook)

2. stone models of the Edicule. The only example known so far was found in Amsterdam in 1977 (Fig. 43). It came from a seventeenth-century cess-pit in an excavation carried out by the City's Archaeological Research Department at Egelantiersstraat 162/168 (invent. nr EGS1–3; now on loan to the Museum for Religious Art, Het Catharijneconvent, Utrecht, Inv. no. RMCC m 314).[59] The model, which was found in fragments but has since been restored, is carved in a pink limestone probably from the Jerusalem/Bethlehem area. It measures 13.2 cm high by 17 cm in length. Comparison with fifteen representations of the Edicule made between the

fourteenth and eighteenth centuries shows that the Amsterdam model represents the Edicule as it was rebuilt in 1555. Since the model could not have been based on any single one of the known illustrations of the Edicule, it seems certain that it was made in Jerusalem and that the stone is of local origin. Because it is a three-dimensional object, the product of careful observation and precise carving, the Amsterdam model provides in many ways the most satisfactory known representation of the Edicule as it stood from 1555 to 1808. It seems inconceivable that it is unique: other examples will surely come to light either in excavations or unidentified in museum collections.

3. wooden models of the Church of the Holy Sepulchre which can be dismantled (Figs 44–5) to reveal a model of the Edicule, the cupola and roof of which can be removed to reveal the interior of the Chapel of the Angel and the Tomb Chamber (Figs 46–7). The Edicule models are often missing from the Rotunda, but the number in collections suggests that they were made for sale as separate items. The production of these olive-wood models, inlaid with mother-of-pearl and ivory and/or bone, seems to have begun at Bethlehem at the end of the sixteenth century, probably under Franciscan influence,[60] but whether they are the result of the availability of copies of Amico's drawings of 1593–7 prior to publication (see below no. 4)[61] or are a separate and parallel development (and therefore have an independent value as evidence), as the stone model (no. 2) suggests, has yet to be established. There are two types of model of the church, a small, chunkier, darker, less elaborately decorated type, and what seems to be the more normal type, larger, lighter, and very elaborately decorated (Figs 44–5). Whether these are of different date, the product of different workshops or simply of different quality and therefore cost is not yet known. Dating depends on the date by which examples had reached European collections: a model of the church complete with a model of the Edicule was brought back to Moscow from Palestine in 1653 by the Russian traveller Arsenii Sukhanov, and is preserved today at New Jerusalem near Moscow;[62] models of the Edicule now in the Van de Poll-Wolters-Quina Foundation at Zeist in the Netherlands were obtained in Jerusalem in 1669;[63] a model of the Church of the Holy Sepulchre with the Edicule was in the Danish Royal Cabinet by 1674;[64] and a model of the church in the British Museum used by Willis in his study of the Church of the Holy Sepulchre[65] was formerly in the collection of Sir Hans Sloane (1660–1753).[66] It must have been such a model of the Edicule which (possibly in the 1670s) led Sir Christopher Wren to draw a parallel between the 'small Models of Wood, garnished with Mother of Pearl, of the holy Sepulchre at *Jerusalem* . . . usually made for Sale to Pilgrims and Foreigners' and the models of the shrine of Diana made by the silversmiths of Ephesus.[67]

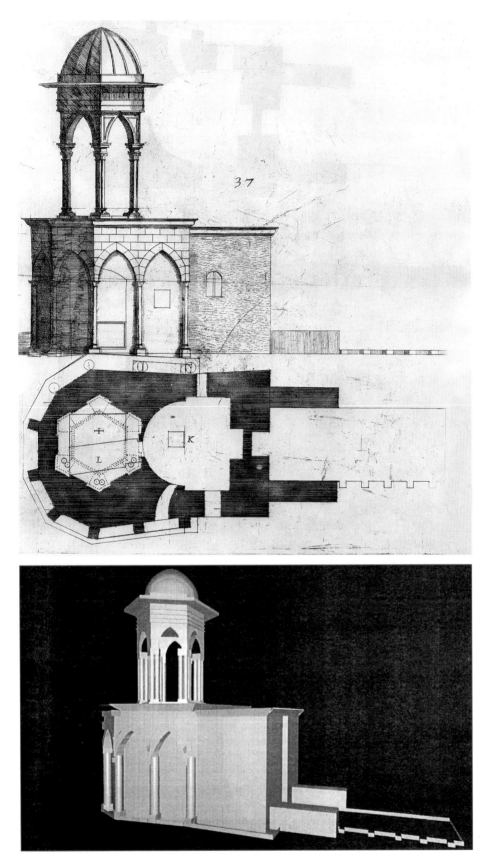

Figs 48 and 49. Bernardino Amico, plan and south elevation of the Edicule drawn in 1593–7: Fig. 48, engraving by A. Tempesti from Amico's Trattato delle piante et imagini de i Sacri Edificii di Terra Santa (Rome, 1609), Pl. 37, cf. p. 19 (see here p. 46, no. 4). (British Library: 60.h.10). Fig. 49, digital visualization of Amico's survey of the Edicule based on his Trattato (Florence, 1620), Pl. 33, cf. Chapter 33 (see here p. 46, no. 4, and p. 13). (Engineering Surveying Research Centre, City University, London)

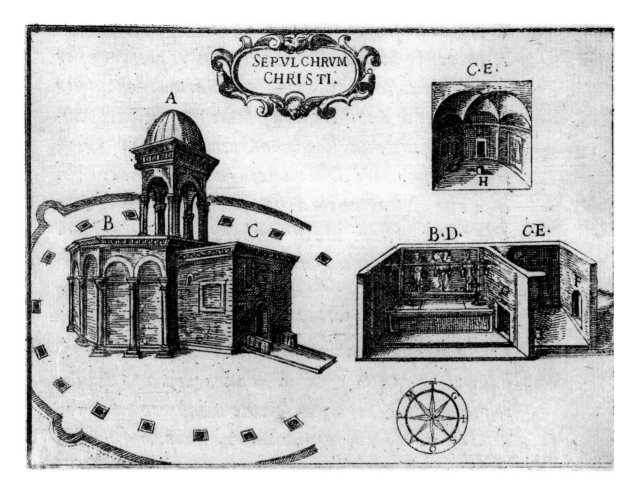

Fig. 50. Giovanni
Zuallardo, the exterior of
the Edicule from the south-
east, with the longitudinal
section of the Tomb
Chamber (BD) and the
Chapel of the Angel (CE)
looking north, and the
interior of the Chapel of
the Angel looking west
(CE), drawn in 1586:
engraving by Natale
Bonifacio from Zuallardo's
Il devotissimo viaggio
(Rome, 1587), p. 207. See
this page, no. 4. (Bodleian
Library, University of
Oxford: Antiq. e.I. 1587.4)

4. measured surveys: whatever manuscript plans may remain to be found, the only printed versions are based on measurements taken by Bernardino Amico during his time in Palestine in 1593–7. Two editions were published, Rome 1609 [the dedication dated 1610] with the original drawings engraved by A. Tempesti or Tempesta (1555–1630) (Fig. 48), and Florence 1620 [the colophon dated 1619] with new engravings in a smaller format by J. Callot (1592–1635). A translation of the second edition with a substantial introduction by Bagatti reproduces Callot's engravings.[68] The unit of measurement used in the text and for the scales shown on some of the drawings has caused much confusion.[69] This is partly because Amico or his editor changed the unit of measurement between editions from the 'ancient Roman palm' (equivalent to 0.2234 m) to the ordinary palm 'which is in use in the Kingdom of Naples' (equivalent to 0.2637 m), making *canne d'architettura* of ten palms equivalent to 2.234 m and 2.637 m respectively.[70] Amico's measuring rod may also have been inaccurate,[71] but a more serious problem is that the scales on Callot's reduced engravings in the 1620 edition no longer correspond to Amico's text,[72] the latter not having been changed to match the change in scale. Amico

Fig. 51. Cornelis de Bruyn, the Edicule from the southeast, detail from his view of the interior of the Rotunda drawn in 1681: engraving from his Reizen (Delft, 1698), Pl. 144. See p. 48, no. 5. (Bodleian Library, University of Oxford: 20601 c.3)

claims that his plan of the Edicule may be 'minutely measured according to its scale' and that 'those who delight to handle the compass will not find the least point of difference or error between' the plan and the relief in perspective.[73] But this claim is difficult to reconcile with his admission that in the elevations of the Edicule, he made the external columns and their bases, 'uguali, parte per negligenza, parte per abbelire il disegno' ('I have made them equal, partly through idleness, partly to beautify the design').[74]

5. engraved views: these exist in considerable quantity, but have to be used with caution for many are simply reproductions of earlier engravings, with or without acknowledgement and with varying degrees of reworking.[75] The three most important sets, each independent of the other, and in the case of Amico and de Bruyn based on original drawings by the authors themselves, are as follows. Giovanni Zuallardo, in Jerusalem in 1586, published a plan, elevation, and internal views of the Edicule (Fig. 50),[76] the source of which is not yet known. Amico's *rilievi* and elevations were prepared in 1593–7 (Fig. 48).[77] They must be read in the light of his own admissions about

them (see above, no. 4) and the perhaps over-stringent comments of Willis.[78] Cornelis de Bruyn (1652–1726/7, sometimes known as Le Bruyn) made his drawings on the spot in 1681 and tells us something about how he set about each one. The engraved plates prepared for the first (Dutch) edition of 1698 were used for all subsequent editions with the addition of Italian titles which may suggest the nationality of the otherwise apparently unknown engraver. De Bruyn provides a view of the Rotunda with the Edicule (Fig. 51), a detailed view of the east face of the Edicule (Fig. 52), and an uncharacteristically stylized and inadequate longitudinal section, possibly reflecting the difficulty of making records inside the Edicule.[79] The engravings published by these three authors were reprinted again and again during the seventeenth and eighteenth centuries, sometimes reworked to a degree which makes their parentage difficult to recognize.

Fig. 53. Elzear Horn, coloured ink drawing of the Edicule from the south, dated 5 December 1729, from his Elucidatio Terrae Sanctae. (Vatican, Biblioteca Apostolica, Cod. lat. 9233, Tomo II°, f. 57r)

Fig. 54. Elzear Horn, coloured ink drawing of the interior of the Edicule from the south, showing the Chapel of the Angel and the Tomb Chamber, not dated but a pair with Fig. 53 of 5 December 1729, from his Elucidatio Terrae Sanctae. (Vatican, Biblioteca Apostolica, Cod. lat. 9233, Tomo II°, f. 58v)

6.   drawings: many of these doubtless remain to be discovered, particularly from the later part of the period. The most important so far published are by Elzear Horn (c. 1691–1744), a Franciscan, who was in Palestine from 1724 until his death. His manuscript, in three volumes with drawings on 227 pages, is in the Vatican Library (MS 9233). It has been twice edited, but only in excerpts and with a limited number of the drawings, principally because many of these are copied from printed sources.[80] Horn's drawings of the Edicule are independent of earlier

Fig. 55. Thomas Shaw, the cupola over the Edicule looking north, detail from his drawing of the Edicule in 1722. See this page. (Bodleian Library, University of Oxford: MS. Add.D.27, f.219^v-220^{ar})

sources and of the first importance, with a plan, north and south elevations (both with and without ornaments), a longitudinal section and a detail of the cupola (Figs 53–4).[81] Examples of the kind of drawings which may still be found are in the manuscript notes made by Thomas Shaw (1694–1751) during his visit to Palestine in 1722 (Fig. 55).[82] The second of these provides a view of the architecture and Renaissance decoration of the cupola over the Edicule which is more detailed than any other yet noted.

7. oil paintings on wood or canvas: these are rarely mentioned but there is a series of *proskynitaria* or pilgrim souvenir paintings in oil on canvas which show a kind of bird's-eye view of Jerusalem with vignettes of the principal shrines, all of which include the Edicule. One of the earliest is an Armenian Catholic version painted after 1674 and now in Iran.[83] Fourteen Greek Orthodox versions have been recorded in Coptic churches in Egypt, with further examples in Cyprus (1), Tinos (2), Hydra (2), Iraq (4), and Geneva (1).[84] About half of these are probably of eighteenth- or early nineteenth-century date, and so depict the Edicule of 1555. The remainder presumably show the Edicule as rebuilt in 1809–10. Their value as evidence is dependent on their condition, which is often poor, and on the availability of good

Fig. 56. Silver *artophoria* (containers for the Holy Bread) in the form of models of the Edicule. Height 7 cm, length 14.4. Before 1808. See p. 51, no. 9. (Athens, Benaki Museum, Acc. nos TA 321, TA 322)

reproductions, but they comprise a different and independent tradition of representation and therefore deserve consideration.

8. representations are also found on pottery, for example on an eighteenth-century maiolica basin from the workshop of Boselli in Savona, Liguria,[85] now in the museum of the Studium Biblicum Franciscanum, Jerusalem. This piece bears the arms of the Franciscan Custody of the Holy Land, at whose order it was presumably made. Here again there may be others, but such views are probably all derived from printed sources and may therefore have little independent evidential value.

9. silver containers for Holy Bread (ἀρτοφόρια) modelled on the Edicule as it was before 1808 and opening to reveal a cross-wall and a metal plate representing the burial couch (Fig. 56).[86] The overall shape presumably derives from engraved views (see above, no. 5), but the models are of Greek workmanship and come from Kermir in Cappadocia.

(Above left)
Fig. 57. The Edicule, apparently showing the 'Lenten ornaments', wall-painting in the northern narthex of the Theotokos Church, Monastery of Mar Saba, mid-19th century. See p. 52. (Photograph John Crook)

(Above right)
Fig. 58. David Roberts, The Shrine of the Holy Sepulchre, lithograph (Holy Land i (1842), [Pl. 10]), after an original drawing in pencil and watercolour dated 'April 18th 1839'. See p. 52.

THE EDICULE FROM 1809–10 TO THE PRESENT DAY

This Edicule survives today, but the visual sources for its appearance in the nineteenth century are still important both for the information they provide for

its original appearance and ornaments and for the problems in the use of visual sources which they reveal. It is not necessary to list these sources here, but the advent of photography should be noted. The first daguerreotypes were taken in Jerusalem in December 1839. Photographs of the outside of the Church of the Holy Sepulchre were taken as early as 1850,[87] but the earliest photographs of the Edicule at present known to me, by definition interior views, were taken by Zangaki in the 1870s or just after (Fig. 59).[88]

A nineteenth-century painting in the south-east corner of the northern narthex of the Theotokos Church in the Monastery of Mar Saba shows the immense quantity of lamps and other ornaments used to dress the outside of the Edicule (Fig. 57).[89] Drawings and photographs show these 'Lenten ornaments' whose use by all three communities was discontinued in 1920 lest their combined weight, which was said to be over 7,000 lb, should bring down the outer cladding of the structure then already bulging badly outwards.[90] These illustrations also reveal the painted decoration of the cupola, now smoke-blackened and almost indecipherable, and the use of a pair of great painted cloths rigged over the east face and Entry of the Edicule to keep off the rain which came through the oculus of the dome of the Rotunda. This remained open to the sky until provided with a cover when the dome was rebuilt in 1868 (see below, p. 108).

These cloths are a feature of David Roberts's lithograph of the Edicule from the east, based on a drawing he made on 18 April 1839 (Fig. 58).[91] This is certainly the best-known nineteenth-century view of the Edicule, being at first sight both the most competent and by far the most convincing. Yet it is also extraordinarily inaccurate in almost all the details of its architecture. Roberts's view provides a cautionary note on which to end this survey of the visual evidence for the form and decoration of earlier Edicules.

CHAPTER 3

THE TOMB AND THE EDICULE FROM THE BEGINNINGS TO THE DESTRUCTION OF 1009

The structural sequence of the tomb is conventionally divided into six distinct periods (Figs 64 and 66):

1. The construction and 'use' of the original rock-cut tomb until buried under the fill of Hadrian's works in 135
2. The tomb buried under Hadrian's works from 135 until uncovered in 325/6
3. The Edicule created by Constantine around the tomb, until its virtual destruction by the Caliph al-Hakim in 1009
4. The Edicule as rebuilt in the early eleventh century, embellished by the Crusaders, and later stripped and in decay, with only minimal repair, until its rebuilding in 1555
5. The Edicule as rebuilt 'from the first foundations' by Boniface of Ragusa in 1555, until it was damaged by fire in 1808
6. The Edicule as rebuilt by the Greek architect Komnenos in 1809–10, which survives today.

The sections which follow deal with each of these stages, setting out the principal problems of interpretation and indicating the changes in the fabric of the Edicule. Special attention is given to the evidence for the rock-cut tomb, both that which is described in the Gospels and that which was discovered in 325/6 and is still at least in part preserved within the Edicule (see also below, pp. 109–19).[1]

THE TOMB OF CHRIST IN THE GOSPELS AND LATER

For the original tomb in which Joseph of Arimathea laid Jesus's body on the evening of the day of crucifixion in 30 or less likely 33[2] we have the direct evidence only of the Gospels. It is probable that none of the writers witnessed the events of that day and no surprise therefore that the accounts they provide are not entirely consistent. The texts of the Synoptic Gospels (Matthew, Mark and Luke) describe the crucifixion and burial in broadly similar terms, but John is more detailed, not least about the tomb itself.

The accounts are quite short: Matthew (Mt) 43 verses (27.32 to 28.8); Mark (Mk) 36 verses (15.20 to 16.8); Luke (Lk) 41 verses (23.26 to 24.10, and 24.22–4); and John (J) 44 verses (19.17 to 20.18). The evidence they provide for the location and nature of the tomb may be summarized as follows.

Jesus was taken out (Mt, Mk, J) [i.e. of the gate of the city, cf. Hebrews 13.12,13] to a/the place called Golgotha, which means the place of a/the skull, where they crucified him (all Gospels). Multitudes stood by watching (Lk), or passed by and derided him (Mt, Mk), and many read the title over his head, 'for the place . . . was near the city' (J). A rich (Mt) member of the council (Mk, Lk), Joseph of Arimathea (all Gospels), took away his body (J). In the place where he was crucified there was a garden and in the garden (J) a tomb (Mk), a new tomb (Mt, J), where no one had ever been laid (Lk, J). In this, Joseph's own new tomb (Mt) which he had hewn out of rock (Mt, Mk, Lk), he/they (Mt, Mk, Lk/ J) laid Jesus (all Gospels). And Joseph rolled a stone to/against the door of the tomb (Mt, Mk).

[The next morning] the women (Lk), the two Marys and Salome (Mt, Mk), went to the tomb (all Gospels). They found the stone rolled away (Mk, Lk, J). It was very large (Mk). An angel [had] rolled back the stone and sat upon it (Mt).

[Peter and another disciple came out (i.e. of the city)] and went toward the tomb (J). Reaching the tomb first, the other disciple stooped to look in (J). Peter and the disciple went into the tomb (J), and then went back to their homes (J) [i.e into the city].

Mary stood outside and stooped to look into the tomb (J) and saw two angels sitting where the body of Jesus had lain, one at the head and one at the foot (J). The [three] women entered the tomb (Mk, Lk) and saw a young man sitting on the right side (Mk), *or* two men stood by them (Lk). The women went out (Mk) and departed (Mt) and returning from the tomb told this to the apostles (Lk).

The essential 'facts' seem to be these. The tomb was outside the city in a cultivated area (κῆπος 'garden'), and was in the place, i.e. presumably not far from the place, of crucifixion. It was the tomb of a rich man, previously unused, new-cut in the rock and closed by a large stone which could be rolled to or against, i.e. across, the door. To look into the tomb, it was necessary to stoop, suggesting a low door. Within there was room for at least five persons, two of whom might be sitting. On the right-hand side it was possible to sit where the body of Jesus had lain.

These few 'facts' are about as much as can be extracted from the Gospel accounts. They can only be interpreted in the light of existing knowledge of contemporary Jewish burial practice in the Jerusalem area and, for logical reasons, must *not* be explained in terms of the possible form of the tomb inside the present Edicule (see above, p. 15). What is clear is that the kind of tomb suggested by the Gospel accounts *is* consistent with what is now known of contemporary practice in the Jerusalem area: i.e. a rock-cut tomb, a low entrance closed by a moveable stone, and a raised burial couch within. The difficulty is perhaps that such a tomb is too simple: burial couches on more than one side, long narrow rectangular niches or loculi (*kokhim*) in which a body might be inserted at right-angles to the walls of the tomb, and multiple chambers are commonplace. The absence of such features may be due to the sparseness of the Gospel accounts: they may not be mentioned because irrelevant, but that does not mean they were not there. In a new tomb, however, they are not perhaps to be expected. It was only with time that additions were needed, and the more complex Jerusalem tombs are clearly the product of successive generations.[3]

The burial couch implied on the right-hand side has usually been taken to mean that there were an arcosolium – a shelf cut in the rock wall below a shallow arch (see below, pp. 110–13).[4] But if there were more than one bench, it is unnecessary to postulate an arcosolium (or arcosolia) rather than burial benches of the usual kind ranged along the walls. It may even be possible to suggest that the reference to the right-hand side might be taken as implying that there were benches on more than one side, since otherwise there would be no need to be specific. We cannot be certain, therefore, of the precise kind of tomb implied by the Gospel accounts, but the few details we have are entirely consistent with what we now know of contemporary tombs.

The traditional interpretation of the tomb as having a single arcosolium on the right-hand side and a rolling stone smoothly dressed and of almost mechanical perfection[5] is heavily influenced by the supposed form of the tomb discovered in 325/6 and now located beneath the Rotunda. At least one tomb chamber apparently similar to this view of the tomb implied by the Gospel accounts has been reported in the Hinnom Valley, immediately south of Jerusalem (pp. 102, 114). But if we limit ourselves strictly to what can be derived from the Gospel accounts, a wider range of possibilities emerges, with a correspondingly wider range of parallels readily available in the contemporary rock-cut tombs of the Jerusalem area.

The only other possible references to the place of crucifixion in the period before 135 are in the Epistle to the Hebrews and perhaps in Revelation. The Epistle to the Hebrews was certainly written before 96, possibly before 70, and conceivably before 64. The direct statement in 13.12 that Jesus 'died outside the city' may be independent of the Gospel accounts as we have them, although the author was not himself among those who had heard Jesus (2.3). The verse is in any case the only explicit statement of what has otherwise to be inferred from the Gospels, even from John 19.20. The possible reference in Revelation 11.8 is discussed below, p. 64.

Although there has been no lack of surmise, nothing whatever is known of the later history of the Tomb of the Gospels in the period down to 135.[6] Adjacent tombs[7] were presumably emptied[8] when the occupied area of the city was extended northwards in 41–4 (Fig. 60B; see below, p. 58). But whether or how this expansion, or the wars and sieges of 66–70 and 132–5, affected the tomb is quite unknown.

The foundation of Colonia Aelia Capitolina by Hadrian in 130/1,[9] on the ruins of the city destroyed in 70, brought major changes to the area. But here we have a logical difficulty. The evidence for Hadrian's works relates to the tomb discovered in 325/6, the tomb which lies today beneath the Rotunda of the Holy Sepulchre. The view that this tomb is the same as that described in the Gospels depends upon Eusebius' assumption that they were one and the same (see below, p. 66). Everything learnt about the site by modern archaeological and topographical investigation shows that this could be the case, but there is no proof. In describing here the effect of Hadrian's works upon the site, it has to be clear that we are talking of their effect on the site of the tomb now located beneath the Rotunda and not necessarily therefore upon the tomb described in the Gospels.

There is a further difficulty. The sources for the effect of Hadrian's works on the tomb are not contemporary with Hadrian. They relate to the moment nearly two hundred years later when the tomb as we have it was revealed by the removal of Hadrian's works. They impute to Hadrian a desire to conceal and supplant the sites of the crucifixion and burial of Jesus which is more likely to reflect fourth-century assumptions about pagan attitudes to Christianity than second-century reality. Eusebius (260/5–339) was nevertheless a contemporary observer of Hadrian's buildings as they still existed in the 320s, of their removal and of what was revealed beneath them, and as such is a witness of outstanding importance. When his account of contemporary events disagrees with information given by Jerome (c. 347/419–20), who had not been born at the time of Constantine's works, Eusebius's version is normally to be preferred.

According to Eusebius's *Life of Constantine*,[10] the whole site had been covered with a great quantity of earth and paved with stone, and on this a temple to Aphrodite had been erected over the 'sacred cave', i.e. the tomb. Jerome adds the information that this situation had lasted about 180 years, from the time of Hadrian to the reign of Constantine (actually about 190 years), but asserts that it was a statue of Jupiter which had stood over the place of Resurrection (i.e. the tomb) and a statue of Venus on the rock of the Cross (*in loco resurrectionis simulacrum Iovis in crucis rupe statua ex marmore Veneris*).[11] By the time Jerome wrote this letter *c.* 395 knowledge of the previous situation seems already to have become confused. This confusion may be due to Eusebius who wrote his *Life of Constantine*, in which the temple is attributed to Aphrodite in 337/9, more than a decade after its demolition. The coins of Aelia Capitolina – by contrast, strictly contemporary evidence – depict neither Venus nor her temple.[12] They show two different temples of Tyche, however,[13] and it seems possible that Eusebius chose to identify one of these with Venus to heighten the supposed defilement of the site. For Jews and Christians, Tyche was a 'bearable' pagan deity who appears on coins of Agrippa II; Aphrodite/Venus was an abomination.[14]

The contribution of archaeology to this enquiry is very limited. There is evidence for the existence of a large building of Roman date on the site now occupied by the Church of the Holy Sepulchre,[15] but it is doubtful if it can be precisely dated or more closely identified, except as a monumental public structure. There is certainly insufficient evidence to establish the former existence of a raised podium, let alone of a temple, on the site of the tomb, were it not for the evidence of Eusebius.[16]

Hadrian's works, whatever their exact nature, are conventionally and reasonably dated to the period after the suppression of the Bar Kokhba Revolt in 135.

This estimate of Hadrian's works and their effect on the site now occupied by the Church of the Holy Sepulchre represents the position reached by the early 1990s. In 1993 a radical new proposal was put forward, the implications of which for the development of the site of the Holy Sepulchre have not yet been thought through. In that year Doron Bar suggested that the Tenth Legion camp had not been on the south-western hill, within the lines of the former First Wall, as shown on Fig. 60C. He argued that the camp had lain instead to the north, within the limits of Aelia, occupying the area between the western wall of the city as it was in AD 70 (the Third Wall), and the line of the Second Wall (Fig. 60B). In terms of the plan of Aelia, this would be the area west of the Roman cardo where many scholars have placed the west forum and the adjacent temple and/or basilica.[17]

Only the implications of this suggestion for the site of the Holy Sepulchre can be considered here. First, the extensive levelling of the area may have been undertaken not in 135 or later for Hadrian's works, but to prepare the site for the legionary fortress in the years after 70. Second, although Hadrian may well have dedicated a temple within the fortress in 130/1, it seems most unlikely that a temple within a military camp would have been dedicated primarily to Aphrodite/Venus: as we have already seen, there are numismatic grounds for questioning such a dedication.[18] Third, following the departure of the Tenth Legion from Jerusalem at the end of the third century (see below, p. 62, n. 44), the site would have been to some extent deserted and free for redevelopment, a context in which the demolition of a major public building, even a temple, is easier to understand.

These implications depend on the proposition that the Tenth Legion camp did lie to the north, within Aelia, like the military camps at Bostra, Dura Europos and Palmyra.[19] They carry with them the further implication that the information given by Eusebius and Jerome about the site of the Holy Sepulchre has to be carefully controlled. This is not perhaps surprising, for Eusebius wrote his *Life of*

Opposite:
*Fig. 60. The topography
of Jerusalem: A, before
c. AD 41–4; B, AD 41–4 to
AD 70; C, in the Roman
period, c. 135–c. 325;
D, in the Byzantine period,
4th–7th century AD. After
Stern ed. 1993, ii, maps on
pp. 718, 758, and 769,
with modifications.
(Drawn by Steven Ashley)*

Constantine two centuries after the foundation of Aelia, and Jerome added his comments sixty years later still. Their record of contemporary events demands respect; their statements about the distant past are another matter entirely.

What Eusebius has to say about the excavations and what was revealed may be broadly correct, even if economical. His attribution of the demolished temple to Aphrodite may be open to question, even if it is likely that he had seen the building before it was removed. But Eusebius says nothing about Hadrian. It is Jerome, even further removed in time, when the site had been changed out of recognition by Constantine's new buildings, who provides the additional information that the temple was built by Hadrian. Jerome gets the time elapsed slightly wrong. He also says that it was a statue of Jupiter which stood over the tomb, rather than a temple to Aphrodite, and adds that a statue of Venus had stood on the rock of the Cross (see above, p. 56). We do not know what Jerome's sources were, and the discrepancies suggest that either they or his use of them was muddled. There seems little to rely upon in what Jerome says on this matter, if other and contemporary sources, whether written, numismatic or archaeological, point in a different direction.

It is too early yet to reach any firm conclusions on the implications of this new view of the location of the Tenth Legion camp. The need, above all, is for secure archaeological information from the north-western part of the Old City, the Christian Quarter.

THE EDICULE BETWEEN 135 AND 325

The Gospels imply that the crucifixion and burial of Jesus took place outside the city walls. When Bishop Makarios of Jerusalem sought the burial place in 325/6, he excavated a site within the walled city and located a tomb that he and others accepted as the burial place of Christ, and which has ever since been the focal point of the Church of the Holy Sepulchre in its successive forms (see below, p. 65). We now know that there is no real conflict in the two accounts. Although no part of the Second Wall has yet been identified with certainty, all scholars seem agreed that Kenyon's Site C and Lux's excavations under the Redeemer Church provide good evidence that the area of the Church of the Holy Sepulchre was outside the city until the construction of the Third Wall by Herod Agrippa in AD 41–4 (Fig. 60A and B).[20] The traditional sites of the crucifixion and burial have remained within the city ever since.

We have no specific record of why Makarios chose this spot. It has usually been assumed that he was relying on a tradition preserved within the Christian community in Jerusalem.[21] And it has sometimes been argued that his choice, apparently in stark opposition to the Gospel account, is a powerful argument in favour of the survival of precise topographical knowledge of the location of the sites of the crucifixion and burial since their disappearance beneath Hadrian's structures in 135. Parrot, for example, declares 'C'est donc bien que la tradition était contraignante et que c'était *là* et *non ailleurs*' ('The tradition was compelling: it was *there* and *nowhere else*').[22]

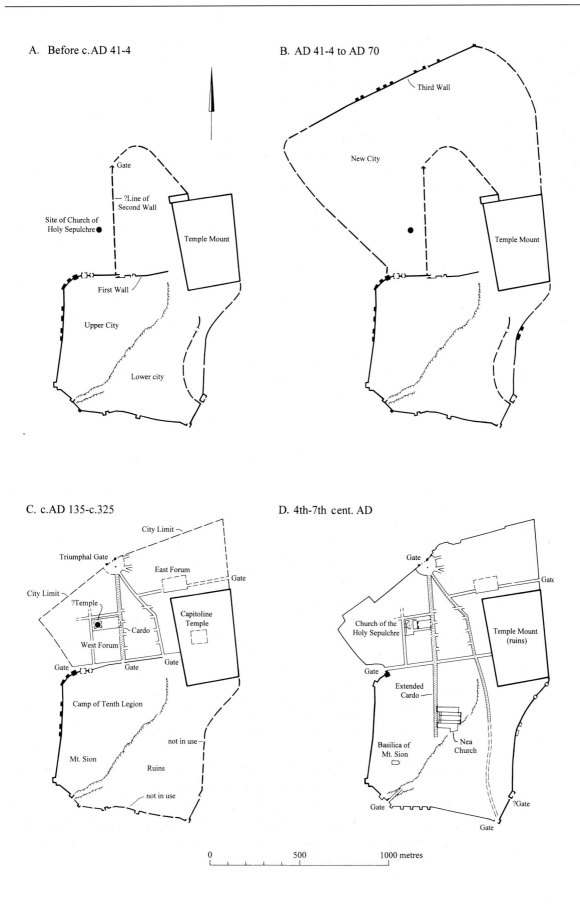

A. Before c. AD 41-4

Gate

?Line of Second Wall

Site of Church of Holy Sepulchre ●

First Wall

Temple Mount

Upper City

Lower city

B. AD 41-4 to AD 70

Third Wall

New City

Temple Mount

C. c. AD 135-c. 325

City Limit

Triumphal Gate

East Forum

Gate

City Limit

?Temple

Cardo

Capitoline Temple

West Forum

Gate

Gate

Gate

Camp of Tenth Legion

not in use

Mt. Sion

Ruins

not in use

D. 4th-7th cent. AD

Gate

Gate

Church of the Holy Sepulchre

Temple Mount (ruins)

Gate

Extended Cardo

Basilica of Mt. Sion

Nea Church

Gate

?Gate

Gate

0   500   1000 metres

In the years between 135 and 325/6 there are two contemporary witnesses to the existence of knowledge of the site of the crucifixion, the sermon *Peri Pascha*[23] by Melito of Sardis who died towards the end of the second century, to the significance of which in this context Canon A.E. Harvey was the first to draw attention,[24] and the *Onomastikon* of Eusebius, written probably before the close of the third century.

The text of *Peri Pascha*, a dramatic work of Greek rhetoric possibly composed between 160 and 170, survives essentially intact, with versions of varying completeness in Coptic and Georgian, fragments in Syriac, and a Latin epitome.[25]

The sermon begins after the reading of the Passover narrative of Exodus 12 and shows how that text is to be seen in the light of Christ, the true Passover lamb, the Jewish festival becoming the Christian Easter. In the second half of the sermon, after describing the death of Jesus as the slaughter of the paschal lamb, Melito asks, 'And where has he been murdered?', and replies, 'In the middle of Jerusalem'.[26] Two hundred lines further on Melito repeats his charge three times:

> you killed your Lord in the middle of Jerusalem.

> Listen, all you families of the nations, and see!
> An unprecedented murder has occurred in the middle of
>   Jerusalem,
>   in the city of the law,
>   in the city of the Hebrews,
>   in the city of the prophets,
>   in the city accounted just.
> And who has been murdered? Who is the murderer?
> I am ashamed to say and I am obliged to tell.
> For if the murder had occurred at night,
>   or if he had been slain in a desert place,
>   one might have had recourse to silence.
> But now, in the middle of the street and in the middle of
>   the city,
>   at the middle of the day for all to see,
>   has occurred a just man's unjust murder.[27]

In the first three of these four statements[28] the Greek wording is identical, ἐν μέσῳ Ἰερουσαλήμ with minor variations of no importance in the Georgian and Syriac versions. The fourth statement is in different words (for variants see below):

> νῦν δὲ ἐπὶ μέσης πλατείας καὶ ἐν μέσῳ πόλεως.[29]

The critical points are two: Melito's emphasis on placing the site of the crucifixion in the middle of Jerusalem and his use of the word πλατεῖα. Melito's choice of site can probably be explained only by the assumption that he had learnt that the site was *then* believed to be in the middle of the city (possibly echoing Revelation 11.8: see further below, p. 64). Melito went to the East at some point in his life to investigate the canon of the Old Testament and it may have been in the course of this journey that he obtained information about the site of the crucifixion.[30] But we do not know whether the sermon was written before or after this journey, nor if he visited Jerusalem, and so we cannot be sure whether he obtained his information on the spot or at second hand. Melito must in any case have known that the Gospel of St John, which he certainly uses, placed the execution near to, i.e. outside, the city (19.20), and that the other Gospels implied this, and that there was therefore a conflict between these accounts and the site he chose to emphasize. His choice heightened the drama of his sermon: we must beware of applying a modern preference for topographical scholarship. What mattered then and now is that in Melito's day the site was apparently pointed out in the middle of the city.

Melito's words in Line 704 may suggest a more precise location, even though the text of this line is somewhat corrupt. The Greek manuscripts (Hall's Sigla A and B) seem to imply the phrase ἐπὶ μέσης πλατείας and this appears at first sight to mean 'in the middle of the street', but the meaning of the word πλατεῖα, which occurs only here in *Peri Pascha*, deserves closer inspection. This noun is really the feminine of the adjective πλατύς, 'broad, wide', with ὁδός, 'road' to be supplied,[31] hence 'wide street, highway'. This seems to have been its normal meaning in Hellenistic and Roman times.[32] Eusebius uses the word to refer to the colonnaded cardo immediately east of the Church of the Holy Sepulchre,[33] but on occasion, as in the Septuagint text of Nehemiah 8.16, πλατεῖα appears also to mean 'open place, plaza, square', as can the corresponding Hebrew feminine noun,[34] and as does πλατεῖα in Modern Greek. The corresponding Latin word appears sometimes to have this meaning. An inscription of AD 151, strictly contemporary with Melito, records the paving of a 'platea', apparently the open space or 'piazza' just outside the south gate of Timgad in Numidia in North Africa. An earlier inscription, of the reign of Domitian (81–96), from the East, from Antioch in Pisidia in Asia Minor, seems to name the open space in front of the propylea leading to the principal temple 'The Square of Tiberius' (*Tiberia platea*).[35] Three possible interpretations must therefore be considered in establishing Melito's meaning.

If the phrase was originally in the plural, ἐν μέσαις πλατείαις, as the Coptic, Georgian and Syriac (S²) versions may suggest,[36] the meaning is presumably a general one, 'in the middle of the streets', and simply reinforces the second half of the line: 'in the middle of the streets and in the middle of the city'.

If the phrase was in the singular, as the surviving Greek MSS suggest, the straightforward translation 'in the middle of the street' has no obvious meaning, unless, as Canon Anthony Harvey has suggested to me, πλατεῖα is here a street name, like the 'street called Straight' (Acts 9.11), possibly with reference to the cardo, the north-south street of Aelia (Fig. 60C). In Melito's time this would be the northern half of the line shown on the Madaba Map, for the southern extension of the Roman cardo was not laid until the time of Justinian (527–65) (Fig. 60D).[37] But, unless Revelation 11.8 can be taken this way (see below, p. 64), there is no other specific tradition that Jesus was crucified in or by a street, even if it seems likely that the route from the gate by which he left the city did pass close by the site of the cross (see above, p. 54). Are we to suppose that by Melito's time some spot literally in the middle of a street was pointed out as the site of the crucifixion?

A simpler view is that Melito is using πλατεῖα to mean 'open place, plaza, square' rather than 'street' in the strict sense, and is reflecting a rather precise tradition that in his time the site of the crucifixion was believed to lie in the centre of an open space in the middle of Aelia Capitolina. If so, Melito may here reflect the Jerusalem tradition which guided the search undertaken on Constantine's orders a hundred and fifty years later, for it was in the area of a temple within or adjacent to what may have been a public open space that Bishop Makarios excavated in 325/6. πλατεῖα might here apply to the open space of the temple temenos,[38] but we are not told, and Melito was unlikely in the context of a sermon to refer to the presence of a pagan temple.

When Melito wrote in the second half of the second century, possibly in 160/70, only a generation had passed since Hadrian's works had changed for all time the topography of the area in the angle between the First and Second Walls (Fig. 60B, cf. Fig. 60C). Assuming that these works were Hadrian's, rather than those required by the construction of the Tenth Legion camp after 70 (see above, pp. 57–8), a number of people still alive will have remembered the broad outlines of the vanished landscape now covered by the immense dumps required to level the site (Fig. 61).[39] They may have found it difficult to recall precisely where within the new complex the earlier landmarks had lain, but they may have remembered something of their nomenclature. A complex train of argument and textual emendation led Vincent[40] and Simons[41] to the suggestion that the land in the angle of the First and Second Walls was known in the time of Nehemiah (3.8, 8.16), in the second half of the fifth century BC, as 'The Square'. Avigad's discoveries from 1969 onwards in the Jewish Quarter[42] have confirmed the 'maximalist' topography of Vincent and Simons, although so large an area was never occupied in the time of Nehemiah. Whether or not Vincent and Simons are correct, the Septuagint translation uses the word πλατεῖα for what in the Vincent-Simons argument would be this spot. The topographical issues are difficult and contentious, but the suggestion raises the possibility, no more, that Melito, who would have known the Septuagint text of Nehemiah, as well as its ancient Jewish form as a single text with Ezra,[43] in using πλατεῖα reflects not only the open space of his day but a much earlier Jerusalem description, perhaps even a place-name.

Towards the end of the period between 135 and 325/6 there is a second contemporary witness to the survival of knowledge of the place where Christ was crucified. In his description of the discoveries of 325/6 and of Constantine's buildings Eusebius failed to mention Golgotha, but in his *Onomastikon*, probably compiled in the 290s,[44] he placed Golgotha 'in Aelia, to the north of Mt Sion':

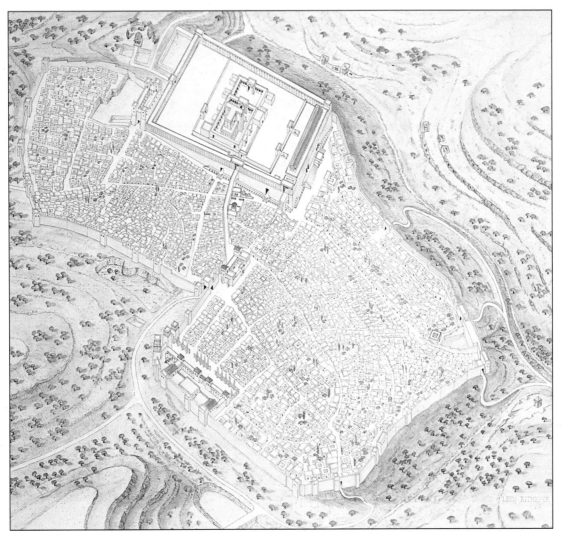

Γολγοθά «κρανίου τόπος», ἔνθα ὁ Χριστὸς ἐσταυρώθη. ὅς καὶ δείκνυται ἐν Αἰλίᾳ πρὸς τοῖς βορείοις τοῦ Σιὼν ὄρους.[45]

Golgotha, 'place of a skull', where the Christ was crucified, which is pointed out in Aelia to the north of Mount Sion.

This use of Aelia rather than Jerusalem has no particular significance,[46] but a location 'in Aelia', rather than 'outside' or even, as seen from Mt Sion, 'beyond' Aelia, is certainly significant. Eusebius described a site as being in the suburbs of Aelia when he wanted to.[47] Thus, his location of Golgotha 'in Aelia to the north of Mt Sion' appears to reflect a continuation of the tradition explicit in Melito. This is even more striking because Eusebius used here, as repeatedly elsewhere, the word δείκυται, 'is shown', 'is pointed out', with the clear implication that there was something to be seen.[48] Jerome's translation of Eusebius's entry on Golgotha seems to confirm this:

Golgotha locus Caluariae, in quo saluator pro salute omnium crucifixus est.

Fig. 61. Reconstruction of Jerusalem in the time of Christ, bird's-eye view looking north-east (cf. the air photograph, Fig. 2). The re-entrant to the left shows the area outside the First and Second Walls as it may have been in the period before AD 41–4. Although inevitably conjectural in parts, this reconstruction helps in following the discussion on p. 62. It does not show the Third Wall of AD 41–4, nor attempt to indicate what development if any may have taken place between the Third and Second Walls in the period between AD 41–4 and the destruction of the city in AD 70. (Drawn by Leen Ritmeyer)

et usque hodie ostenditur in Aelia ad septentrionalem plagam montis Sion.[49]

Golgotha, place of Calvary [*i.e.* skull], in which the saviour for the salvation of all was crucified. And up to this day it is shown in Aelia to the north [*literally*, on the north side] of Mount Sion.

By the time Jerome wrote Golgotha had indeed, in the eyes of contemporaries, been revealed. What there was to see of the rock of Golgotha before 325/6 is a question which cannot now be resolved. In his elegant reconstruction of the Roman temple constructed over the tomb Dan Bahat has shown how the summit of the rock could have been visible in the court of the temple;[51] but this can be no more than reasonable surmise.

It has recently been suggested that Eusebius's words mean that Golgotha was 'in Aelia near the northern parts of Mount Zion', and that it 'would be stretching "the northern parts of Mount Zion" rather far to assume that Eusebius is referring to the site of the temple of Venus'.[52] On this is built a whole new theory that Constantine shifted the traditional location of Golgotha northwards to the site of the temple.[53] This will not do. The Greek (and Jerome's Latin) means 'north of Mt Sion' and no more.[54] Moreover, in the late third century, a location 'in Aelia' probably still carried a specific meaning, i.e. within the Roman colony, and was thus clear to the north of the north slopes of Mt Sion (Fig. 60C). In 333 the Bordeaux pilgrim had to leave Jerusalem to climb Sion,[55] and in the later fourth century the church on Sion still lay outside the perimeter of Aelia, to the south.[56] Third, the theory implies that a location previously pointed out (δείκνυται) was moved in the actual construction of the very building intended in part to mark its spot, although authenticity of place, not least of Golgotha, was a key element in, for example, the Jerusalem rite of baptism.[57]

The site chosen for the excavations of 325/6 remains, however, the decisive evidence for the survival of knowledge of the site of the crucifixion as a topographical location (Eusebius) as distinct from a rhetorical device (Melito).

There remains to be considered one other possible reference to this tradition. In Revelation 11.8 the bodies of the two witnesses 'will lie in the street of the great city which is allegorically called Sodom and Egypt, where their Lord was crucified'. While it is clear that Jerusalem here 'is not simply the literal Jerusalem, any more than Babylon is simply Rome', and that 'the interpretation of the entire passage must be symbolic',[58] the earthly Jerusalem is nevertheless identified with the great city, and the choice of words is precise, to the extent that the word used is πλατεῖα, as in Melito.[59] If the text has not been adjusted at this point to conform to the situation after 135, the phrase appears to take the tradition of the location of the site back to the time in the late first century when Revelation was written, when the site of the crucifixion already lay within the Third Wall erected in 41–4, and before the construction of the cardo. Melito quotes from Revelation elsewhere in *Peri Pascha*,[60] but we cannot assume that in his references to the crucifixion he was influenced by the text of Revelation rather than by independent evidence of the same tradition.

THE EDICULE BETWEEN 325/6 AND 1009

Eusebius's account of the discovery of the tomb in the course of excavations undertaken following the Council of Nicaea in 325 and his description of Constantine's church, the Martyrion, with its associated structures have been the subject of many detailed discussions over the last century and a half (Figs 62, 63A).[61] In recent years discussion has focused on the curious fact of Eusebius's apparent failure to mention Golgotha or the finding of the True Cross, and upon the contrasts between his writings and those of Cyril.[62] These studies have gone far to clarify the silences, hidden meanings and changes in focus of Eusebius's words as he distilled his thought in the *Theophany* (shortly after 324)[63] and addressed in turn the congregation at the dedication of the Holy Sepulchre (17 September 335),[64] the emperor on his thirtieth jubilee in Constantinople (25 July 336)[65] and posterity.[66] In the context of the tomb, we have three limited themes to pursue: why its discovery was a surprise, what was found, and what was done.

Makarios, bishop of Jerusalem (314–33), may have taken the leading role, asking the emperor in person at Nicaea in June/July 325 for 'permission to destroy the temple of Venus in the quest for the tomb of Christ'.[67] Once the fill covering the site had been removed, the cave, ἄντρον, i.e. the tomb, immediately appeared, παρ' ἐλπίδα πᾶσαν, 'contrary to all expectation', 'altogether unhoped for', 'against all hope'.[68] This phrase has given rise to some discussion,[69] but should probably be taken at face value. The landmark, because in some way visible and able to be pointed out, was Golgotha (above, p. 63). Neither Eusebius in the *Onomastikon* nor Melito in *Peri Pascha* mentions the tomb, but the Gospels make it clear that the places of crucifixion and burial were not far apart (above, p. 54). Nevertheless, the tomb had not been seen for nearly two hundred years and Makarios and Eusebius can have had little reason to suppose that it would really have survived and be found. In exactly the same way, government officials faced with the discovery of the Rose Theatre in London in 1989, demolished three centuries earlier, admitted that they had not expected to find anything, although they knew that it was the right site. Makarios dug more in hope than expectation and was, to Eusebius's surprise, proved 'right'.

What was found? Eusebius and Cyril (bishop of Jerusalem, *c.* 351–86) provide but a very few details. Eusebius says only that what was found was a cave (ἄντρον); he says nothing else about its appearance as first seen. It is Cyril, who may himself as a boy have seen the cave when first uncovered,[70] who provides in his *Catechetical Lectures*, delivered in 348 or 350, a few more details. There was originally an outer hollowed-out rock (προσκέπασμα, σκέπη, literally, a covering in front of, a shelter) before the entrance to the sepulchre, but this had been cut away to make room for the imperial adornment.[71] This hollowed-out place in front of the tomb was presumably an open and unroofed or partly unroofed forecourt or ante-chamber cut in the rock face (Fig. 64A). It is a feature often seen in Jewish tombs of the period before 70[72] and Cyril himself adds that it was usual in front of tombs in the area (ἐνταῦθα). When Cyril spoke, the stone that

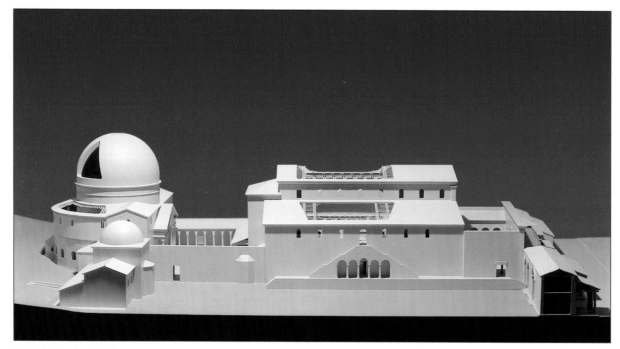

Fig.. 62. Constantine's
Church of the Holy
Sepulchre, as dedicated
335, with the Rotunda of
the Anastasis (the
Resurrection) as completed
in the later 4th century,
looking north. Model by
the late H.R. Allen on the
basis of working drawings
by Sheila Gibson, 1987.
(Tower of David Museum,
Jerusalem)

had closed the tomb was still lying before the entrance.[73] Cyril also asserts that traces of the garden in which the tomb originally lay could still[?] be seen.[74] This may mean that patches of soil which had once been cultivated were visible near the tomb. Such areas of cultivated soil are often seen even today among the rock-cut tombs around Jerusalem, and the clean soil would have been readily distinguishable from the overlying fill of the temple podium.

Eusebius hailed the cave thus uncovered as 'the august and all-holy monument (μαρτύριον, literally 'proof', 'testimony') of our Saviour's Resurrection'.[75] He gave no reasons for this confident assertion. Was it obvious that this was the tomb of the Gospels and if so how? Many answers might be suggested, but there is no way of knowing which if any are true. Some scholars have thought that it was because, among a number of tombs uncovered (see above, p. 56, n. 7), this one appeared to conform to the type of tomb implied by the Gospels and, being close to the rock identified as Golgotha, was at once accepted as the authentic tomb. This might be so, and the assumption need not be wrong. But there could have been more. During the period from the crucifixion down to 135 the tomb probably remained accessible and – more particularly before 70 – could have been marked in some way, possibly with cut or painted graffiti which were legible in 325/6 and left no doubt in the minds of those (for Eusebius was not the only one, and perhaps not the first) who made the identification. Graffiti are the earliest evidence for the identification of the tomb of Peter in the Vatican cemetery.[76] The possibility of their presence on the remains of the tomb in Jerusalem must be high among the points to be examined when the remaining elements of the rock-cut structure are uncovered in any forthcoming restoration of the Edicule.

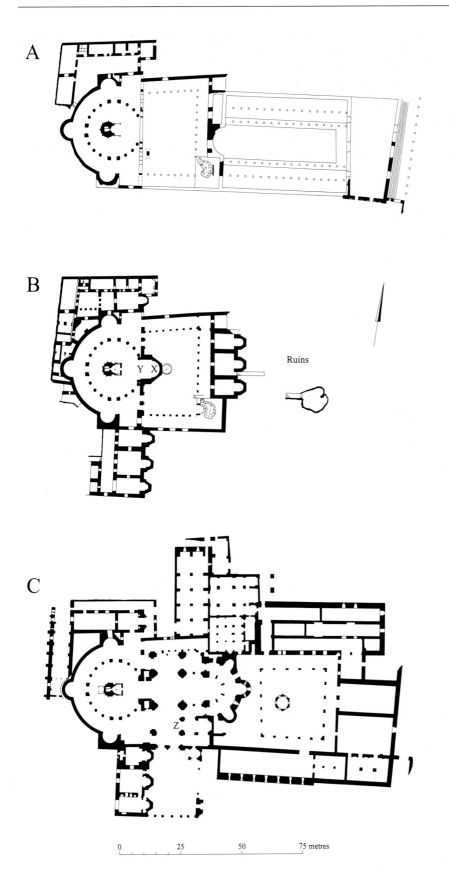

A

B

Ruins

Y X

C

Z

0   25   50   75 metres

Fig. 63. The structural
development of the Church
of the Holy Sepulchre:
A, Constantine's
Martyrium, the Court
before the Cross, and the
Edicule, as dedicated 335,
with the Rotunda of the
Anastasis (the Resurrection)
as completed in the later
4th century; B, as rebuilt in
the 11th century and
completed by Michael IV
Paphlagon c. 1040
(X marks the supposed
position of the Genoese
Golden Inscription of 1105,
Y the supposed position of
the inscription Praepotens
Genuensium Praesidium);
C, as reconstructed by
the Crusaders in the
12th century and
completed by 1167/9
(Z marks the position of the
inscription recording the
consecration of the Calvary
chapels in 1149). (After
Corbo 1981; Ousterhout
1989, 1990a; and Clapham
1921; with modifications.
Drawn by Steven Ashley)

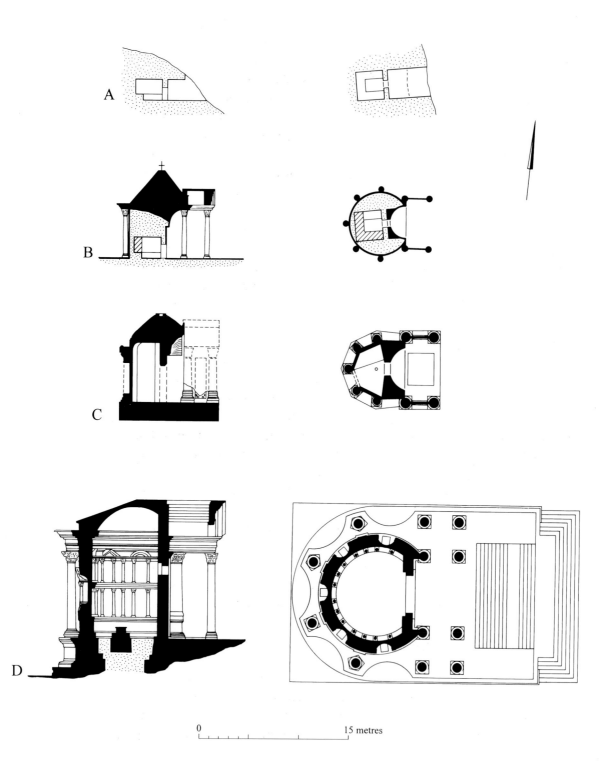

0   15 metres

Fig. 64. The creation of Constantine's Edicule (left, sections; right, plans). A, the rock-cut tomb, a new reconstruction; B, Constantine's Edicule erected around and over the tomb freed from the surrounding rock; C, the Narbonne model enlarged to the same scale (cf. Fig. 16); D, the Round Temple at Baalbek to the same scale (see p. 69, n. 82). The hatched areas in the section and plan at B indicate masonry which may have been inserted to fill in parts of the original tomb when Constantine's Edicule was constructed (see p. 118). (C, after Lauffray 1962; D, after Krencker 1923. Drawn by Steven Ashley)

What was done to the tomb thus discovered? Writing shortly after the discovery in 325/6, Eusebius recorded his astonishment that it was then possible to see the rock containing the tomb 'standing erect and alone in a level land, and having only one cavern within it'.[77] Cyril describes (above, p. 65) how the ante-chamber of the tomb had been cut away in the course of the works. From these accounts we can see how the ground (which was sloping down to the east, as we know from observations of the rock surface below the Rotunda floor[78]) had been cut back, leaving only the rock actually containing the burial chamber to rise as an isolated block from a level surface. This now free-standing feature Constantine 'embellished with choice columns and an abundance of ornament, making the venerable cave gleam with shining decorations'.[79]

There have been several attempts to establish the form and appearance of the Edicule constructed by Constantine to enclose the rock-cut Tomb Chamber thus released from the surrounding rock. The sources are many and varied (see above, pp. 21–8) and Dr John Wilkinson has set out his resulting reconstruction in both drawings and a model.[80] A slightly different, architecturally more canonical, version has been drawn by Terry Ball for Père Coüasnon,[81] and a new attempt drawn by Steven Ashley for the present project appears in Figs 64 and 66.

In essence, the Edicule consisted of two parts (Fig. 64B). In front was a porch of four columns with a pediment and a gabled roof. Behind was the Tomb Chamber, freed on all sides from the living rock, rounded or polygonal outside, covered with marble, decorated by five columns with semi-detached bases and capitals, and surmounted by a conical roof of tapering panels, topped with a cross. These elements correspond to the descriptions of pilgrims and to the various contemporary representations (see above, pp. 21–8). They seem also to be reflected in the Narbonne model (Fig. 64C; see above, p. 22 and Figs 16 and 76), although as noted there is reason to believe that this may be a relatively crude and architecturally uncanonical version of a structure which in the original must have been a work of highest quality.[82]

Our purpose here is to follow the major events in the subsequent life of this and successive Edicules down to 1809–10, and in particular to examine the question of how much of the original rock-cut Tomb Chamber enclosed in Constantine's Edicule may survive, for this is a key question in planning any investigation which may take place when the restoration of the present Edicule is undertaken.

It may, however, be worthwhile to consider briefly the question of the authenticity of the tomb uncovered in 325/6. It can certainly be regarded as a Jewish tomb of the Second Temple period, but is it the tomb in which Jesus was buried? The position is well put by an Israeli scholar, the former City Archaeologist of Jerusalem, Dan Bahat:

We may not be absolutely certain that the site of the Holy Sepulchre Church is the site of Jesus' burial, but we certainly have no other site that can lay a claim nearly as weighty, and we really have no reason to reject the authenticity of the site.[83]

Since the heated debates of the nineteenth century, controversy about the authenticity of the site has played little part in serious academic discussion. Increasing knowledge of the topography and archaeology of the north-western quarter of Jerusalem and of the site of the Holy Sepulchre Church in particular, although still very inadequate in both content and quality, has raised no serious obstacle to acceptance of the authenticity of the site (Fig. 60).

Recently, however, there have been two new suggestions. The first is that Constantine, wishing to destroy the pagan temple and to replace it with a new Christian temple in honour of the 'saving sign', the cross, relocated the site of Golgotha to the north, proof of his choice being 'clinched when an empty tomb was discovered and heralded as being that belonging to Christ'.[84] As we have already seen (above, p. 64), this suggestion relies upon a misreading of Eusebius's entry on Golgotha in the *Onomastikon*. The assumption that the site of Golgotha, still pointed out in the late third century, could be moved and yet retain public acceptance, betrays a profound misconception of the importance of traditional location in the organization of sacred space.[85]

The second suggestion builds on the first. 'As in Rome, Antioch, and perhaps Constantinople, Constantine's first ecclesiastical construction in Aelia was to be a cathedral.' A site was selected, several buildings including a temple were demolished, and

> only in the course of leveling the area . . . was the rock-cut tomb . . . serendipitously revealed . . . and immediately identified as the locus of Jesus' entombment and resurrection. What was initially begun as an episcopal complex became, in addition, a great martyrium'.[86]

Basing herself on Taylor's thesis, dismissing Bahat and others 'who have been tempted to argue that the site was identified by local tradition' as 'rationalist apologists', omitting to mention Melito and Eusebius's *Onomastikon*, Wharton proposes 'a less historically improbable reading'.[87] In doing so she warns readers to take more seriously Eusebius's own acknowledgement that the site of the Passion 'had remained unknown for a long series of years'. But these are in fact Constantine's words in his letter to Makarios as quoted by Eusebius,[88] and the subject of the sentence is not the site of the Passion but τὸ γνώρισμα, identified by some as the wood of the cross itself, a famous *crux criticorum*.[89] The Greek does not say this was unknown, but that it was long hidden (ὑπὸ τῆ γῆ πάλαι κρυπτόμενον τοσαύταις ἐτῶν περιόδοις λαθεῖν).[90] There is nothing here to contradict Dan Bahat's balanced assessment of the probable authenticity of the site.[91]

The rock-cut chamber enclosed by Constantine's Edicule seems to have survived entire until 1009. There is no evidence that his Edicule did not also survive, but it can scarcely have remained unscathed. The roof of the Rotunda was burnt by the Persians in 614[92] and again by rioters in 966,[93] and had been damaged by an earthquake early in the ninth century.[94] But we have no certain knowledge either of any damage done to the Edicule or of any repairs which may have been required.

The descriptions of the Edicule given by pilgrims during the period down to 1009[95] thus probably reflect in all essentials (if not in the detail of ornaments) the Edicule created by Constantine.[96] Some doubt has arisen, however, from the words used by Willibald, as reported by Hugeburc, to describe the basic shape of the tomb as he saw it at the end of 724:

> Illa sepulchra fuerat in petra excisa, et ille petra stat super terram et est quadrans in imo et in summo subtilis; et stat nunc in summitate illius sepulchri crux.[97]

> The tomb had been cut out of the rock. And that rock stands above the ground, and it is square *in imo* and slender above. And there stands now on top of the tomb a cross.

The problem lies in the words *est quadrans in imo*. First, since the subject of *est* is unclear, the phrase might describe the tomb or the rock, i.e. the inside or the outside of the monument. Second, what does *in imo* mean? This has given great difficulty. Many commentators have taken the phrase as a whole to mean that the exterior of the Edicule as Willibald saw it was square below.[98] And this view has led some to argue either that the lower part of the Edicule was always square outside;[99] or that its plan was modified at some stage, perhaps after the Persian attack of 614;[100] or that *quadrans* can mean polygonal.[101] Lauffray, by contrast, refused to believe that the Edicule was ever square externally, preferring to take the phrase to refer to the portico alone or to a rectangular plinth at ground level.[102]

As long ago as 1849 Willis took the phrase to have a quite different meaning, noting crisply that *quadrans in imo* 'refers to the square form of the chamber within' (Fig. 14).[103] There can be no doubt that Willis was right. Indeed, the Tomb Chamber is still today *quadrans in imo*. Not only does this reading avoid all the difficulties, but *in imo* occurs again in this meaning in Adomnán's description of the placing of the lamps over the burial-couch (see below, p. 111).

It might be argued that the elegant chiasmus, *quadrans in imo et in summo subtilis*, with the deliberate contrast of *in imo* and *in summo*, demands the translation 'square below and slender above'. If this view were to prevail, it still does not necessarily imply that the 'square below' was external, even if that seems the obvious meaning. Further evidence is provided by comparing the Narbonne model of the ?fifth century (Figs 16 and 76) with Adomnán's description of the Edicule *c.* 683 as *rotundum*, and Bernhard's *IX columnas in circuitu sui* of *c.* 870.[104] All three deal with the exterior of the same structure: it is hardly likely that it can have been rebuilt as a square some time between *c.* 673 and 724 and rebuilt again before *c.* 870 in the form it apparently had in the fifth century. If Willibald's description refers to the interior it does not contradict them.

There is thus no need to assume a change in the basic shape of the Edicule between the late seventh and the late ninth centuries, and no need to suppose that the form of the Edicule built by Constantine did not survive unchanged until 1009.

The churches of Jerusalem were untouched by the Arab conquest of the city early in 638,[105] but were not so fortunate in 1009.[106] In that year the Fatimid Caliph of Egypt, al-Hakim bi-Amr Allah (996–1021) ordered Yaruk, governor of Ramla, 'to demolish the church of the Resurrection and to remove its (Christian) symbols, and to get rid of all traces and remembrance of it'. Yaruk's son and two associates 'seized all the furnishings that were there, and knocked the church down to its foundations, except for what was impossible to destroy and difficult to grub up to take away'. Al-Husayn ibn Zahir al-Wazzan 'worked hard to destroy the tomb and to remove every trace of it, and did in actual fact hew and root up the greater part of it'.[107]

It has not previously been realized that Adémar of Chabannes, writing at Angoulême in 1028/9, preserves what seems to be an eye-witness western account of this destruction.[108] Raoul de Couhé, bishop of Périgueux, reported (*retulit*) on his return from Jerusalem in 1010 *que viderat ibi nefanda*, 'the abominable things he had seen there'.[109] These *nefanda* can only refer to the destruction of the church and tomb in September 1009 described by Adémar in the previous chapter. This contains a rather precise description of the attack on the tomb:

> lapidem monumenti cum nullatenus possent comminuere, ignem copiosum superadiciunt, sed quasi adamans immobilis mansit et solidus.[110]

> when they were unable by any means to reduce the tomb [*monumentum*] to rubble, they also tried a great fire, but it remained like adamant, immovable and intact.

Although the last clause may contain an echo of Virgil (cf. *Aeneid* vi, 552), and is in any case an exaggeration, the use of heat to split and reduce the limestone from which the original tomb was hewn provides a circumstantial detail which would have been practical, and may have left traces of reddening to be observed when the Edicule receives its now inevitable restoration.

Rodulfus Glaber provides a second, and independent, western account of the destruction, perhaps derived from Ulric, bishop of Orléans (1021–35), who was at Jerusalem in 1025/8 (probably 1027) and *quid uiderit nobisque narrauerit, non pretermittendum uidetur miraculum*, 'told us what he had seen, not omitting the miracle [of the Holy Fire]'.[111] According to Glaber, al-Hakim's agents used iron hammers to try to break up the hollow structure of the tomb (*concauum sepulchri tumulum ferri tuditibus quassare temptantes*), but failed (*minime valuerunt*).

Although the reference to 'iron hammers' is perhaps a gloss – what else would have been used? – the general tenor of the remark is clear. These three independent accounts, preserved independently by Yahya, Adémar, and Glaber, are consistent, whether they derive from Muslim officials, Christian Arab sources, or western clerics: the rock-cut tomb was not completely destroyed. Some part, perhaps much, survived.

Constantine's church of the Martyrion (Figs 62, 63A, cf. Fig. 63B) was almost totally destroyed, never to be rebuilt, but even of this church the eastern wall and doorways still stand in part to a height of 4.6 m.[113] The outer wall of the Rotunda of the Anastasis survived to over twice this height, 'almost right round the whole edifice', 'all round the Rotunda', to the underside of the internal and external cornices.[114] The roof and the interior of the Rotunda with its columns and piers were brought down, the rubble itself probably encumbering and thus protecting the lower parts of the outer walls: these were thus, it seems, 'impossible to destroy'. To some extent this rubble may also have protected the lower parts of the Edicule and rock-cut tomb within. Here, as Yahya reports, ibn Zahir destroyed 'the greater part', leaving the implication that he did not destroy all, whether of the rock or of Constantine's enclosing Edicule. As a comparison of the descriptions made before and after 1009 shows[115] the rock-cut roof and much, perhaps all, of the west and east walls were removed, but the south wall and the burial couch survived, and possibly part of the north wall, in so far as this did not form part of the north side of the burial couch itself. The way in which the western half of the medieval Edicule reflected what we now believe to be the form of Constantine's Edicule also suggests that there was something left from which to start again.[116] Only detailed investigation and record when restoration is undertaken will perhaps show just how much did survive al-Hakim's attack.'

CHAPTER 4

THE BYZANTINES AND THE HOLY SEPULCHRE IN THE ELEVENTH CENTURY

The 547 years of the medieval Edicule are both the least known and the best documented in its history. The sources are rich and varied (above, pp. 28–40), but have never been subject to the same detailed analysis as those for Constantine's Edicule, and do not include any one source as detailed as the Narbonne model for the earlier or Amico's drawings for the later Edicule. To complicate matters, the medieval Edicule went through a series of changes during these five and half centuries which appear to have modified significantly its form and appearance. The currently accepted account of the history of the rebuilding of the Church of the Holy Sepulchre following the destruction of 1009 provides an even greater difficulty, and to that we must turn first before dealing with the Edicule.

REBUILDING THE CHURCH

As early as 1012, only three years after its destruction, the Christians of Jerusalem were able to begin repairing and rebuilding the church of the Resurrection. The work was done initially by the order or at the invitation of the Bedouin Emir Al-Mufarrij ibn al-Djarrah who had seized Ramla and made himself for the moment master of Palestine. Ibn al-Djarrah supported the work, restoring several parts of the church 'dans la mesure de ses moyens et de ses forces'.[1] In 1014, five years after the destruction of the church (*post quinquennium euersionis templi*), al-Hakim's mother Maria, a Christian whose brother Orestes had been Patriarch of Jerusalem (984–1005), began 'to rebuild with well-dressed squared stones the Temple of Christ destroyed by her son's order' (*reedificare Christi templum, iussu eius filii euersum, politis et quadris lapidibus*).[2]

The Christian rites were, however, still subject to harassment. In November/December 1020, at the request of Patriarch Nikephoros I of Jerusalem

(1020–36), whom he had just appointed, al-Hakim ordered that the Christian liturgies should be allowed to be celebrated without hindrance 'in the enclosure of the church known as the Quyâmah [the Resurrection] and on its ruins'.[3] In 1023, two years after al-Hakim's death, Nikephoros went to Constantinople on the instruction of late caliph's sister, Sitt al-Mulk, to report to Basil II (976–1025) on the restoration and rebuilding of the Church of the Holy Sepulchre and the other churches in Egypt, Palestine and Syria, and to begin negotiations for the renewal of trade between Egypt and Byzantium. Sitt al-Mulk's death interrupted the discussions and Nikephoros returned to Palestine in April or May 1024.[4] His report to Basil may be taken to mark the completion of a significant stage in the rebuilding of the Holy Sepulchre: the work had apparently lasted some ten years, from 1012 to 1023.

Western evidence for this first stage of the rebuilding, like that for the destruction itself, can be shown (as we shall see) to derive from first-hand sources, principally from returning pilgrims and a Greek monk who came with them.

The volte-face by the Caliph al-Hakim, the very man responsible for ordering the destruction of the Church of the Holy Sepulchre, was known in the West at the latest by 1027 when the Angoulême pilgrims who formed part of the great pilgrimage which left for Jerusalem in the autumn of 1026 and attended the ceremony of the Holy Fire at Easter 1027, returned home. The pilgrims included William IV Taillefer, count of Angoulême, and several members of Adémar of Chabannes' monastery of St Cybard: Abbot Richard (who died on the outward journey at Selymbria [Silivri] on the Propontis), Giraldus Fanesin, his lay advisor, and Amalfredus who was made abbot on their return in June 1027.[5]

They brought back with them a Greek monk of Sinai, Symeon, who for political reasons travelled by a different route. Symeon reached Angoulême at about the same time and stayed there over the winter of 1027–8 before moving on to Rouen, and then in 1028–30 going on pilgrimage to Jerusalem with Archbishop Poppo of Trier.[6] Symeon is almost certainly the source, as Robert Lee Wolff has shown, of Adémar's information about the murder of the emperor Nikephoros Phocas (969), about al-Hakim's supposed abortive attack on the Monastery of Mt Sinai (c. 1012), about Basil II's campaigns against the Bulgarians (1001–18) and about the Norman invasion of Apulia and their defeat at Cannae (1018).[7]

Symeon had served for seven years as a guide for pilgrims in Jerusalem, perhaps in c. 1012–18, before becoming a monk first at Bethlehem and then at Mt Sinai. Later he was sent as a messenger from the monastery of Mt Sinai to Duke Richard of Normandy, and it was on this journey that he met the pilgrims of 1027 at Antioch.[8]

Symeon is thus the obvious person to have told Adémar what had happened at Jerusalem after the destruction of 1009, and to have drawn a comparison between the Church of the Holy Sepulchre before and after the event.[9] Adémar wrote:

[Rex Babilonius] . . . jussit reaedificari basilicam sepulchri gloriosi. Tamen redincepta basilica, non fuit amplius similis priori nec pulchritudine nec magnitudine . . .

[The king of Babylon: i.e al-Hakim of Cairo] . . . ordered the basilica of the Holy Sepulchre to be rebuilt, and the work was begun, but it was not comparable to its predecessor in either beauty or size . . .[10]

Pilgrimage to the Holy Sepulchre seems indeed to have begun again after only a very short break following the destruction of 1009. As we have seen, Symeon appears to have been a pilgrim guide there from *c.* 1012–18; the Irish St Coloman died *en route* at Stockerau near Vienna in 1012;[11] Adalgerius, a future abbot of Conques, made the journey before 1019;[12] and Giraud, Audebert's successor, was beheaded *in via Sancti Sepulcri* in 1022.[13]

These early journeys and the later mass pilgrimages of 1026–7 and 1035, at which pilgrims are known to have attended the ceremony of the Holy Fire, demonstrate that the church and the tomb had been put back into liturgical order within a few years of 1009. At Easter 1027 Richard, abbot of Saint-Vanne at Verdun, saw the Fire appear in a single lamp at the tomb.[14] At some time between 1025 and 1028, probably at this same Easter of 1027, Ulric, bishop of Orléans, saw the Fire appear in one of the seven lamps hanging at the tomb, as he told Rodulfus Glaber. Ulric bought this lamp and its oil from a certain Jordanus, supposedly patriarch of Jerusalem, for a pound of gold, and took it back with him to Orléans.[15] Hugh of Flavigny's long account of Abbot Richard's participation throughout the liturgies of that Holy Week is remarkable for the normality of its context: his description, especially of the events surrounding the Holy Fire, might have been written of any Holy Week down to modern times (cf. Fig. 103).[16]

An analysis of forty-eight pilgrimages known to have taken place in the 160 years between 940 and 1099 shows no obvious interruption after 1009 which cannot be explained by the Byzantine closure of the route for three years in 1017–18,[17] or by the difficulties in the Mediterranean which led by 1026–7, and even before, to the opening of a land route via Hungary.[18]

Jerusalem Pilgrimages by Decade, 940–1099[19]

940–9	One	1020–9	Five (2 large)
950–9	One	1030–9	Three (1 large)
960–9	One	1040–9	Two
970–9	One	1050–9	Seven (1 large)
980–9	Two	1060–9	One (1 large)
990–9	Three	1070–9	Two
1000–9	Nine	1080–9	Three
1010–19	Three	1090–9	Four

These repeated pilgrimages, the numbers and rank of those involved,[20] the many donations they made for restoring the House of God (*domui Dei restaurande plurima detulerunt munera*),[21] for example the pound of gold given by Ulric of Orléans, and the even more remarkable hundred pounds of gold said to have been sent by Duke Richard II of Normandy *Hierosolimam . . . ad sepulchrum Saluatoris*,[22] all suggest that the reconstruction of the Holy Sepulchre from 1012 onwards cannot have been negligible.

The ritual of the Holy Fire required at least the removal of al-Hakim's rubble from the remains of the rock-cut tomb. The hanging of lamps over the tomb suggests a ceiling or at least an enclosure with high walls from which to suspend them. There can be little doubt that the Edicule was in fact actually rebuilt at this time. It was not a large structure and the site was full of stone ready to hand from the demolition of 1009. But could the Rotunda of the Anastasis, the church of the Resurrection itself, have been reroofed? As we have already seen, the outer walls of the Rotunda survived to a height of 11 m or more (see above, p. 73). Clearly, the rubble must have been cleared away to uncover the level floor on which processions could move; temporary roofs could have been erected around the inside of the Rotunda, supported by the surviving or re-erected columns and piers of the ambulatory. This, with the rebuilt Edicule, would have been sufficient for both the daily and the special liturgies. It is possible, however, that much more was done, that the Rotunda and its roof were rebuilt, together with some of the other buildings, as perhaps Yahya suggests when he describes the work begun by Ibn al-Djarrah in 1012. The use of squared stone in the work begun by Maria, al-Hakim's mother, in 1014 and the years which elapsed before her daughter, al-Hakim's sister, ordered Patriarch Nikephoros to report to the emperor at Constantinople in 1023, suggest a major undertaking. It should be regarded as the substantive first phase of the post-Hakim reconstruction.

The evidence reviewed here means that the nature and extent of the works said to have been carried out by the Byzantine Emperor Constantine IX Monomachos (1042–55) must be reassessed (Figs 63B, 65). These works can no longer be regarded as the definitive reconstruction following the events of 1009. They are at most the second phase of an operation which began in 1012, thirty years before.

More or less normal relations between Byzantium and the Fatimids were apparently re-established in 1027,[23] but it was not until 1037–8 that there was a formal agreement between the emperor Michael IV the Paphlagonian (1034–41) and the caliph al-Mustansir (1036–94).[24] One of the conditions was that the church of the Resurrection should be rebuilt at the emperor's expense. Syriac and Arabic sources record that workmen and 'a vast quantity of silver and gold' were sent, but they differ in assigning the treaty to the years AH 427 (5 November 1035 to 24 October 1036) or AH 429 (14 October 1037 to 2 October 1038).[25]

It is, however, usually asserted that most of the assistance came in the time of the emperor Constantine IX Monomachos (1042–55), and that the work was completed in 1048.[26] Whenever the source of this view can be traced, it appears to be based on William of Tyre.[27] But William was born *c.* 1130 and was only writing from *c.* 1165 onwards, more than a century after the event. He appears not to have known Greek or Arabic, and himself noted that for these periods he was 'informed solely by traditions' (*solis traditionibus instructa*).[28] Internal evidence also shows that William's account has to be regarded with caution, not least because his date of 1048 is based on inconsistent indications (fifty-one years before the 'liberation' of the city, i.e. 1048, and thirty-seven years after the destruction of the church, i.e. 1046). Moreover, he makes Constantine (1042–55) the successor of Romanos (III, 1028–34), omitting Michael IV, Zoe, and Michael V, and appears to attribute (and has been taken by all writers to be attributing) the work to patriarch Nikephoros (1020–36) while dating its completion to 1048.[29] He does not in fact quite say this, but rather that Nikephoros was patriarch when a mission to Constantinople was successful in obtaining the emperor's support for the rebuilding. Only after this did '*they* [my emphasis] build the church of the Holy Resurrection which is now in Jerusalem' (*eam que nunc Ierosolimis est Sancte Resurrectionis edificaverunt ecclesiam*). It appears in fact that Nikephoros did send a mission to Constantinople towards the end of the reign of the caliph al-Zahir (died 1036), and that an agreement was subsequently made between the emperor Michael IV and the caliph al-Mustansir, as noted above, in 1037–8, hence William of Tyre's reference to Nikephoros who appears to have died before the mission's final success. If this is correct, the second phase of the eleventh-century rebuilding began *c.* 1037/8 in the reign of Michael IV. How long did it continue and of what did it consist?

There is only one almost contemporary Byzantine historian who mentions the rebuilding of the Holy Sepulchre and whose work survives. John Skylitzes lived in the second half of the eleventh century and his *Chronicle* goes down to 1057. Skylitzes recorded that the emperor Romanos III (1028–34), 'getting in touch with him [i.e. the caliph al-Zahir (1021–36)], strove eagerly to take the rebuilding [of the Church of the Holy Sepulchre] in hand; but his death intervened and his successor completed the work [i.e. Michael IV (1034–41)].' Skylitzes has nothing to say about the church in his chapter on Constantine IX Monomachos.[30]

Skylitzes' account is entirely consistent with the only other independent early witness, Yahya ibn Sa'id of Antioch, who died *c.* 1066 and whose *History* survives down to 1027. Yahya, a Melchite, was an 'astute well-placed' Christian Arab observer.[31] Towards the end of his *History* he describes how Romanos III treated with al-Zahir for the conclusion of peace, the first condition being that the emperor should rebuild the church at his own expense, that he should appoint a patriarch to Jerusalem and that the Christians should rebuild all the destroyed churches on Fatimid territory. In exchange, Romanos offered to release Muslim prisoners.[32] Negotiations were interrupted by the death of Romanos in 1034, but Yahya notes that they recommenced under his successor Michael IV and lasted three-and-a-half years. He will, he writes, describe the clauses of the treaty under the year concerned, but the account of this year is not preserved in any of Yahya's surviving manuscripts. Delayed by Romanos' death in 1034 and al-Zahir's in 1036, the treaty was only finally concluded between Michael IV and the new caliph al-Mustansir in 1037/8.

The Byzantine historians of the next generations either copy Skylitzes,[33] or say nothing about the Holy Sepulchre.[34] Chroniclers who wrote later still seem to be repeating a different version in which Michael IV begins and completes the negotiations and undertook the work: none attributes the rebuilding to Constantine IX.[35]

Why then did William of Tyre say that it was done by Constantine? Was he informed by one of those *traditiones* to which he refers in his Prologue (see above, p. 78), perhaps derived from an inscription or a mosaic in the church? If so, no trace of it has come down to us. It seems more likely that he was relying on the dates he was told. The Crusaders frequently used the year *from* their liberation of Jerusalem in 1099 as a means of dating: the dedication of part of the Church of the Holy Sepulchre in 1149 was recorded in an inscription as having taken place on the fiftieth anniversary of the capture of the city.[36] A dating clause 'before the liberation' seems to reflect this usage. The rebuilding, William wrote, was fifty-one years *before* the liberation, i.e. 1048. If the date was, for example, sixty-one years before (LXI instead of LI), or 1038, it would agree with the evidence of the sources nearest in date to the event, and would be twenty-nine (XXIX) not (as William had it) thirty-seven (XXXVII) years after the destruction. One can play endless games with the corruption of Roman numerals, but it is clear that the scope for error is considerable.

Whatever actually happened, it is most probably here that the solution lies. William was given a date, or a count back from 1099, which corresponded to a year or years which he knew fell in the reign of Constantine IX Monomachos, and he assumed that this meant that Constantine was responsible for the rebuilding. The earlier sources should now be accepted, both their positive witness in favour of Michael IV as the emperor who completed the reconstruction of the Church of the Holy Sepulchre, and their common silence on the role of Constantine IX Monomachos.

If the reconstruction was indeed complete before the death of Michael IV in 1041, it explains how it was that the Persian traveller Nasir-i-Khusrau, a strictly contemporary witness, saw the church in the spring of 1047 in what sounds like its fully restored state: 'a most spacious building . . . capable of containing eight thousand persons . . . built, with the utmost skill, of coloured marbles, with ornamentation and sculptures, inside . . . everywhere adorned with Byzantine brocade, worked in gold with pictures . . . There are also pictures [i.e. mosaics] of the Prophets.'[37] The evidence of Nasir-i-Khusrau supports the view that the church was already fully restored before the traditional date of 1048 (Fig. 65).

It is more difficult to establish in detail what was done in this second phase of the work, but it is significant that while the first phase (1012–23) was local in inspiration, the second (*c.* 1037–8 to *c.* 1040) was Byzantine and imperial. This distinction may reflect precisely what Professor Robert Ousterhout identified in his study of Constantine Monomachos and the Holy Sepulchre: 'two teams of masons . . . two workshops [which] operated independently for the most part . . . each group of masons built in the technique and materials with which it was

Fig. 65. The Byzantine Church of the Holy Sepulchre as rebuilt in the 11th century and completed by Michael IV Paphlagon c. 1040. X marks the supposed position of the Genoese Golden Inscription of 1105; Y the supposed position of the inscription Praepotens Genuensium Praesdium. (Enlarged from Fig. 63B; drawn by Steven Ashley)

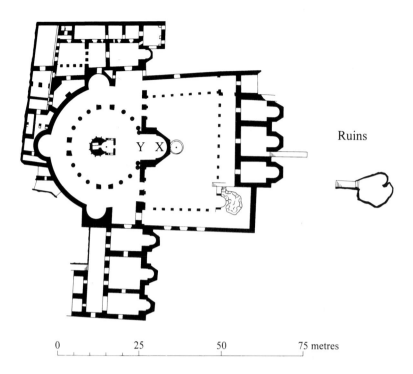

Ruins

```
0              25              50              75 metres
```

most familiar'.[38] Professor Ousterhout saw these teams as working contemporaneously, 'under the direction of a head architect from Constantinople'. It is now the question whether a new analysis will in fact allow their work to be seen as two successive structural phases.

It may be that this is not the answer, and that the two teams were indeed contemporaneous, in which case another solution or solutions will have to be sought, for unless the works of 1012–23 were swept entirely away, remains of them must survive to be identified in the present structure.

The works of the second structural phase may of course have consisted essentially in the decoration with mosaic and sculpture of buildings already reconstructed in the first phase, including the Rotunda, or they may have included the reroofing of the Rotunda (a difficult technical task) as well as its subsequent decoration. A further possibility is that the projecting bema and apse were added to the east side of the Rotunda in this second phase (Fig. 65).

In a recent review of the evidence of eleventh- and early twelfth-century western writers Dr John France has drawn attention to the 'surprising paucity of references to the destruction of the Holy Sepulchre in 1009'.[39] It was, he suggests, 'an event which had passed out of human memory by the time of the First Crusade'.[40] Explanations for this silence might be sought in the poor communications of the age, in the lack of a sense of 'western Christendom' and in a feeling that Jerusalem did not occupy 'a high place in the minds of the men of that time', that it was 'a distant and sacred place, but not one which concerned many people for most of the time'.[41] 'It would now seem appropriate', he concluded, 'to start to reconsider the place of Jerusalem in contemporary piety and, therefore, its influence upon the calling of the First Crusade.'[42]

The structural history of the Church of the Holy Sepulchre in the eleventh century may suggest an alternative explanation. Rebuilding started within three years of the destruction. The Rotunda, much of which survived, and the site of the tomb were quickly put into some sort of order. Pilgrims were arriving again almost at once. Within eighteen years at the very most the ceremonies of Easter Week, including the descent of the Holy Fire, were celebrated as before. True, Constantine's great basilica, the Martyrium, had gone, never to be rebuilt, but the places that had always been the goal of pilgrims, Golgotha and the Life-giving Tomb, were readily accessible (Fig. 65).

This seems a more likely explanation for the silence of western writers about the destruction of 1009. Some of the damage had been made good within a few years, and throughout the rest of the century pilgrims flocked to Jerusalem as never before. The event of 1009 was not mentioned, not because it had passed out of memory, nor because men did not care, but rather because architectural history was not relevant. It seems difficult to find in this any evidence that Jerusalem loomed less in contemporary piety, or that its influence on the calling of the First Crusade was less than has been supposed. The primary objective of the crusade, however much debased in the event, was 'To deliver Christ's tomb'.[43]

THE BYZANTINE EDICULE

This reconsideration of the darkest period in the architectural history of the Holy Sepulchre has brought us directly back to the Edicule itself. The splendour of the Rotunda as Nasir saw it in 1047 must imply that the Edicule (which he does not mention, perhaps for religious reasons) was by then fully reconstructed. It probably had been by 1027. As Wilkinson observes, the Christians in the Holy Sepulchre 'required a monument with the same structural characteristics as before . . . to carry out their daily liturgy', and this 'surely resulted in a structural continuity'.[44] If we add to this the very short space of time, possibly no more than three years, which may have elapsed between the destruction of 1009 and the restoration of some sort of order in the period 1012–23, and the certainty that at least the lower part and thus the plan of the tomb survived in the rock, there can be no surprise that the form and functional elements, if not the decoration, of the Constantinian monument were reflected in the Byzantine Edicule (Fig. 66A, B). This was the Edicule the Crusaders found when they first entered the Church of the Holy Sepulchre in the evening of 15 July 1099.

To understand what was done in rebuilding the Edicule in the eleventh century it is necessary to make use of sources from the period after 1099. This means taking care to distinguish the Byzantine work from what the Crusaders did to the Edicule after 1099.

Like its Constantinian predecessor, the eleventh-century Edicule comprised two principal elements: a rounded western structure enclosing the burial chamber and a narrower rectangular eastern compartment providing the entry to the tomb (Fig. 66B). Four elements forming part both of the present Edicule of

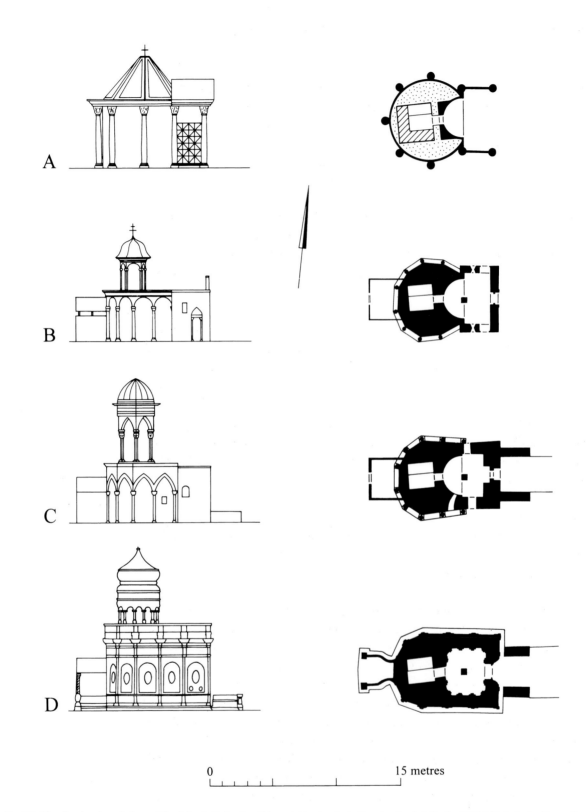

Fig. 66. The structural evolution of the Edicule (left, elevations; right, plans). A, Constantine's Edicule, 325/6-335; B, the Byzantine and medieval Edicule, c. 1012–40 with later modifications; C, the Edicule rebuilt 1555; D, the Edicule rebuilt 1809–10. For the hatched area in the plan at A, see the caption to Fig. 64. For B and C, see p. 88. (Drawn by Steven Ashley)

1809–10 and of the Edicule of 1555 appear for the first time in connection with this medieval monument:

1. an enclosed eastern compartment (now the Chapel of the Angel), fully integrated with the rounded western structure
2. a cupola carried on pillars and set on top of the western structure, over the burial chamber
3. a chapel attached to the west end of the Edicule, now the Coptic Chapel
4. benches flanking the entry in front of the door of the Edicule.

The cupola (2) and western chapel (3) are first recorded in the twelfth century. The benches (4) are shown in the views of Reuwich (drawn 1483), Baumgartner (1498), van Scorel (drawn 1520) and von Borculo (1538) (see above, p. 37, nos 3 and 4, Figs 32, 34, 36–8), but the date they were first installed is not yet known.

The evolution of the eastern compartment (1) is more difficult to follow. The compartment derives from the open vestibule covered by a gabled roof supported on four columns forming the front of Constantine's Edicule (Figs 64B and 66A). The spaces between the columns to north and south were closed by low railings, and the space to the east by a double gate. The vestibule was thus a railed porch and in no sense a walled structure.

Daniel the Abbot said of this compartment in 1106/8 that there were 'three doors in the chamber, cunningly fashioned like a grille[?], and through these doors come the people to the tomb of the Lord'.[45] Sixty years later, c. 1170, John of Würzburg wrote

the square place before the tomb is a porch with two gates. Through one the people are sent in who are going into the monument and the tomb, and the other is an exit for the people to leave. In this porch are the guards of the Sepulchre. There is a small door towards the choir.[46]

The guards were thus in the porch, controlling the people coming in through the north gate, visiting the tomb and leaving through the south gate, as Theoderic writing at the same time (1164/74) makes clear.[47] All three writers mention the stone on which the angel sat and John of Würzburg and Theoderic note that it was inside the porch. Theoderic also records that the three doors were three feet wide and seven feet high and that the north and south walls (and perhaps, by implication, the east wall as well) were 'little' (parvi parietes). These descriptions suggest that the eastern compartment was still relatively open. It was nevertheless substantial enough to carry mosaics. The west wall was apsidal and covered by a conch, as in the Constantinian Edicule (Figs 64B, 66A) and in the Narbonne Model (Figs 16 and 76, cf. Fig. 64C). Over the low entrance to the Tomb Chamber there was a mosaic showing the entombment and the angel with the three Marys at the empty tomb. Over the lintel of the door an inscription ran round the apse.[48] Theoderic adds that this whole small room, which was too cramped to hold more than twelve people, was decorated with the same very delicate mosaic. Thus the porch, while still seeming relatively open, was apparently solid enough to carry mosaic work on the interior faces of its three outer walls, 'little walls', as Theoderic called them, each containing a door seven feet high.

The basic form of the eastern compartment with its three doors was thus in being by 1106/8 (Daniel) and by c. 1170 it was elaborately decorated on the interior with mosaics. It is the plan of the Edicule at this stage in its development which was copied full-size(?) at Eichstätt c. 1160 (Fig. 28); see above, p. 31, and below, pp. 97, 113).[49] According to Wilkinson, who gives no source,[50] the two side doors were walled up by the Muslims after the surrender of the city in 1187. Yet the north door, or at least its outline, can still be seen in the lower part of the fourteenth-century drawing reproduced in Fig. 39. Whenever exactly the walling-up took place, it turned the porch into the fully enclosed room with a single entrance from the east, the form of which survives in the rebuilding of 1809–10.

The cupola (2) over the Tomb Chamber is mentioned by Daniel in 1106/8. It was supported on pillars and covered with gilded silver plates, and carried on top a silver figure of Christ, larger than life, 'made by the Franks'.[51] The Eichstätt copy of c. 1160 is crowned by a rebuilt version of this cupola, carried on a hexagonal ciborium supported by six columns (Fig. 28).[52] John of Würzburg and Theoderic both mention the cupola, Theoderic recording (by 1174) that it was then topped by a gilded cross on which was a gilded dove.[53] At Augsburg a copy of this cupola built in 1507–8 still survives (Fig. 31).

The chapel (3) attached to the west end of the Edicule is first mentioned in 1102/3.[54] It contained the parochial altar and is described by Theoderic:

> at the head of the tomb towards the west there is an altar surrounded by iron walls [i.e. grilles], doors and locks, with lattice work of cypress decorated with various pictures, and a roof of the same material similarly decorated above the walls. . . . There is a line going round the iron wall containing . . . verses.[55]

This chapel, or a later version of it, appears on Santo Brasca's sketch plan of 1480, on Reuwich's woodcut based on a drawing of 1483, and on Konrad von Grünenberg's drawing of 1487 (Figs 35–7), see above, p. 37, no. 4), and in later views such as Fig. 51. In 1537–9, when the Franciscans were imprisoned in Damascus,[56] the chapel was apparently taken over and perhaps reconstructed by the Copts,[57] and has remained in their possession ever since. The structure of their present chapel (Fig. 67) corresponds so remarkably to Theoderic's description of the chapel in the twelfth century as to suggest that its traditional form and materials were retained when the chapel was rebuilt between 1809–10 and 1818 (see below, p. 105).

The origin of the benches (4) flanking the entrance to the Chapel of the Angel cannot yet be dated. As we have seen (p. 83), they first appear in illustrations of the late fifteenth century. Their function appears to have been to accommodate the guardians controlling entry to the tomb (cf. Fig. 58). Once the north and south doors had been closed, and entry restricted to the single entry to the east, the guardians would have taken post outside this entry rather than inside the Chapel of the Angel, as before (see above, p. 83). The benches were probably therefore installed at some date after the walling-up of the north and south doors of the Edicule and may originally have been provided for the use of the Muslims who held the keys of the Edicule from 1187 until the Franciscans secured them, either in c. 1333–5[58] or a century later.[59]

We can now attempt a tentative outline of the architectural form of the Edicule as rebuilt in the eleventh century (Fig. 66B). Some time before 1106/8 the Tomb Chamber was rebuilt and enclosed in a rounded structure decorated externally with eight columns carrying an arcade of rounded arches. Since the rock-cut roof of the Tomb Chamber had been destroyed by al-Hakim, it was now possible in constructing a domed roof over the tomb to leave an opening for the practical purpose of allowing the smoke of the lamps to escape, and perhaps for the metaphysical purpose of accommodating the descent of the Holy Fire on Easter Saturday (Fig. 39); see below, p. 138).[60] Since, however, the dome of the Rotunda was open at the top, allowing the rain to pour in, the new opening over the Tomb Chamber was covered by building a cupola on a hexagonal ciborium of six columns (or six pairs of columns) to keep the water out. The rectangular eastern compartment was rebuilt as a more substantial structure than before, with 'small' walls rather than columns, and the opportunity was taken to provide gates in the north and south walls, as well as to the east, to regulate the flow of pilgrims – an innovation presumably dictated by experience.

The form of the Edicule as thus rebuilt has survived the reconstructions of 1555 and 1809–10 to a remarkable degree (Fig. 66), but when was the rebuilding carried out? The limiting dates are 1009 and 1106/8.[61] The splendour of the Rotunda as rebuilt by Michael IV Paphlagon and described by Nasir-i-Khusrau in 1047 suggests that the Edicule, the *raison d'être* and focus of the Rotunda, and structurally a much less demanding work, was already complete. It is of course not impossible that the Crusaders had again reconstructed the Edicule between 1099 and 1106/8 when Daniel the Abbot described it, but there is no evidence for this and it seems unlikely: why, if the Crusaders had reconstructed the whole, did Daniel specifically describe the silver figure of Christ on top of the cupola as 'made by the Franks'?

The treatment of the burial couch in the Tomb Chamber was also changed in the initial reconstruction. The upper surface of the rock-cut bench was 'now' covered with marble, and the vertical face protected by a marble slab pierced by three circular holes through which pilgrims could touch and even kiss the rock itself.[62] The reason for this marble cladding was perhaps two-fold: to conceal the damage done by al-Hakim's agents, and to prevent the removal of further pieces of rock by pilgrims. This arrangement of three 'port-holes' was to become almost a symbol of the tomb (Fig. 41); see above, pp. 31, 37–40, nos 1, 5, 7 and 8) and was to be immensely influential in the design of shrines throughout Europe. An exact parallel survives today in the marble slab covering the face of the rock couch in the Tomb of the Virgin in the Kidron Valley, which can probably be dated to the second quarter of the twelfth century.[63]

The date at which the burial couch was first covered with marble and the slab with three 'port-holes' erected against its face is thus a matter of more than local importance: the iconography of a whole class of Russian grave memorials appears, for example, to have been influenced by the image of the three holes,[64] while in the west they continue for centuries to be shown on objects great and small, both on major works of art such as the Cherves (Charante) tabernacle of c. 1225[65] and on items of relatively mass production such as English medieval alabasters of the fifteenth century.[66]

The existence of these late representations of the three holes also raises the question of how long they remained visible on the tomb itself. The holes are never mentioned in descriptions of the sixteenth century and later, but when did they disappear?

The account of the Abbot Daniel who visited Jerusalem in 1106/8 is the earliest certain surviving witness to the existence of the 'port-holes'.[67] Jachintus the Presbyter, whose description perhaps belongs to the late or even middle eleventh century, appears to mention them, but more work needs to be done to establish the date of his visit and to clarify his meaning.[68]

The earliest certain visual evidence for the three holes seems at present to be the reverse of the seal of Warmund (patriarch of Jerusalem, 1118/19 to 1128; see above, p. 39, no. 7).[69] From this time onwards representations multiply, in Crusader art and on Crusader artefacts, and they spread rapidly across Europe (Fig. 41); see above, pp. 31, 37–40).[70]

The three holes are recorded for the last time as still visible in descriptions of the fourteenth century, the latest so far noted being that by Fra Niccolò da Poggibonsi in the spring of 1347.[71] They do not appear, except in a quotation from an earlier source, in Felix Faber's account of his visits in 1480 and 1483: it is clear from his search for any sign of the living rock that there were then no holes giving a view of the rock of the burial couch (see below, p. 114).[72] The reason seems to be that the covering of the couch was remodelled by the Franciscans at some date in the first half of the fifteenth century to make the place more convenient for the celebration of the mass.[73] Previously a removable wooden altar had been used, as it is again today and has been for many years (see below, p. 129).

This remodelling explains why the 'port-holes' do not appear in descriptions of the fifteenth[74] and first half of the sixteenth centuries, or in large-scale copies of the Edicule made at this time.[75] Their non-appearance in the engravings of Bernardino Amico, based on drawings made in 1593/7 (see above, p. 46, no. 4), or in descriptions[76] and on large-scale copies of the second half of the sixteenth century and later,[77] has (when considered at all) been put down to the changes made by Boniface of Ragusa in 1555. It now seems clear that the changes to the cladding of the burial couch were made at least a century earlier.

Fig. 67. The Coptic Chapel built against the west end of the Edicule between 1809–10 and 1818, looking north-east. Cf. Fig. 84 and see p. 105. (Photograph John Crook)

The problem is complicated by a description of the tomb made by an anonymous English pilgrim in 1345, two years before da Poggibonsi.[78] The English account describes (?uniquely at this period) the marble slab forming the top of the burial couch, but says nothing of the treatment of the vertical face. Da Poggibonsi does the reverse, describing the vertical face but not the top. The two accounts are not at variance, they are complementary, but they provide a good example of the problems of interpreting medieval descriptions and the danger of using negative evidence. Putting the two together, the English traveller tells us that in 1345 the tomb was

> decoratum quodam lapide porphirino habente labia per latera, et unam virgulam in medio in eodem lapide sculptam

> 'decorated with a porphyry slab, that had lips on the sides, and in the middle of the slab there was cut a streak',[79]

while da Poggibonsi adds that 'in the front of those slabs of marble of the Sepulchre are three round windows, through which one can see better the Holy Sepulchre'.[80] The English pilgrim's description of the slab over the burial couch tallies so exactly with the slab still there today (Figs 1 and 101) that there can scarcely be any doubt that they are one and the same.[81] But if it is the same slab, what did the Franciscans do in the fifteenth century to change the covering of the burial couch and make it more suitable as a place on which to celebrate mass? Obviously, there is still more to learn from pilgrim descriptions of the later Middle Ages. At present we can only note the problems and accept that one result at least of the Franciscan changes was to remove the vertical slab with three holes, or perhaps to leave it in position and cover it by placing another slab in front.

The 'port-holes' were thus a feature – perhaps the defining feature – of the medieval Edicule, and it seems probable that they disappeared in the later fourteenth or fifteenth century. It is less clear when they were first installed. The obvious moment might be after the destruction of 1009, as part of the Byzantine rebuilding of the earlier eleventh century (see above, pp. 81–5). This may be correct and, if Jachintus really does refer to the 'port-holes' in the late eleventh century, must be correct. But there is another possibility. On the eve of the Crusaders' conquest of Jerusalem in 1099, the Greek patriarch and a Syrian bishop removed at least some of the rock of the burial couch to prevent it falling into Crusader hands.[82] The Crusaders recovered it and swore to protect it, and the cladding of the burial couch could have been renewed as a result of this episode, i.e. between 1099 and the time Daniel saw it in 1106/8.

There remains another and as yet unresolved problem. After 1555, the rectangular front part of the Edicule was narrower externally north–south than the rear component, around which there was an arcade of ten columns (Fig. 66C; cf. Fig. 48). The evidence from before 1555 is conflicting. The copies at Eichstätt and Görlitz (cf. Fig. 32) show the front part wider than the adjacent in-curving section of the rear component (cf. Fig. 66B), but the San Vivaldo copy and some of the drawings show the reverse (Figs 29, 34–5), and others are equivocal (Figs 36–7, 39). Similar problems arise over the number of columns, perhaps only eight rather than ten before 1555 (Fig. 66B). These inconsistencies probably result from the difficulty of drawing a shape so complex as the Edicule. More evidence is needed for a final solution.

CHAPTER 5

THE CRUSADERS AND THE HOLY SEPULCHRE IN THE TWELFTH CENTURY

THE EDICULE

Whatever the Crusaders may have done to the Edicule itself between 1099 and 1106/8 – and it seems they may have done very little – by that date they had erected a silver figure of Christ on top of the cupola. This was later removed, possibly because it was tarnishing under the open dome, and replaced by a gilded cross topped by a gilded dove, both presumably impervious to the weather. The cupola was likewise covered with plates of gilded silver and the flat roof of the Edicule with sheets of gilded copper.

The problem of what exactly the Crusaders did do to the Edicule has been muddled by a suggestion that seems to have begun with Vincent and Abel but has recently received widespread acceptance. Vincent and Abel suggested that the cupola and marble cladding of the Edicule were replaced in a better style in 1119 and that at the same time the interior was decorated with mosaics.[1] In claiming this, they relied upon G. Mariti's *Istoria dello stato presente della città di Gerusalemme* published at Livorno in 1790. Unfortunately, the date 1119 is a mirage and the renovation a myth. Never checked back to their source, but often repeated, Mariti's words were used by Corbo in 1981 to support his view that the Edicule had been 'rifatta completamente dai Crociati nel 1119',[2] and to attribute to this restoration fragments of sculpture found in the 1960s and 1970s.[3] Folda drew attention to Corbo's 'archaeological reconstruction drawings' showing a total change in the ground plan of the Edicule brought about by the supposed works of 1119,[4] and pointed out that most of the sculptures illustrated by Corbo must be dated to the middle or third quarter of the twelfth century, rather than 1119, but he did not question Corbo's basic assumption.[5] The new Grove *Dictionary of Art* also follows Corbo, writing that 'the aedicule of the Holy Sepulchre was completely renovated in 1119' and claiming that 'the Sepulchre itself was enclosed in a sumptuous aedicula, constructed of marble and intricately carved'.[6]

All this is wrong, partly because Vincent and Abel went beyond what Mariti had said, and partly because the reference which Mariti gives in a footnote on p. 142 of his book has been overlooked. This refers to p. 63 of Cherubino Ghirardacci's *Historia di Bologna* of 1596 which shows that the date 1119, given in a column on the left-hand side of the page, refers to the election of Pope Callistus II (1119–24), and not to what follows. Ghirardacci's text continues:

Roberto, & Rengherio fratelli in questo tempo habitauano in casa di Tancredi, & Boemondo Signori di Antiocha, che erano all'impresa di terra santa, & Rengherio fu quello, che della scultura dilettandosi, ad instanza di Balduino intagliò le lettere sopra l'Altare del santissimo sepolchro, che è di marmo, cioè. *Præpotens Genuensium præsidium.* [At this point in the right-hand margin is the name *Rengherio Renghieri*

Fig. 68. The Crusader Church of the Holy Sepulchre as reconstructed in the 12th century and completed by 1167/9. Z marks the position of the inscription recording the consecration of the Calvary chapels in 1149. (Enlarged from Fig. 63C; drawn by Steven Ashley)

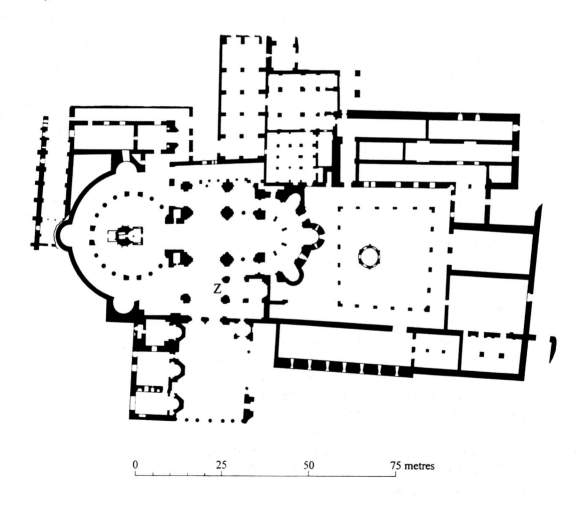

0   25   50   75 metres

The brothers Robert and Rengherio were dwelling at this time in the house of Tancred and Bohemond, lords of Antioch, who were engaged on the matter of the Holy Land. Rengherio was the one who in excellent carving on Baldwin's orders cut the letters above the altar of the Holy Sepulchre in marble, thus: GENOA: MIGHTY BASTION!

This is not the famous Golden Inscription dated 26 May 1105 which Baldwin I of Jerusalem (1100–18) is said to have ordered to be written in letters of gold in the apse of the Church of the Holy Sepulchre (*in truina sepulcri*) setting out the aid Genoa had given in the conquest of the Holy Land and the grants made to her in gratitude (Figs 63B, 68 at X).[7] *Præpotens Genuensium præsidium* is a second, quite separate inscription, said to have been written in golden letters on the arch above the altar (*in muro arcus supra altare*) (Figs 63B, 68 at Y).[8]

It has never proved possible to discover Ghirardacci's source for claiming that this Genoese motto was carved by a Bolognese sculptor. In his *Liguria trionfante* published in Genoa in 1643 Epifanio Ferrari dismissed the claim with contempt as an attempt to glorify Bologna.[9] In 1890 Carlo Malagola, director of the Archivio di Stato di Bologna, reported after an exhaustive search that before the time of Ghirardacci he could find no mention of Renghiero Renghieri nor of the inscription he had cut, whereas all later mentions were clearly derived from Ghirardacci. Ghirardacci had been, he suggested, motivated by 'un falso sentimento di gloria cittadina'.[10]

And so it appears that there is no reason to believe that a Bolognese sculptor called Rengherio ever existed, let alone that he carried out the renovation of the Edicule in or around 1119. There is nothing here to show that the Crusaders ever undertook its wholesale reconstruction, nor to suggest that they rebuilt its cupola, although they might have renewed the cupola at some later date, possibly when the life-size figure of Christ which they had erected before 1106/8 was replaced by the gilded cross, and the cupola covered with plates of gilded silver.

Thus the Rengherio story provides no support for the view that the Crusaders encased the Edicule in marble, but some time in the first half of the twelfth century (at any rate before *c.* 1170), they did cover the interior with mosaics, and it was perhaps at this time that the eastern compartment became more solidly enclosed. At least fourteen Latin inscriptions were now placed around the exterior, in the Chapel of the Angel and in the Tomb Chamber, and around the ironwork enclosing the altar built against the west end of the Edicule.[11] In the middle of the century the Byzantine emperor Manuel I Comnenos (1143–80) covered the burial couch with gold.[12]

Fig. 69. The Crusader facade of the south transept of the Church of the Holy Sepulchre with the dome over the crossing, now the Katholikon, looking north. Taken on the Friday of Holy Week 1990, during the sermon in the Parvis by the Greek Orthodox Patriarch. (Photograph Martin Biddle)

THE BUILDING OF THE CRUSADER CHURCH

The changes the Crusaders made to the Edicule have to be seen in the context of what they did to the church itself. The individual elements are clear enough (Figs 63C, 68). The Crusaders rebuilt the chapels around Calvary and extended the Byzantine church east across the previously open court – the 'Court before the Cross' of Constantine's original buildings and of their Byzantine successors (Fig. 63A and B). Into the open court they inserted in the finest late Romanesque style a choir with an ambulatory and three radiating chapels, the whole linked to the Rotunda around the tomb by a crossing covered by a dome and flanked by transepts to north and south. The grand façade of the south transept incorporated the double portals of the principal entrance to the new church (Fig. 69). West of the entrance rose a five-story campanile. And to the east, on the site of Constantine's Martyrion basilica and its atrium, emerged the entire complex of buildings necessary to house the prior and canons of the Augustinian Priory of the Holy Sepulchre in Jerusalem – cloister, chapter house, refectory, kitchen, dormitory and their vaulted substructures. Below the cloister, from the centre of which the drum of its cupola now emerged, was the Chapel of St Helena and the adjacent and yet lower Chapel of the Invention of the Cross.

If the separate elements are clear enough, their chronology is much less so. We can leave to one side the campanile, the priory buildings, and the Chapel of St Helena, which are not our direct concern here and which in any case require detailed reconsideration in the light of new discoveries and increasing knowledge of Crusader architecture and architectural decoration.[13] We are left with the buildings around Calvary and the extension of the church eastwards.

It is usual to date the completion and consecration of these works to 15 July 1149, the fiftieth anniversary of the capture of the city by the Crusaders.[14] It is notorious, however, that William of Tyre makes no mention of such a dedication.[15] And it has become increasingly obvious that parts of the church and some of its sculpture belong not to the 1130s and 1140s but to the 1150s and later.[16]

This date of 1149 derives from a Latin inscription in rhyming hexameters once painted in gold letters on the wall above or around the arch which led to the Chapel of Golgotha (now the Chapel of Adam) below the northern of the two chapels on Calvary. The inscription was thus above the second arch on the right as one entered the south transept by the main doors (Fig. 68 at Z). The text was already very damaged when it was recorded 'below the upper cornice (*sub coronide fastigii*) of Mount Calvary' by Quaresmius in the early seventeenth century (Fig. 70), but in 1860 de Vogüé recognized that John of Würzburg had recorded the first four lines *c.* 1170, and was thus able to offer a reconstruction of the whole text.[18] The same four lines and a crucial fifth containing the name of the Patriarch Fulcher (1146–57) were recorded by Theoderic writing before 1174, but his account was not published until 1865,[19] and was not therefore available to de Vogüé, to confirm his identification of the patriarch involved.

The first five lines, here taken from Theoderic, are safe enough, but there are clearly problems with Lines 6–10 for which we have only the degraded text as

```
·.··.·.··.·.··.·.··.·.··.·.··.·.· SPNMSARA
                                         I
·.··.·.·) D I M · S·.·.· SED DOMIAC
S·AR CIRCVM SVPER·.·.·.·.·
                              I
ALVIChERICO PATARChA·
                         I
CVI· TNC. QVRT· PATAR-
Ch AVS·.·.·.·.··.· SEMEL VN·
AB VRBE QVAE SIMILIS
              ERANT
P VR (·.·.·.··.·.··.·.··.·.··.·.··.·.··.·
EXORT DNINV MERABAN-
TVR S.IMVL ANN·.·.·.·.
·.··.·.··.·.··.·.··.·.··.·.· VINDE-
CES·.··IVDICES·.·.·.·   .
```

Fig. 70. The fragmentary surviving text of the inscription on the west face of Calvary recording the dedication of the Calvary chapels in 1149, as recorded by Francesco Quaresmius between 1616 and 1634 and published in 1639. (After Quaresmius 1989, 266, where the inscription which appears in Quaresmius 1639, ii, 483, divided between the foot of Col. a and the top of Col. b has been combined into a continuous text, with the omission of two lines composed entirely of dots at the beginning, and marks of abbreviation above T, I, and V in the fourth line from the end.)

recorded with obvious errors by Quaresmius (Fig. 70). Line 6, however, provides the fourth year of Fulcher's patriarchate, and since this began on 20 February 1149, the date must be 15 July 1149, as de Vogüé saw.[20] With this clue, Lines 7 to 10 can be reconstructed with some probability from the scraps recorded by Quaresmius. The text of the inscription follows, as reconstructed by de Vogüé with revisions by Thomsen and myself, the words supplied printed in *italic*.[21]

Est locus iste sacer, sacratus sanguine Christi,	1
Per nostrum sacrare sacro nichil addimus isti.	
Sed domus huic sacro circum superedificata	
Est quinta decima Quintilis luce sacrata	
Cum reliquis patribus a Fulcherio patriarcha,	5
Cuius tunc quartus Patriarchatus *annus*;	
Septem septies capta et semel unus ab urbe,	
Quae similis pu*ri fulgebat stamine auri,*	
Ex ortu Domini numerabantur simul anni	
Undecies *centum et quadraginta novemque*	10
. . . iudices . . .	

The reconstructed text can be translated:

This place is holy, sanctified by the blood of Christ,   1
By our consecration we add nothing to its holiness.
But the house built around and above this sacred place
Was consecrated on the fifteenth day of July,
With other fathers present, by Fulcher the patriarch,   5
Who was then in the fourth year of his patriarchate,
The fiftieth year since the capture of the City,
Which then shone like pure gold.
From the birth of the Lord there were numbered
Eleven hundred and forty and nine years.   10
[Indiction date?]

De Vogüé was notably cautious in assessing the significance of this inscription.
The new church was consecrated on 15 July 1149, but that did not mean that it
was

> . . . entièrement achevée; tout porte à croire, au contraire, qu'à cette époque
> aucun des travaux intérieurs n'était commencé; mais il est certain que la
> bâtisse proprement dite était terminée. La consécration a pu se faire, et le
> culte continuer à se célébrer dans l'ancienne abside de la rotonde, tandis que
> la décoration du nouveau chœur s'exécutait, que l'on sculptait les
> chapiteaux, et qu'on recouvrait les murs de mosaïques.[22]

> . . . completely finished. To the contrary, everything leads one to believe that
> at this time none of the internal works had been started. But it is certain
> that the structure itself had been finished. The consecration had been held,
> and the cult continued to be celebrated in the ancient apse of the Rotunda,
> while the new choir was decorated, the capitals carved, and the walls
> covered with mosaics.

De Vogüé went on to show that this was what the documents in the cartulary of
the Priory of the Holy Sepulchre seemed to suggest. From 1102 up to 1167 the
altars and sanctuaries mentioned were always the same from one charter to
another: the Holy Sepulchre, the Cross, and two other altars. But in a charter of
1169 and from then onwards there were added to these, the high altar in the
choir, the Prison and its altar, the Invention (i.e. the Chapel of the Invention of
the Cross) and its altars, the parochial altar at the *caput* (i.e. at the back) of the
Holy Sepulchre, the patriarchal throne which is behind the high altar, and the
Compas which is in the middle of the choir. It is clear, as de Vogüé noted, that
the charter of 1169 reflects the church as we know it today, for the *Compas*, the
Middle of the World, is now inside the church, whereas previously it was outside
in the court east of the Rotunda and its Byzantine apse, and the Prison and the
Invention of the Cross are now seen as communicating directly with the interior

of the building. Between 1167 and 1169 the documents appear to begin to reflect a profound re-arrangement of the church.

Already 140 years ago de Vogüé adduced further evidence to the same effect. The first four kings of Jerusalem, up to Fulk of Anjou, who had died in 1143, were buried beside the piers of the arches supporting the Calvary chapels. When Baldwin III died in 1163 he was buried between the piers on the south side of the crossing of the Crusader church.[23] Second, the Genoese Golden Inscription placed in the then still existing apse of the Byzantine church in 1105 (Figs 63B, 65 at X, with the golden epigram perhaps at Y) was destroyed in the time of King Amalric (1163–74), certainly no later than 1169 and possibly by 1167, for in one or other of those years Pope Alexander III wrote to Amalric and to the patriarch and other prelates of the kingdom and to the master of the Temple requiring the reinstatement of the inscription which Amalric had allowed to be destroyed.[24] If one rejects the view, as surely one must, that this was done to diminish the glory of Genoa, it can only have taken place when the Byzantine apse was demolished to open up the Rotunda to the new east end. In other words, as in countless churches of the west, the old work had been allowed to stand while the new work was erected around it. Only at the last minute was the old work taken down and the two parts of the church united with the least possible interruption to worship. The evidence suggests that this took place between the accession of Amalric in 1163 and the years 1167 or 1169.

The inscription above the arch of the Chapel of Golgotha has more to tell. It is not a record of the dedication of the whole church. The text is quite explicit. It refers to *locus iste sacer*, 'this holy place consecrated by the blood of Christ', in other words to the place of crucifixion, the place where his blood was shed. Nothing is said about the tomb, the place of his resurrection. Moreover, if Theoderic's description of the position of the inscription is correct, it stood above the entrance to the Chapel of Golgotha, below the Chapel of the Elevation of the Cross, in precisely the place where pilgrims were shown in the rock red streaks said to be the blood of Christ.

Some have argued that the phrase *domus huic sacro circum superedificata* in Line 3, 'the house built around and above this sacred place', refers to the church as a whole, but it is in reality a precise and accurate description of the complex of chapels on two levels that still surround the Rock of Calvary. And the location of the inscription on the front of Calvary supports this limited reference. One has only to recall the Golden Inscription of Genoa to see that there were more prominent places in which an inscription commemorating the completion and dedication of the whole church could have been set up.

This interpretation of the inscription as recording the dedication of the Calvary chapels in 1149 is not new. Already in 1921 Thomsen had identified it as giving the day in July 1149 'an dem die Kalvarienkapelle der Kreuzfahrer geweiht wurde' ('on which the Crusaders' Calvary chapel was consecrated').[25] But somehow this identification has been overlooked, and the text has come instead to be taken as recording the dedication, and hence the essential completion, of the Crusaders' reconstruction of the Church of the Holy Sepulchre.

The Crusaders seem in fact to have approached the reconstruction of the Church of the Holy Sepulchre with a circumspection amounting almost to timidity, perhaps because they had found a church barely sixty years old, of considerable size, and decorated throughout with the finest mosaics and painting (see above, p. 79). Initially all they seem to have done was to place a silver figure of Christ over the Edicule. If the inscription on Calvary means what it says, it was to be half a century before they had completed the chapels which ever since have enclosed the Rock, and another fifteen years or so before the great work of the choir, crossing and transepts was completed and dedicated. No record of such a final dedication appears to survive. It is not mentioned by William of Tyre, perhaps because it took place before his return from Europe to the kingdom in 1165.[26]

There are a number of pointers in this direction, as we have already seen. The cartulary of the Holy Sepulchre suggests that changes in the arrangement of the altars had taken place by 1169. The Genoese began their complaints against the removal of the Golden Inscription in 1167 or 1169, claiming that it had been destroyed by King Amalric whose reign began in 1163. The burial of Baldwin III between the southern piers of the crossing in 1163 indicates that the structure of the Crusader church must by then have been substantially complete.

The coins of King Amalric provide a further indication.[27] Shortly after the beginning of his reign in 1163 a new type of denier was issued showing on the reverse the distinctive shape of the conical 'dome' over the Rotunda of the Holy Sepulchre. Although the Rotunda had appeared before on Crusader seals (see above, p. 39, no. 7), this was the first time it had been shown on the coins: the Tower of David was the device used by Amalric's predecessor, Baldwin III.[28] Professor Michael Metcalf was the first to suggest that this change in coin type was perhaps to be associated with the changes in the Church of the Holy Sepulchre in the period 1167–9 deduced by de Vogüé from the charters of the church.[29] If, as now seems the case, these changes reflected the completion and final consecration of the Crusaders' work on the church in the early years of Amalric's reign, between 1163 and 1167–9, the change in the coins has an even clearer motive. It might be objected that Amalric's deniers show the Rotunda of the church rebuilt over a century before and not, for example, the new dome over the Crusader crossing. But it was the Rotunda with its distinctive conical roof that was the symbol of the church, used on seals since the early days of the kingdom of Jerusalem. It was quite unlike the dome of the Templum Domini (the Dome of the Rock), and on the principle of *pars pro toto* stood for the church of Christ's Resurrection.

One might have expected that the accounts of pilgrims and others who visited the Holy Sepulchre in the course of the twelfth century might have thrown some direct light on these problems. But architectural history was not one of their concerns, and precise description not part of their purpose. An additional problem is that many of the surviving accounts are difficult to date,[30] and they frequently rely without acknowledgement on earlier and undatable materials. The best accounts come from the beginning of the period, before the Crusader church was built (Jachintus, Saewulf, Daniel the Abbot), and from the later years when it was complete (John of Würzburg, Theoderic, John Phocas). But are there any accounts from the middle years of the century which can help? The problem is that these accounts tend to have been dated by whether or not they appear to reflect the Crusader church as completed, so it has been believed, in 1149.[31]

The one account which is clearly relevant is that preserved in Arabic by Muhammad al Idrisi whose 'Geography' was completed in 1154.[32] Idrisi's description, probably taken from an informant or earlier writer of unknown date and language, is particularly important for what it says of the entrance to the Holy Sepulchre from the north and west, from what is now Christian Quarter Street, and of the Rotunda and its decoration. It is much less clear when it comes to the rest of the church. To the east of the Rotunda was the 'very large church in which the Roman Franks have mass'. Idrisi (or rather his source) continues, 'to the east of this church [my emphasis, cf. Fig. 63B], somewhat to the south, is the prison in which Christ was incarcerated, and the place of the Crucifixion'.[33] There are difficulties with this, notably the phrases 'very large church' and 'somewhat to the south', which fit well neither the Byzantine nor the Crusader church (cf. Figs 63B and C, 65 and 68), but until Idrisi's source is identified and his use of it controlled, or at least until we have a critical edition of Idrisi, his description cannot be taken as evidence that the Crusader choir and ambulatory were in existence by 1154.[34]

For John of Würzburg, who visited Jerusalem about 1170, the choir was then *adjectionem novae ecclesiae*, 'the addition of a new church'. He continues with repeated emphasis, *illud novum et de novo additum aedificium*, 'a new structure and recently added . . . in which the high altar is consecrated in honour of the Anastasis, the Holy Resurrection.[35] These words might refer to a building finished twenty years before, but their reiterated emphasis reflects better a completion in the decade before his visit.

This reconstruction of the structural history of the Crusader Church of the Holy Sepulchre provides a context for the Crusaders' work on the Edicule. The accounts by John of Würzburg c.1170 and by Theoderic before 1174 show that the Edicule had by then reached its fullest development. The Chapel of the Angel was walled on three sides and had three doorways, the interior of both the Tomb Chamber and the chapel were covered with mosaics and other ornamentation, and there were inscriptions in Latin both within and without (see above, p. 91). It is the structure of the Edicule at this stage in its development which is seen in the large-scale copy erected at Eichstätt in Bavaria about 1160 (see above, pp. 31, 84). How much earlier the Edicule had reached this form we do not know. The fact that the supposed refurbishment of the Edicule in '1119' has proved to be an illusion does not mean that works of which we have no knowledge had not by then been begun or even completed.

But the Edicule which the Crusaders found in 1099 was, like the Rotunda and apse, a relatively new structure. There can have been no immediate need to do anything substantial. Daniel's account suggests that by about 1106 all the

Crusaders had done to the Edicule was to place a silver figure of Christ on top of its cupola.

A possible solution which may be offered as a working hypothesis is that the Crusaders' first significant works in the church were concentrated on the two holiest sites, Calvary and the Edicule. Only when these were completed was attention turned to the much greater task of the choir and transepts. If this is correct, the Edicule may have been embellished with mosaics and the cupola and other elements reworked at about the same time that the works of Calvary were in progress, that is to say in the 1140s.

To sum up: the idea that the Crusader Church of the Holy Sepulchre was consecrated on 15 July 1149 is based on one source and only one, the inscription on the façade of Calvary. But this inscription refers only to the consecration of the *domus* of Calvary, the Calvary chapels. To the contrary, there are several independent reasons for placing the completion of the Crusaders' church in the 1160s, and more particularly in the period between the accession of Amalric in 1163 and 1167/9. This proposal resolves many problems of dating and sequence in the architectural history of the Church of the Holy Sepulchre. To control, refine and correct this attempt to discriminate the broad outlines of the structural history of the church in the time of the Latin kingdom of Jerusalem will require a minute analysis, stone by stone, of the standing structure. It will also involve a reconsideration of the art-historical problems presented by the decoration of the church in stone and mosaic, and of the liturgical implications resulting from this proposed dating and the consequent changes in our understanding of the structural development of the church.

By 1187 the decoration of the Edicule had reached a peak of magnificence it has never since regained. That autumn, the silver covering the exterior was stripped off and minted into coins to pay the knights and sergeants defending the city, the new coins bearing a representation of the Sepulchre they were paid to defend (see above, p. 37, no. 6). Jerusalem surrendered to Saladin on 2 October 1187. None of the buildings was looted. The Church of the Resurrection was closed for three days while its future was discussed. In the end it was decided to follow the example of the Caliph Omar who on his capture of the city in 638 had confirmed the Christians in their possession of the church. It was not therefore demolished as some had advised, but left in the hands of the Eastern Christians from whom the Crusaders had seized it eighty-eight years before. Four Syrian priests were permitted to remain in the church.[36]

CHAPTER 6

THE EDICULE IN LATER MEDIEVAL AND MODERN TIMES

Under the truce concluded between King Richard of England and Saladin in 1192, Christian pilgrims were to be free to go up to Jerusalem. Hubert Walter, the bishop of Salisbury, who led the third group to go that autumn, requested Saladin

> that at the Tomb of the Lord, which he had visited and where the divine rites were only occasionally celebrated in the barbarous manner of the Syrians, the sacred liturgy be permitted to be celebrated somewhat more becomingly by two Latin priests and the same number of deacons, together with the Syrians, and that they be supported by the offerings of pilgrims.[1]

Saladin agreed and the bishop appointed the priests and deacons. But when a little later an embassy from the Byzantine Emperor Isaac Angelus asked that control of the Holy Sepulchre should revert to the Orthodox Church, Saladin refused. No one sect would be allowed to dominate, 'like the Ottoman Sultans after him, he would be arbiter of them all'.[2]

Saladin's successors were not so tolerant; pilgrims found themselves required to pay considerable fees. By 1217 Thietmar found the church 'without lamps, without honour, without reverence, and always shut unless opened to pilgrims on payment of fees'.[3] But in 1229 the Crusaders recovered Jerusalem for ten years under the terms of a treaty between the Emperor Frederick II and the Sultan al-Kamil. On 17 March Frederick entered the city. The next day, a Sunday, he went to attend mass in the Church of the Holy Sepulchre, but not a single priest was there, and he crowned himself.[4] The Crusaders' hold on the city was never strong during these years. Following the expiry of the treaty in 1239, the city remained uneasily in their hands until the summer of 1244.

In June that year ten thousand Khwarismian horsemen swept down from the north-west, and broke into Jerusalem on 11 July. The citadel held out until it was surrendered under safe-conduct on 23 August, the terms of which were broken.

No mercy was shown. The Khwarismians entered the Church of the Holy Sepulchre, broke open the tombs of the kings, slaughtered the Christians who had taken refuge in front of the Edicule, decapitated the priests who were celebrating at the altars, and

> in sepulchrum resurrectionis Dominicae manus sacrilegas extendentes, illud multipliciter deturparunt, tabulatum marmoreum, quod circumcirca erat positum, funditus evertentes . . . Columnas vero sculptas, quae ante sepulchrum Domini erant ad decorem positae, sustulerunt; illas in Christianorum contumeliam ad sepulchrum sceleratissimi Machometi, in signum victoriae, transmittentes.[5]

> laying sacrilegious hands on the tomb of the Lord's resurrection, they defiled it in many ways, overturning from its base the marble cladding placed around it . . . The carved columns placed in front of the tomb of the Lord for decoration they removed, sending them as a sign of victory to the tomb of the evil Mohammed, to the disgrace of the Christians.

These events, formally recorded by those in the best position to know the facts, may have been exaggerated from the despair of the moment and the need to rouse sympathy in Europe. But the details of the damage done to the Edicule are precise. They also go far to explain the condition of the Edicule as it is first visible to us in drawings, constructed of blocks which seem stripped of any proper covering (Figs 34, 36–7, and cf. Figs 51–4 for the continuing situation after 1555).

For the next three centuries until 1555 the Edicule seems to have been in continuous decay. Although the Franciscans had secured sole rights in the Edicule by the early fourteenth century, they did not recover its keys from the Muslims for another century. There is no record of repairs, perhaps because these were forbidden, but at some stage the north and south doors of the Chapel of the Angel were walled up (see above, p. 84; and cf. Figs 39 (lower) and 66B).

This Edicule of the Middle Ages, the goal of countless pilgrims, was depicted in many different media and described with varying degrees of precision and detail by many writers (above, pp. 20, 28). A detailed analysis of this evidence, most of which relates to these centuries of decay, will be undertaken on another occasion. Our purpose here and in Chapters 4 and 5 has been to set out the evidence for the nature, date and subsequent alteration of a structure which now appears to be in origin a Byzantine work of the first half of its eleventh century rather than, as previous commentators have thought, a Crusader operation of the twelfth.

The Edicule that faced Boniface of Ragusa in 1555 was thus the sadly decayed survival of a structure by then some five-and-a-half centuries old.

THE RENAISSANCE EDICULE

The reconstruction of the Edicule by Boniface of Ragusa in 1555 has been described as 'minor in scope'.[6] In fact, although he reused some earlier elements in approximately their original positions (see below, p. 116), Boniface's work appears to have involved the demolition of the structure and its reconstruction *a primis fundamentis*, as Vincent and Abel note: 'l'édicule du moyen âge est complètement rasé pour faire place à une nouvelle construction'.[7] The Edicule drawn by Bernardino Amico in 1593/7 and that viewed by all subsequent visitors until 1808 was thus a Renaissance building of the mid-sixteenth century (Figs 43, 46–56; cf. Fig. 66C), and not the decaying remains of a Byzantine structure elaborately decorated by the Crusaders.

Boniface was appointed Custos of the Holy Land in 1551 at a time of great difficulty for the Franciscan community, recently expelled from its convent on Mt Sion.[8] During the eight years of his first custody, Boniface not only secured a new site for the convent but also undertook the restoration of several of the Holy Places including, in the Church of the Holy Sepulchre, the Stone of Unction and the Edicule.

Fifteen years later in 1570, when he was bishop of Stagno, Boniface issued a solemn open letter describing his work on the tomb.[9] According to Boniface, the Edicule was in a state of collapse in 1555 when Pope Julius III (1550–5), urged on by the Holy Roman Emperor, Charles V, and his son King Philip of Spain, instructed him to undertake the restoration (*quam primum refici instaurarique*), supported by imperial funds made available through Francisco Varga, Charles's ambassador to Venice:

> Cum igitur ea structura solo aequanda necessario videretur, ut, quae instauranda denuo moles erat firmior surgeret diuturniorque permaneret, ea diruta, sanctissimi Domini Sepulchrum in petra excisum nostris sese oculis aperte videndum obtulit . . . Cum vero lamina una alabastri ex iis, quibus Sepulchrum operiebatur . . . super iis sacrosanctum Missae mysterium celebraretur, necessitate urgente commovenda esset, apparuit nobis apertus locus ille ineffabilis, in quo triduo Filius hominis requievit.[10]

> It was therefore necessary to take the structure down to the ground so that the rebuilt fabric should rise stronger and last longer. The demolition brought forth clearly to our very eyes the sepulchre of the Lord Most Holy cut out of the rock . . . When we had to remove one of the alabaster slabs covering the Sepulchre, [one of those] on which the holy mystery of the Mass is celebrated, there appeared laid open to us that ineffable place on which the Son of Man lay for three days.

Boniface also described his work on the Edicule in two passages of a manuscript entitled *Liber de perenni cultu*, written about the same time by order of Pope Pius V (1566–72) and published in 1573.[11] Prepared when Boniface was about to set out on a mission to King Philip of Spain, the text confirms and adds to his letter of 1570.

According to the *Liber*, Boniface opened the tomb on 27 August 1555, by which time Julius III, the instigator of the restoration, had died and Pope

Paul IV (1555–65) had been elected. In this version the work was paid for by King Philip:

> a primis fundamentis ipsum sanctum locum instauravi, et lucidissimis marmoribus decoravi.[12]

> I restored that holy place from the very foundations and decorated it with slabs of shining marble.

Boniface adds that this is recorded on a marble slab in the altar of the Column of the Flagellation in the Chapel of St Mary in the Church of the Holy Sepulchre.[13] In his commentary on the life of Boniface, Cipriano da Treviso[14] uses rather different words: 'Sepulchrum novis ac pretiosis marmoreis tabulis undequaque texit ac tholum quo operiebatur resarcivit'. These words appear to reflect an old misconception, corrected by Horn,[15] that Boniface renewed the dome of the Rotunda. What they surely mean is that he rebuilt the cupola over the Edicule, as its Renaissance decoration shows (Figs 52, 55).

Because Boniface had seen the remains of the original rock-cut tomb within the Edicule, he was able to draw a parallel with a tomb he had seen south of the city at Acheldama. Here were shown the caves in which the apostles had supposedly hidden after Jesus' arrest. Boniface thought (*ut reor*) correctly that these were ancient tombs cut in the rock and afterwards used by hermits:

> ibi ego inveni sepulchrum quoddam simile omni ex parte sepulchro, in quo iacuit Christi corpus, quod et fratribus ostendi, ut gaudeant, et posteris suis, et peregrinis ad Terram Sanctam adventantibus ostendant. Ego hoc potui peroptime scire, quia corporis Dominici locum vidi, quando . . . ipsum sanctum locum instauravi.[16]

> I found there a tomb similar in every way to that in which Christ's body lay. I pointed this out to the [Franciscan] brothers that they might rejoice and show it to their successors and to pilgrims coming to the Holy Land. I was very well able to know this, for I saw the place of the Lord's body . . . when I restored that holy place.

The surviving architectural evidence for Boniface's restoration of the Edicule and his evidence for the original form of the rock-cut tomb are considered below (pp. 120–1, 124; pp. 114, 116).

During the centuries following Boniface's restoration, the Edicule began again steadily to decay (Figs 51–4). Some of the blocks of his marble cladding were removed, others became detached. No repairs were possible and on special feasts the Franciscans took to concealing the unsightliness of the structure by covering the exterior with elaborate silken hangings.[17] In May 1728 the Franciscans were able to carry out some restoration of the interior of the Tomb Chamber. The work seems to have been of very short duration and was presumably limited to refixing marble slabs. It was observed by Father Elzear Horn,[18] and what he saw led him to the view that the Tomb Chamber was not cut in the living rock but built of large cut stones mortared together. Since Horn did not record which of the marble slabs he saw removed, we cannot tell what he was looking at, but one can still see that the west and east walls are constructed at least partly of cut stone, not rock (see below, pp. 122–4), while Boniface before him and Maximos Simaios after him independently recorded rock-cut elements. If Boniface and Simaios were describing the north and south walls (as Simaios explicitly says he was), and Horn was referring to the east and west walls, and perhaps only to their middle or upper parts, there is no inconsistency in their accounts. Unlike Boniface and Simaios, Horn presumably did not have the opportunity to examine the structure down to ground level.

THE FIRE OF 1808 AND THE REBUILDING
OF THE EDICULE

In 1808 the Church of the Holy Sepulchre was extensively damaged by fire. The roof of the Rotunda collapsed on to the Edicule, destroying the cupola and much of the marble and limestone cladding, but leaving the interior relatively undamaged. The door of the Edicule survived the fire and is preserved today in the Museum of the Greek Orthodox Patriarchate.[19] Blackened and slightly charred near the bottom on the outside but otherwise intact, the door seems to have protected the interior from the worst effects of the heat and smoke, although half the hangings in the Chapel of the Angel were scorched.[20]

Several accounts of the fire of 1808 and the subsequent rebuilding of the church and Edicule were written from the differing points of view of the various communities and by independent contemporary commentators, although the latter were not themselves eye-witnesses.[21] Two of the most important sources are the memorandum by the Greek Maximos Simaios, who observed the work throughout,[22] and the inscriptions on the Edicule itself.[23]

In March 1809 the Greek Orthodox community obtained from Sultan Mahmud II (1809–39) a firman authorizing them to restore the church. The work was completed over the following year under the direction of a Greek architect from Istanbul, Nikolaos Ch. Komnenos.[24] The 'Ch.' stands for χατζῆ, Turkish 'haci', a pilgrim, in this case one who has made the pilgrimage not to Mecca but to Jerusalem.[25]

Nikolaos Komnenos (1770–1821), a native of Mitylene, worked in Istanbul from the 1790s restoring the church of the Zoodochos Pege (Balíklí Kilesi) in 1797 and 1807[26] and the church of the Panagia (the Virgin of Pera), and constructing other large public and private buildings.[27] Inscriptions in the Holy Sepulchre (e.g. no. 20 in the Edicule, Fig. 71) consistently describe him as βασιλικός, 'basilikos', presumably with the meaning 'soultanikos' (the sultan often being designated 'basileus', as Professor Donald Nicol points out to me), suggesting an imperial or state practice the nature and extent of which remain at present unknown. He was generally known as Komnenos κὰλφα (Fig. 71), a

Fig. 71. Inscription 20, on the east wall of the Tomb Chamber, recording Nikolaos Komnenos (1770–1821) of Mitylene, architect of the reconstruction of the Church of the Holy Sepulchre and the Edicule, 1809–10. (Photograph John Crook)

Turkish word meaning 'master builder', and an inscription in the Rotunda of the Holy Sepulchre, over the triumphal arch opening into the katholikon, described him as Ἀρχιτέκτων, 'architect'.[28] Komnenos was an early member of the Filikí Hetairía, the more or less secret society working for Greek independence, and was murdered by the mob in Istanbul together with the Patriarch Gregorios V and members of the Greek community on 21 April 1821, the day after news of the Greek Revolt reached the City.

All accounts are consistent in claiming that Komnenos, with the support of the patriarch, had volunteered his services for the reconstruction of the Church of the Holy Sepulchre.[29] He left Istanbul on 3 May 1809 and had completed the work by 13 September 1810, a remarkably short period given the extent of what had to be done. According to contemporary documents the work was carried out by 'Romaic' (i.e. Orthodox) builders from the patriarchate of Jerusalem supervised by Komnenos and Drakon, a master-mason from Rhodes.[30] The latter is not mentioned in the inscriptions on the Edicule. These record the master-mason Antonoglu Potos from the village of Agios Stephanos in Caesarea (no. 8), the mason Lazos son of Theodore from the village of Loudros, and the plasterer Kouloumoglu Potos (no. 7), all from Cappadocia.

Komnenos' restoration of the Church of the Holy Sepulchre was extensive, involving both the katholikon, its eastern apse rebuilt with a distinctive shell-shaped (μύαξ) roof (Fig. 72), and the Rotunda. The columns and piers of the Rotunda, calcined in the fire, were cased in plastered rubble; the dome was rebuilt and the interior completely redecorated. The central inscription at the top of the east front of the Edicule claims that the entire κουβούκλιον (shrine) was rebuilt from the foundations in March 1810 (no. 1), and the year is repeated several times elsewhere (nos 9b, 10b, 16d, and 20: Fig. 71). Only the marble cladding of the Tomb Chamber and the lowest course of the exterior were left in position (see below, pp. 120–1). The Chapel of the Angel, the vaults over the Tomb Chamber and over the chapel, the exterior walls and the cupola were rebuilt in the new style. Maximos Simaios recorded in some detail what was revealed in the course of the work (see below, pp. 115–16).

The Coptic Chapel seems to have been omitted in the rebuilding of 1809–10. The architectural detail of the west end of the Edicule continues uninterrupted behind the chapel, which is straight-jointed against the Edicule and differs slightly from it in the profile of its mouldings (Figs 67 and 84). The Coptic Chapel must, however, have been erected before 1818,[31] and it appears on the plan of the Edicule drawn in 1825 by the architect J.J. Scoles and used by Willis for Fig. 8 in his Pl. 2 (see here Fig. 14).[32]

Komnenos' work has not commended itself to non-Orthodox critics (e.g. Figs 58–9, 72). Structurally it was not a success, except in the important sense that it saved the building from collapse until a thorough restoration at last became possible in recent years.[33] The dome of the Rotunda had to be rebuilt in 1868, and Komnenos' repairs to the walls and piers were seriously weakened by the earthquake of 1927. In the following years the whole structure had to be strapped and scaffolded by the Public Works Department of the Mandatory

Fig. 72. The eastern apse of the Church of the Holy Sepulchre with its distinctive shell-shaped roof, by Nikolaos Komnenos 1809–10, looking north-west. (Photograph Martin Biddle)

Fig. 73. The decayed state of the stonework of 1809–10 on the north face of the Edicule (Bay GH, cf. Fig. 9.1). (Photograph John Crook)

Fig. 74. The north-east angle of the Edicule showing Plinth 1 (lower) and Plinth 2 (upper) beneath the base moulding of 1809–10, looking south-west. The outward bulge of the lower part of the east front is clearly visible by reference to the west end of the north bench and to the steel shoring of 1947. (Photograph John Crook)

Government of Palestine. The beams and girders remained until the church was comprehensively restored in 1968–79 (see above, pp. 7–9).[34]

The present Edicule has been the subject of particular abuse, but its site and form were dictated by its predecessor (see below, pp. 120–1), while its style belongs to Komnenos' time and empire and is not without its own interest as an example of Ottoman, specifically Istanbul, baroque (Figs 6–8, 11, 90–3). But here too structural defects have had their impact. Until the dome was again rebuilt in 1868 and the central opening provided with a cover, rain poured down through the *oculus* of the dome on to the Edicule (Fig. 58). The water rotted the iron cramps holding the blocks of the Edicule together, with the result that the weight of Komnenos' upper works – the vaults over the two chapels and the cupola over the Tomb Chamber (Figs 81–2, 88) – has settled down on what seems to be no more than a cladding of the pre-existing lower walls of the Edicule, forcing the facing stones, no longer retained by their cramps, to bulge outwards (Figs 73–4). The earthquake of 1927 threatened the whole structure with collapse, but it was not until March 1947 that it was strapped together by a cradle of steel girders put in position by the Public Works Department of the British Mandatory Government of Palestine, the last of their works in the Church of the Holy Sepulchre (Figs 8, 11, 74); see above, p. 9). Since then nothing has been done. The present state of the unsupported east and west walls is parlous, elements in the east front having moved as much as 3 cm in the years 1990–3.

CHAPTER 7

NEW INTERPRETATIONS: THE FORM AND SURVIVAL OF THE ROCK-CUT TOMB

Although the present investigation has revealed no new physical evidence for the form or condition of the rock-cut tomb within the Edicule, the associated enquiry into the other sources, and the structural approach which has been applied to their interpretation, make it possible to make some observations which may be of importance when the time comes for restoration and the recording of what may be revealed.

The form and components of the rock-cut tomb contained within the Edicule presumably correspond to what its discoverers in 325/6 would have expected from the Gospel accounts, i.e. a chamber not exceeding a capacity of about five persons, with a low entrance and a burial couch to the right (above, p. 66).

Cyril's evidence on the cutting away of a forecourt, with his touch of personal observation and comparison with other local tombs (p. 65), shows that there was originally a second rock-cut component in front of the entrance to the Tomb Chamber. His evidence does not suggest, however, that there was a fully enclosed rock-cut chamber between the Tomb Chamber and the forecourt, as has usually been assumed, for example in the influential and often redrawn reconstruction by Vincent (Fig. 78).[1] The inclusion of this intermediate chamber is presumably based on the present form of the Edicule, the Chapel of the Angel being taken as its lineal descendant. As we have seen, the present form of the chapel emerged during the Middle Ages on the site of the portico in front of Constantine's Edicule (Fig. 66). If, as seems probable, this portico replaced the προσκέπασμα or σκέπη cut away by Constantine's engineers, there is no space for a fully enclosed rock-cut chamber between the Tomb Chamber and the forecourt.

Fig.. 75. A rolling-stone in its groove: the entrance to the tomb of Queen Helena of Adiabene ('The Tombs of the Kings'), Jerusalem, mid-1st century AD, looking south-east. (Photograph Martin Biddle)

In the absence of this chamber, the tomb becomes a much less complex affair, but simple rock-cut tombs are in fact the norm in the Jerusalem cemeteries of the Second Temple period.[2] About half the known tombs have open, rock-cut forecourts.

Only four tombs, all of élite status, are known to have been closed by a geometrically perfect circular stone rolling in a specially prepared groove (Fig. 75),[3] but the use of a roughly dressed stone to seal the entrance was a common feature, and such a stone could be trundled up to and across the entrance. We should not assume, as did Vincent and Abel,[4] that the tomb of the Gospels, and hence the tomb within the Edicule, was provided with a geometrically perfect stone rolling in a groove. In the Gospels the roundness of the stone is implied only by the use of the Greek verb κυλίω, 'to roll', in compounds meaning 'to roll up to' (Mt 27.60; Mk 15.46), 'to roll away' (Mt 28.2; Mk 16.3; Lk 24.2), or 'to roll away *or* back' (Mk 16.4). The stone is described as 'large' (Mt 27.60) or 'very large' (Mk 16.4), but it is never described as 'round'. Nor is it ever said that the stone was rolled *across* the entrance. Professor Amos Kloner's conclusion that the stone was probably of the less rounded type is almost certainly correct.[5]

The burial shelf or couch and the form of the roof above it provide a further problem. Was the couch set within a niche (an arcosolium), whether covered by a low arch or by a flat ceiling, or was it simply set against one wall of the burial-chamber and thus covered only by the roof of the chamber itself? Here it is essential not to use as primary evidence the form of the burial niche as it was rebuilt in masonry in the eleventh century following al-Hakim's destruction in 1009 (see below, p. 113).

The only visual evidence for the form of the Tomb Chamber before 1009 is provided by the Narbonne model (Figs 16 and 76, see above, p. 22, no. 2; cf. Fig. 64C). Here the interior of the Tomb Chamber was carved through an opening formed for this purpose in the rear of the model (Fig. 76). The plan of the Tomb Chamber is correct in angling the face of the burial couch 'south' of the 'east-west' axis of the model (cf. Fig. 85), but it appears grossly to distort the horizontal angles and dimensions and hence the shape of the chamber (but see below, p. 112). The evidence of the model for the elevation of the interior of the Tomb Chamber may also be unreliable, but the burial couch is at approximately the right height, and the general impression is convincing (Fig. 76). The roof over the burial couch is flat and forms part of the ceiling of the Tomb Chamber as a whole; there is therefore no niche in the wall, let alone a niche covered by a low arch. The ceiling meets the walls in a neatly rounded cove.[6]

The only other evidence for the form of the interior of the Tomb Chamber before al-Hakim's destruction comes from written descriptions. Nine of these provide varying amounts of detail concerning the Edicule (Egeria, Paula, the Breviarius, the Piacenza pilgrim, Sophronius, Adomnán, Hugeburc, Bernard and Photius), but only Paula, Adomnán, Hugeburc and Photius say anything about the burial-couch and only Adomnán and Photius provide any information about the ceiling of the Tomb Chamber or the form of the burial-place. Adomnán says only that 'from the top of a fairly tall man's head, when standing, to the vault of the edicule (*ad illius domunculae cameram*) there was a space measuring a foot and a half',[7] and Photius that it was high enough to take a man standing upright.[8] Adomnán adds that the burial place had been cut into the rock on the north side of the Tomb Chamber in the form of a single shelf seven feet long, 'in the shape of a cave, with the entrance on the side, directly facing the southern portion of the Tomb Chamber, and with a low, man-made roof projecting above (*culmenque humile desuper eminens fabrefactum*)'.[9] Photius provides the strikingly precise description that the rock had been removed to form a parallelepipedal recess (παραλληλεπιπέδῳ σχήματι τυπουμένη) long enough to take a man laid upon it.[10]

Fig. 76. The Narbonne model: the interior chamber with the burial couch to the left, seen through the broken back and columns of the outer wall. Height 1.24 m. Pyrenean marble. ?5th century. See p. 22, no. 2, and cf. Fig. 16 and pp. 69, 110, 149 n. 82. (Photograph John Crook)

Adomnán goes on to specify the position of the twelve lamps which burn over the burial couch day and night, 'four . . . placed low down at the back [as in the tomb today: lit. 'in the deepest place', *not* 'the foot' or 'bottom'] of the sepulchral bed (*in imo illius lectuli sepulchralis loco*): the other eight . . . placed higher up above its right-hand edge [i.e. above the front edge of the couch as seen by the observer, but the right edge in relation to a body lying on it]'.[11] This is what Bede seems to have understood by Adomnán's words, for in quoting them in his own *de locis sanctis* Bede changed the text to read 'quattuor [lampades] intra sepulchrum, octo supra in margine dextro'.[12] This seems to be just what is shown on the most detailed of the copies of the plan which Arculf drew for Adomnán on a wax tablet (see above, p. 26 no. 11, Fig. 25), a source which should be regarded as being in some ways quite independent of the written text it accompanies. Here the burial place is shown (presumably in plan) as a rectangle, with the twelve lamps (apparently in elevation) arranged in two rows, four and eight, the four centred below the eight.[13] Neither in Adomnán's text nor in the copy of Arculf's drawing of the placing of the lamps is there thus any hint of the presence of an arched top to the burial recess, but we must always remember that these descriptions were not intended to give complete architectural details and that simply because no arch is mentioned this does not mean that none was there.

Nevertheless, it is not possible to conclude from the available evidence that the burial couch lay under a low arch. If it did, it may seem surprising that no mention was made of so distinctive a feature, especially since Adomnán used the word *camera* to describe the roof of the Tomb Chamber proper, a noun which does imply curvature, whereas for the top of the burial recess he used the word *culmen*, 'uppermost part, highest point, ridge, gable, roof' with no implication of a curve. In evaluating this evidence, we must bear in mind Adomnán's statement that the Tomb Chamber was devoid of ornament on the inside, and still showed the marks of the workmen's tools.[14] He and all others who saw the tomb before 1009 had its original form directly before their eyes.

Photius' description of the recess as παραλληλεπίπεδος, parallelepipedal, 'with parallel planes or faces', may, however, be decisive in favour of a flat roof over the burial couch. This rare adjective, first recorded in Euclid,[15] has a precise meaning: a solid contained by three pairs of parallel planes, whose six faces are therefore parallelograms, with the opposite faces being parallel and equal.[16] The import of its application to the burial recess can only be that the top and bottom, the two ends, and the back and the plane of the front opening were parallel two and two, even if they were not at right-angles to each other. Since to an observer the top and bottom planes would have been the most obvious, the use of the adjective is strong evidence against an arch and in favour of a flat roof. Photius' scholarship and lexicographical learning give every reason to suppose that he used the word in its precise meaning,[17] as does Byzantine interest in mathematics and geometry.[18]

The word implies that although the planes were parallel two and two, the pairs were not necessarily at right-angles to each other. This is just how the Narbonne model shows the burial couch, with the exception of the two ends (Fig. 76), suggesting that the distortion may not be as great as might otherwise appear (see above, p. 110). The rock-cut Tomb of Mary in the Church of the Virgin in the Kidron Valley displays a similar parallelepipedal form, supposing only that its missing roof was flat.[20]

What was Photius' source? There seems to be no evidence that he ever visited Jerusalem, and he cannot be shown to have used any of the surviving Greek descriptions of the tomb. To the contrary, he says that he had enquired closely into these matters from those who had devoted their life specifically to the care of 'that blessed place'.[21] His informants were probably monks or clergy of the Jerusalem patriarchate whom he met either before or in the course of his fraught and interrupted patriarchate of Constantinople, 858–67 and 878–86.[22] The section of the *Amphilochia* in which Photius describes the tomb seems not in fact to have been written until towards the end or even after the end of his second patriarchate in 886; he died *c*. 895.[23]

To summarize: like most Jewish tombs of the Second Temple period the ceiling of the Tomb Chamber itself was probably more or less flat, but was rounded down at the edges into the walls (Fig. 64A–C). This is what the Narbonne model shows, and is perhaps what Adomnán meant by his use of the word *camera*. The roof over the burial couch may, but need not, have been lower than the ceiling of the burial chamber proper, in which case the burial-place was a recess cut into the north wall. The top of this recess was flat. This is not inconsistent with what is now known of Jewish tombs of the Jerusalem area: arcosolia, burial benches cut in the shape of shelves along the burial-chamber walls, occur in about one hundred of the over nine hundred known tombs of the period, but only sometimes was the ceiling of an arcosolium hewn to form a shallow arch.[24]

In 1009 al-Hakim's agents destroyed 'the greater part' of the tomb (see above, p. 72). The roof and upper part of the walls were certainly removed, as later accounts of the surviving rock-cut elements show (see below, p. 115), so that the subsequent reconstruction will have had to provide a cover for both the burial-recess and for the Tomb Chamber. The form of this reconstruction is uncertain. The seals of the Canons of the Holy Sepulchre and of Peter, prior of the Holy Sepulchre (above, p. 39 no. 7, Fig. 40), show an idealized section of the Edicule with an arch high above the burial-couch. The ?full-scale copy of the Edicule constructed *c.* 1160 at Eichstätt (see above, p. 31, no. 1) has a groined vault carried on haunches which produces in section an arch high above the burial-couch very like that shown on the seals.[25] The idea of this high arch seems to have survived to influence the reconstruction of 1555 (see below),[26] and may in turn be reflected in the curved top of the great marble ikon which stands today over the tomb (Figs 1, 101–2).

By contrast, the coin type SEPVLCHRUM DOMINI attributed to 1187 (above, p. 37, no. 6) seems to show a low arch directly over the burial-couch. This may be a simplified version of the Edicule shown on the seals of Prior Peter and the Canons of the Holy Sepulchre, or even an extreme simplification of the Rotunda shown on these seals overarching the Edicule, but the ?twelfth-century 'replica' of the tomb cut in the rock at Externsteine in the Teutoburger Wald has as its dominant feature just such a low arch over the burial-place (Fig. 77),[27] almost exactly like the arched arcosolia of Jewish tombs. If this is not copied from the contemporary arrangement in Jerusalem, and is not a memory of the tomb before al-Hakim's destruction, where did the idea come from? There seem to be at least three possibilities. First, the Externsteine stone-cutter may have copied a coin or seal brought back from the Holy Land, misinterpreting the image or being misled, if following the coin, by its over-simplification; second, the Externsteine replica might be based on a pilgrim's record of a rock-cut tomb he had seen in the Jerusalem area which was pointed out to him as being like the original tomb of Christ (for such a case, see below, p. 114); or, third, the Externsteine replica might be an accurate representation of the arrangement in the Edicule as it was following the eleventh-century reconstruction. Accounts written by pilgrims in the twelfth century and later do not describe such a low arch. The Eichstätt copy does not have it, and the reconstruction of 1555 made no attempt to reproduce it, but like the Eichstätt copy did have an arch high above the burial couch (see Figs 48 and 54). It must seem unlikely, therefore, that the Externsteine replica with its low arch does faithfully reproduce the arrangement in the Edicule as it was at any stage in its development.

Fig. 77. Externsteine bei Horn, Nordrhein-Westfalen, rock-cut 'replica' of the tomb of Christ, perhaps 12th century: showing the arched recess over a body-shaped burial place sunk into the surface of the shelf. (Photograph Carsten Thiede)

During the later Middle Ages some pilgrims wondered how much of the original rock-cut tomb survived within the Edicule, but few recorded their observations. An exception was the friar, Brother Felix Faber, who during a vigil in the church in 1483 took a candle and 'examined most carefully to see whether I could find any part that was not covered with marble'. Only the west wall of the Chapel of the Angel, 'in which is the door leading into the Lord's sepulchre, was bare; and on holding my light near it I saw a wall cut out of the rock, not made of ashlar work, but all of one piece . . .' though, 'in the upper part there seemed to have been a fracture, which had been mended with stones and cement'. From this he deduced, fairly enough as we have seen, that the tomb had once been partly destroyed, but afterwards restored.[28]

Brother Felix was only able to see what was normally uncovered. When another friar, Boniface of Ragusa, restored the Edicule *a primis fundamentis* seventy-two years later in 1555, he was able to examine what remained of the rock-cut tomb and to compare it with a tomb 'similar in every way' at Acheldama in the Hinnom Valley south of the city (see above, p. 102). Brother Felix had noted this tomb, or one like it, in the gardens near Acheldama in 1483,[29] and it may long have been a well-known place to see.[30] If the Acheldama tomb could be identified, it would show us what Boniface, a careful and precise observer, thought he had seen within the Edicule. There are, however, many rock-cut tombs in the area and by 1639 Quaresmius seems to have had some doubt which tomb Boniface meant (*Id vero antrum illud esse creditur . . .*), describing one whose entrance was like that of the tomb in the Edicule.[31] Either this or another tomb continued to be pointed out at Acheldama throughout the eighteenth century, Mariti, for example, describing one whose interior 'è tutto simile a quello di Nostro Signore'.[32] Tobler suggested two possibilities[33] and Pierotti published a plan of a tomb with a forecourt, antechamber and tomb chamber[34] which might well be the tomb in question were it not for Pierotti's tendency to gild the lily,[35] and for the fact that this tomb seems not to have been seen, at least in the form in which Pierotti drew it, by Macalister.[36] A rock-cut chamber with what looks at first sight to be an arcosolium on the south side and an entrance to the west can be seen today. This tomb may correspond to Macalister no. 39 and to a part of Tobler's no. 13, and might have seemed like the rock-cut tomb in the Edicule, but it is in fact a forecourt opening to the north, with an entrance to a tomb chamber on the south side low down below the 'arcosolium'. The opening to the west is no more than a ?later break into the easternmost part of Tomb no. 38. Until and unless the chamber pointed out by Boniface can be identified, there seems little hope of knowing more precisely what it was he thought he saw within the Edicule in 1555.

In 1728 Father Elzear Horn took the opportunity, during some repairs in the Tomb Chamber to look behind the marble cladding, but was able to see only mortared stonework (see above, p. 103). Following the fire of 1808, however, the Edicule was dismantled down to the top of the external plinth (see below, pp. 120–1) and in October and November 1809 Maximos Simaios recorded what was revealed.[37] The Tomb Chamber appeared as a cave, formed in the rock (μονόλιθος), but the Chapel of the Angel (described as the Chapel of the Sacred Stone) was a masonry structure throughout. The whole surviving part of the Tomb Chamber was cut by chisel in the limestone known as 'meleki' or 'royal', 3 cubits long, 1½ cubits wide and 4 cubits high. The north and south walls were hewn in the rock, but the east and west walls and the roof were built work. The whole floor both in the Chapel of the Angel and in the Tomb Chamber was living rock, not laid nor dug into, but entirely and only natural rock.

Thus far Maximos' description agrees with all we might suspect from the structural history of the Edicule from 1009 onwards (see above, pp. 81–5), particularly in showing that the Chapel of the Angel is a built structure and was never formed in the rock, the forecourt of the original tomb having been cut away when Constantine's workmen isolated the Tomb Chamber from the surrounding rock after 325/6 (Figs 64A, B, 66, 79; see above, p. 65). Maximos' dimensions, given in terms of the πῆχυς or cubit (i.e. the distance from the point of the elbow to the end of the middle finger), were presumably gauged by eye and not measured with a rod. They should not therefore be taken as precise. Even if converted in terms of the longer or royal cubit of 52.3 cm, his horizontal distances seem rather short. His length for the Tomb Chamber converts to 1.57 m, whereas the present tomb-slab is 1.83 m long, and his width, whether for the burial couch or the narrow lower part of the chamber beside it, at 0.78 m compares with the present width of the tomb-slab at 0.94 m. This may mean no more than that the rock-cut elements within the present marble casing are considerably smaller. Maximos' length for the Tomb Chamber (1.57 m) suggests that something may have been lost at one end, possibly in the destruction of 1009, for otherwise the burial couch would have been very short by comparison with contemporary tombs in the Jerusalem area.[38] His observation that the east and west walls were of masonry rather than rock shows how the whole structure might have been shortened in the destruction of 1009.

The height of 4 cubits (2.09 m) given by Maximos is by contrast surprisingly large. It may, however, be reliable, not only because his other measurements seem, if anything, to be underestimates, but also because this was the dimension easiest to judge, being gauged by his own height. We can at least say that one or other of the walls still stood higher than his head, and there seems no doubt from his text that he means this height to be applied to the rock-cut chamber, that is, to the north or south wall or to both.

Maximos' description of the uncovering of the burial couch is less easy to follow.[39] Komnenos opened the west end and encountered an indescribably sweet odour, the 'whole' (i.e. the rock of the burial couch, not the odour; the syntax is confused) rising up to the very 'marble', presumably the burial slab which is still

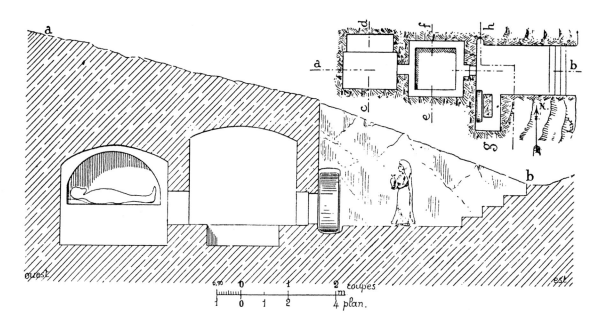

Fig. 78. Reconstruction of the form of the rock-cut tomb described in the Gospels, drawn by Père Vincent. (After Vincent and Abel 1914, ii, Fig. 53)

in place. There was a blocking on the south side consisting of two 'marbles', the outer one presumably represented by the present vertical face of the tomb-shelf (cf. Figs 1, 95, 100, 102). Above 'this' there were two more 'marbles', one above another, each one the same, the upper presumably represented by the present horizontal burial slab. To the east there was a built wall above 'this', and the same to the west. To the north, by contrast, the whole of the sacred grotto was formed of the natural rock.

Maximos' description suggests that only the west end of the tomb-structure was opened, the marble slabs being left in position, and the east end observable from outside, without being dismantled. Sufficient of the rock-cut burial couch seems to have survived to identify its shape. We can perhaps suppose that by this time it looked very much like the rock couch now visible in the Church of the Virgin in the Kidron Valley,[40] battered and hollowed out by centuries of relic-taking. Maximos' description suggests that on top and in front of the burial couch there were two layers of marble cladding. If the outer layer comprised the marble slabs still visible today, the inner layer may be the medieval cladding, which in that case was simply left in position and covered up by Boniface of Ragusa in 1555. There seems no reason to suppose it was not again left in position by Komnenos. If so, it is probably still there.

At this point, it may be useful to summarize the conclusions of this study regarding the original form of the rock-cut tomb preserved within the present Edicule (Fig. 79).

1. The tomb consisted of only two components: an unroofed or partly covered rock-cut forecourt opening by a low entrance into a fully enclosed rock-cut Tomb Chamber (see above, pp. 109–10).

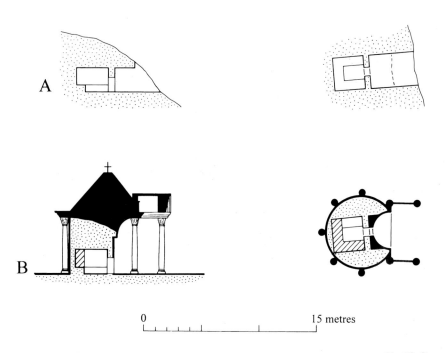

A

B

0   15 metres

Fig. 79. Reconstruction (A) of the form of the rock-cut tomb within the Edicule and (B) of its conversion by the construction of Constantine's Edicule. (Enlarged from Fig. 64A, B; drawn by Steven Ashley)

2. The entrance to the Tomb Chamber from the forecourt was closed by a large stone. There is no evidence that this was round: it is more likely to have been roughly dressed and to have been trundled rather than rolled across the entrance (p. 110).

3. There were probably rock-cut burial couches on two or three sides of the original burial chamber. The form of the chamber as preserved since 325/6, with only a single burial couch, would be quite exceptional (if not unique) among the nine hundred or so rock-cut tombs of the Second Temple period now recorded (see above, pp. 19, 55), while chambers with two or three couches are frequent.[41] A tomb chamber of the form and size proposed here with three couches was found immediately north of the Church of the Holy Sepulchre in 1885, where it formed the inner of two burial chambers.[42]

4. The ceiling of the burial chamber seems to have been flat. There is no evidence that the visible burial couch was set within a niche below the neatly rounded arch of a rock-cut arcosolium (see above, pp. 110–13).[43]

5. The burial chamber was thus a square or rectangular room with a flat roof, with couches ranged along three sides, and with only a limited space excavated to floor level between the couches. This deeper area, sometimes called the 'standing pit', allowed the 'burial attendants, bone gatherers and other visitors to stand upright within the tomb'.[44] Its floor could have been lower than the forecourt and reached by a descent of one or more steps, but there is no evidence for this.

6. On this interpretation, and measuring from the new plan of the present Edicule (Fig. 85), the forecourt will have been no more than 3 to 4 m wide and 3 to 4 m deep from east to west. The Tomb Chamber was perhaps about 2.8 m square and 2 m high. The benches were probably each about 2 m long and 0.8 m wide, with their surfaces about 0.5 m or slightly less above the floor. The area excavated to floor level between the benches will have measured about 2 m from east to west and may have been no more than 1 m wide. It is represented today by the standing area within the Tomb Chamber.

This is the form of the burial chamber shown in Figs 64A and 79. It differs considerably from all previous reconstructions, but has been informed by the mass of new evidence about Jewish tombs of the Second Temple period recovered during the last eighty years. This reconstruction is based strictly upon the evidence of the present structure, upon information recorded by contemporary observers from 325 onwards, and upon the comparative evidence of other tombs in the Jerusalem area. It is independent of the evidence of the Gospels, but is consistent with what they have to say about the form of the tomb (see above, pp. 15, 19, 54–5, 109–10).

Professor Amos Kloner has approached the problem from the different perspective of his unrivalled knowledge of the rock-cut tombs of the Jerusalem area, and has come to very similar conclusions.[45] Our shared hypotheses about the form of the original tomb will be able to be tested if observation and recording is permitted during the inevitable forthcoming restoration of the Edicule.

If the rock-cut tomb within the Edicule was originally of the form suggested here, the action taken by Constantine's agents will have concentrated on preserving the elements mentioned in the Gospel accounts: the stone which closed the entrance, the low entrance through which one had to stoop, and the burial couch to the right on entering (Figs 64B, 79). We know from Cyril that the emperor's workmen cut away the forecourt (see above, p. 65); they may at the same time have reduced the level of its floor so as to eliminate a step or steps down into the Tomb Chamber. The present reconstruction shown in Figs 64B and 79B suggests that they may also have walled up the chamber above the 'unwanted' couches to south and perhaps to west. The thickness of the walls surrounding the present Tomb Chamber leaves ample room for these couches (Fig. 85). It may also be relevant that the west wall of the Tomb Chamber as seen behind the hinged ikon of the Virgin is of masonry (Figs 95–6). This masonry may date from the reconstruction of the west wall of the rock-cut chamber after its destruction by al-Hakim's men in 1009 (p. 73). It is equally possible that these stones represent infilling above a western couch and date from the fourth century, as proposed on Figs 64B and 79B. Only further investigation will settle such questions.

Early pilgrims sometimes remarked that the rock surface of the interior of the Tomb Chamber still showed the marks of the tools with which it had been hewn out, and Arculf even noted the red veins typical of the natural limestone of the site.[46] These descriptions could refer to the ceiling, to the walls above the visible burial couch or to the couch itself. They cannot be taken to imply that the walls were rock-cut all round and did not incorporate areas of masonry infilling. If the infillings were plastered, they would not have been immediately obvious.

This consideration of the evidence for the form and survival of the original rock-cut Tomb Chamber found in 325/6 suggests that much of it still survives inside the Edicule. In part it may even stand to more than the height of a man.[47] Nor has the east wall been entirely destroyed. In 1483, in a careful exploration directed precisely to the question of the degree of survival of the rock-cut tomb, Felix Faber identified part of the rock-cut structure in the west wall of the Chapel of the Angel, beside the door leading into the Tomb Chamber (above, p. 114). There is no reason to dismiss his account, which indicates that in his day some part of the curve of the rock-cut apse forming the west side of Constantine's portico still survived (for this apse, see Figs 9B, 47–8 and cf. Fig. 16; its form is still echoed in the curve of the west wall of the Chapel of the Angel, Fig. 85). There is also evidence in these accounts that the layers of previous Edicules can survive one inside the other like the skins of an onion. They suggest that there is much to be discovered when the time comes for restoration.

CHAPTER 8

NEW DISCOVERIES: THE STRUCTURE OF THE PRESENT EDICULE

As argued above (p. 11), the Tomb of Christ is no exception to the usual rules of structural archaeology. The evidence for the form and character of the present structure recorded in the course of the work of 1989, 1990, and 1992, whether by photogrammetry or by more traditional methods, is displayed as we now understand it in the illustrations accompanying this book, and more particularly in Figs 7–8, 11–13, 64, 66–7, 71, 73–4, 79, 81–2, 84–97, 100–2.[1]

A series of points relevant to the structural history of the present and previous Edicules emerged during this work and are summarized here (cf. Fig. 66).

1. The outer walls of 1809–10 stand on an earlier basal plinth which extends unbroken beneath the benches flanking the Entry (Figs 74 and 89, Plinths 1 and 2, cf. Figs 8, 11, 82, 84 and 86). At the east end of the benches, stone candelabra dated in Arabic '1810' ride up over Plinth 1 and are butt-jointed against Plinth 2 (Fig. 89). Blank panels on the east ends of Course 3 of the benches, now partly hidden behind the candelabra, show that the benches belong to an earlier arrangement of this area. This in turn demonstrates that the plinths belong to an earlier stage of the Edicule. The history of the Edicule suggests that this can only be the reconstruction of 1555 'from the first foundations' (Fig. 66C; see above, pp. 100–2). Contrary to previous belief, therefore, the external ground plan of the Edicule seems to have remained unchanged since at least the mid-sixteenth century. This raises serious questions in relation to the outline of the Edicule shown in Amico's plan based on measurements taken in 1593–7 (Figs 9B, 48; cf. p. 46, no. 4), particularly since Horn's drawings (see above, p. 49, no. 6) and the wooden models of the period (Fig. 46) show a parallel-sided plan such as that which now exists (Fig. 85). If Amico's 'waisted' plan (Figs 9B, 48) is not

simply erroneous, it may represent the structure standing *on* the plinth, omitting the plinth itself. If this is the case, Amico's plan would suggest that the more than half-round shape of the western part of the Constantinian and medieval Edicule survived the rebuilding of 1555 only to be lost in the rebuilding of 1809–10 (Fig. 66).

ii.   The upper course of the plinth is thus also earlier than 1809–10 (Figs 74 and 89, Plinth 2). Its distinctive profile is comparable to the cornice of the Edicule of 1555 (Fig. 52), suggesting that it might be of the same date.

iii.   The stone benches before the entrance (Figs 7–9, 11–12, 74, 85–90) are also earlier than 1809–10 and must therefore have survived the fire of 1808, although the individual stones may have been reset in the reconstruction of 1809–10. There are signs of burning on the stones of the south bench. As already noted, the benches stand on the same basal plinths as the rest of the Edicule and are therefore probably no earlier than 1555 in their present form, but they contain earlier material reused, notably the great reel-and-bobbin cornice seen in Fig. 89.

Fig. 80. The cupboard under the altar of the Coptic Chapel (cf. Fig. 83), showing beneath the shelf the rough stones projecting from the west end of the Edicule. (Photograph Stuart Robson)

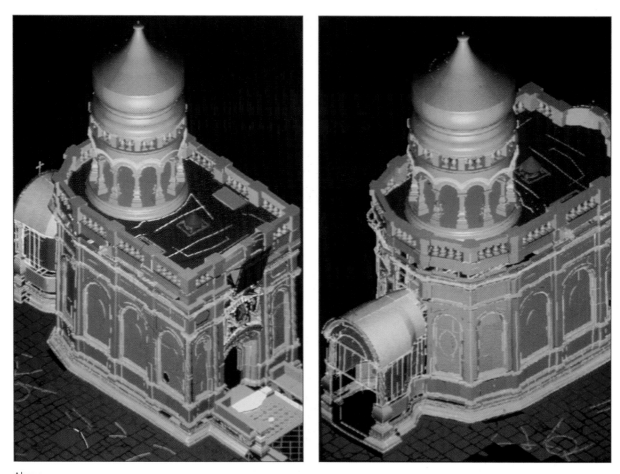

Above:
Fig. 81. Photogrammetric wire-frame 3D computer graphics model of the Edicule, partly surfaced, looking north-west. Isometric projection, some hidden lines still visible, in progress. (Engineering Surveying Research Centre, City University, London)

Above right:
Fig. 82. Photogrammetric wire-frame 3D computer graphics model of the Edicule, partly surfaced, looking north-east. Isometric projection, some hidden lines still visible, in progress. (Engineering Surveying Research Centre, City University, London)

iv.   The marble pavement between the benches in front of the entrance is set at an angle of about 5° to the axis of the Edicule as defined by its external plan (Figs 12, 85 and 90). This alignment is apparently derived from a wall-line just appearing below the white marble step before the entrance (Fig. 90). Although the pavement was laid in 1809–10, the alignment appears to relate to a very much older situation, certainly as early as the Byzantine reconstruction of the Church of the Holy Sepulchre in *c.* 1037/8–*c.* 1040, and possibly earlier.

v.   The sides and roof of the low entry between the Chapel of the Angel and the Tomb Chamber (Figs 93–4) contain work of several periods all earlier than 1809–10 and probably reaching back in part at least to the reconstruction of the rock-cut tomb after its partial destruction in 1009 (see above, p. 118). Limited exploration with a pencil torch behind the upper slab on the north side of the entrance passage suggests the presence here of a masonry wall. The claw- tooled stonework partly concealed by plaster in the roof of the entrance passage (Fig. 94) seems also to be part of a masonry structure rather than natural rock. A masonry wall was seen here by Maximos Simaios in 1809 (see above, p. 115). In 1483 Felix Faber had noted a rock-cut face, with built masonry above, beside this entrance in the west face of the Chapel of the Angel (see above, p. 114).

Fig. 83. The altar of the
Coptic Chapel at the west
end of the Edicule, showing
the cupboard beneath the
altar which covers the back
of the Edicule (cf. Fig. 80).
(Photograph John Crook)

vi.   The alignment of the Tomb Chamber has always been noted as different
      from that of the rest of the visible structure of the Edicule (Fig. 85). It is
      not the same as the alignment of the entrance pavement described in
      (iv), and since it is probably that of the original Tomb Chamber, it
      presumably follows the alignment of the rock-cut tomb of the Second
      Temple period uncovered in 325/6 (cf. Fig. 64A).

Fig. 84. Photogrammetric wire-frame 3D computer graphics model of the south-west exterior angle of the Edicule, at the junction with the Coptic Chapel, showing detail of stone jointing. Isometric projection, hidden lines removed, in progress. Cf. Fig. 67. (Engineering Surveying Research Centre, City University, London)

vii.   Behind a hinged ikon of the Virgin on the west wall of the Tomb Chamber, a rough masonry wall is visible (Figs 95–6). This wall may be part of the Byzantine reconstruction of the eleventh century (see above, p. 118). But it is also possible that it was inserted in 325/6–335 to block up the supposed western bench of the original Tomb Chamber (see Figs 64B, 66A, 79; see above, p. 118). In either case, it is presumably the west wall of built masonry seen by Maximos Simaios in 1809 (see above, p. 115).

viii. The marble cladding of the Tomb Chamber (Figs 95–7, 100–1) was not replaced in 1809–10, the fire not reaching into this part of the structure. The facing probably belongs to the reconstruction of 1555, but parts of it may be earlier. The Greek inscription of

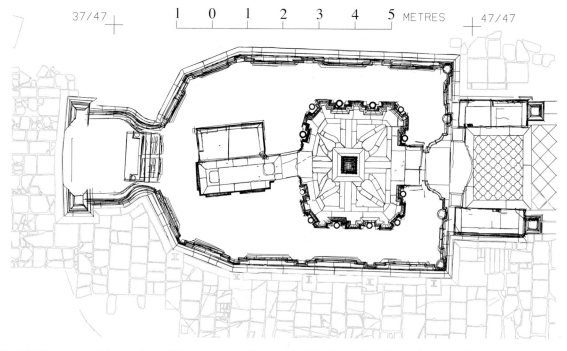

Fig. 85. Photogrammetric wire-frame 3D computer graphics model of the plan of the Edicule showing all lines plotted from a level just below that of the interior floor up to a level just above the surface of the marble slab covering the burial shelf. In progress. (Engineering Surveying Research Centre, City University, London)

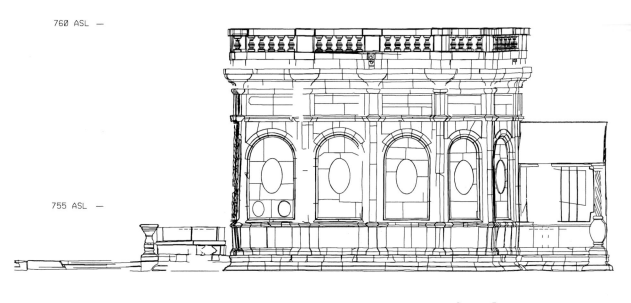

760 ASL —

755 ASL —

1   Ø   1   2   3   4   5   6   7

Metres

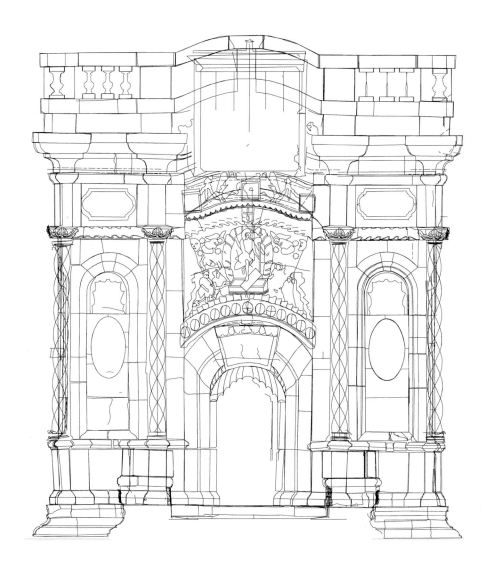

Fig. 86. Photogrammetric wire-frame 3D computer graphics model of the east–west elevation of the north side of the Edicule, from the base of the north candelabrum on the east to the Coptic Chapel on the west. In progress. (Engineering Surveying Research Centre, City University, London)

Fig. 87. Photogrammetric wire-frame 3D computer graphics model of the east elevation of the Edicule, partly surfaced. In progress. (Engineering Surveying Research Centre, City University, London)

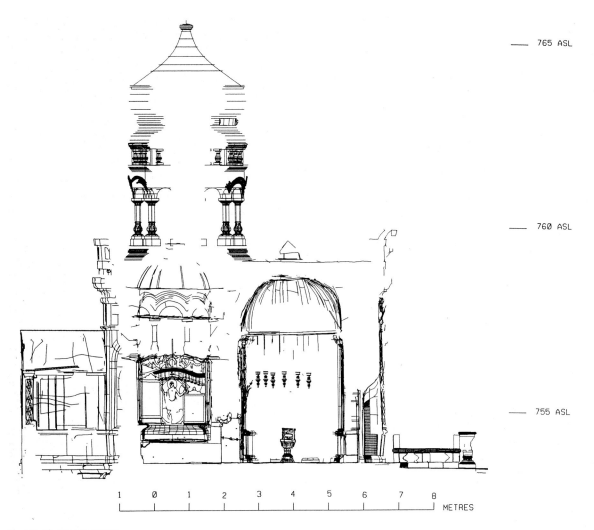

— 765 ASL

— 760 ASL

— 755 ASL

1   Ø   1   2   3   4   5   6   7   8
                                              METRES

Fig. 88. Photogrammetric wire-frame 3D computer graphics model of the west–east section through the Edicule, from the Coptic Chapel on the west to the north bench on the east, showing the Tomb Chamber and the Chapel of the Angel, with their vaults, and the cupola over the Tomb Chamber. In progress. (Engineering Surveying Research Centre, City University, London)

1809–10 (no. 18) high on the east, south and west walls of the Tomb Chamber (Figs 96 and 101) pays no attention to the horizontal jointing of the marble and seems therefore to have been cut on to slabs which were already in position.

ix. The marble slab covering the burial couch appears to have been in position at least as early as 1345 (see above, p. 88). This slab is of a streaked honey-coloured marble found nowhere else in the Edicule. Although at first sight it appears to be composed of several pieces, the slab is in fact one stone. The apparent divisions consist first of an oblique 'cut' across the slab from south to north (Figs 1, 85, 97, 101), and second of a groove, now filled with mortar, which runs along the west and east edges of the slab and all along the front edge, in each case just within the outer margin (Figs 1, 100–1). According to Elzear Horn, writing in the second quarter of the eighteenth century (see above, p. 49, no. 6), these incisions were made when the present covering of the burial couch was made by Boniface of Ragusa in 1555. The intention, Horn says, was to

Fig. 89. The base of the north candelabrum (dated in Arabic figures 1810: Inscription 10b) over-riding Plinth 1 and butting against Plinth 2 and the east end of the north bench, looking south-west. (Photograph John Crook)

Fig. 90. The Entry to the Edicule, showing between the benches the black-and-white floor panel lying at an angle to the rest of the structure (cf. Figs 12 and 85), looking west. (Photograph Stuart Robson)

Fig. 91. The Chapel of the Angel, looking down through the smoke vent, past the fifteen oil lamps, to the floor. The outer door is to the right and the entrance to the Tomb Chamber to the left (cf. Fig. 93). (Photograph Stuart Robson)

Fig. 92. The Chapel of the Angel, looking towards the north-east corner and the opening in the north wall of the Edicule through which the Holy Fire is passed out on Easter Saturday to the Greek Orthodox faithful.
Cf. Figs 86 and 103.
(Photograph John Crook)

deceive the Turks, who, if the slab were entire would have been attracted by its beauty and would have removed it for their own use.[2] Since it now seems that the slab with its diagonal cut and lipped edges was there as early as 1345 (see above, p. 88), this is probably no more than a good story.

x. The shelves of red marble low down above the burial slab on the west, north and east sides appear to have been inserted in 1809–10 (Figs 1, 95–7, 100–2). Candles belonging to the three great communities are placed on them according to strict rules maintained under the Status Quo,[3] and grooves cut into surface of the west (Figs 96, 101) and east (Figs 100–1) shelves mark the line in front of which only the candles, and at times the alms box, of the Greek Orthodox community may be set. A folding wooden altar made to fit precisely into the moulding running along the front edge of these

Fig. 93. The passage leading from the Chapel of the Angel to the Tomb Chamber, with the altar of the rolling stone in the foreground, looking north-west. The visible work is all of 1809–10, except for the iron-cramped marble panels on the north side of the passage, the roof of the passage above (cf. Fig. 94), and the visible parts of the Tomb Chamber beyond. (Photograph John Crook)

Fig. 94. The roof of the passage to the Tomb Chamber, looking upwards, showing (top) the folds of the marble curtain over the entrance to the passage (cf. Fig. 93) and (bottom) the head of the marble arch into the Tomb Chamber (visible below the Komnenos inscription on Fig. 100). Concealed between the marble curtain and arch into the Tomb Chamber is the marble head of an earlier arch and the broken and grease-covered mortar and stone of the earlier wall core. (Photograph John Crook)

Fig. 95. The Tomb Chamber and the burial couch from the passage, showing the contrasting marble cladding of ?1555, the shelf above the burial couch, the ikon of the Virgin covering the cupboard in the west wall, and the treatment of the floor. Cf. Figs 96 and 97. (Photograph John Crook)

Fig. 96. The west wall of the Tomb Chamber, looking west. The cupboard door (with an ikon of the Virgin on its outer face, cf. Fig. 95) is open, showing the blackened wax- and grease-covered wall of rough masonry behind the marble cladding of ?1555. Between the two left-hand candlesticks is the groove cut into the shelf to demarcate the areas used by the Greek Orthodox (to the left) and by the Latins (to the right). Cf. Fig. 100. (Photograph Stuart Robson)

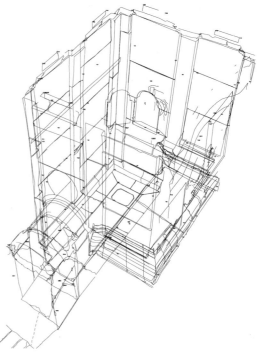

Fig. 97. Photogrammetric wire-frame 3D computer graphics model of the Tomb Chamber, seen from outside its north-east corner, looking south-west, with the entrance passage to the left and the marble slab covering the burial shelf to the right. Isometric projection, hidden lines not removed, in progress. (Engineering Surveying Research Centre, City University, London)

Fig. 98. The Tomb Chamber: looking up at the forty-three lamps which hang above the tomb. (Photograph Stuart Robson)

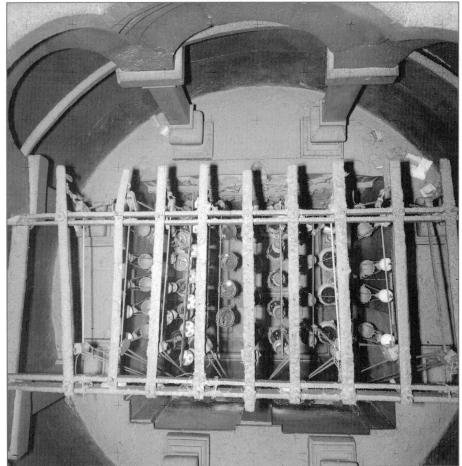

Fig. 99. The Tomb Chamber: looking down through the smoke vent on to the iron grid from which the lamps are suspended. (Photograph Stuart Robson)

Fig. 100. The interior of the Tomb Chamber looking east, through the passage, to the altar of the rolling stone in the Chapel of the Angel. For the inscription, cf. Fig. 71; and for the two-tone cladding, the red marble shelf (the right-hand end used by the Greek Orthodox, the left part by the Armenians), and the treatment of the edge of the burial slab, cf. Fig. 95. (Photograph John Crook)

shelves is placed in position every day for the celebration of the Latin Mass by the Franciscan community.[4] The altar is so constructed that the candles belonging to the three communities, Greek, Armenian and Latin, need not be moved. The eastern shelf was renewed in the 1970s.

xi.   The marble ikon of the Anastasis above the tomb (Figs 1 and 101) dates from the reconstruction of 1809–10: a *tour-de-force* by the Anatolian Greek sculptors who were part of Komnenos' team (see above, p. 105). It replaces a painting of the same subject, of sixteenth-century or even medieval date, which was already badly disfigured by smoke when Horn wrote in the second quarter of the eighteenth century.[5]

xii.   A projecting area of rough stone under the altar of the Coptic Chapel attached to the west end of the Edicule (Figs 80, 83, 85) may be the west face of the Byzantine reconstruction of the west wall of the rock-cut Tomb Chamber noted in (vii), or may even be of earlier date.

xiii.   The plan published here is the first to show accurately the thickness of the walls surrounding the Tomb Chamber and the Chapel of the

Fig. 101. The Tomb Chamber with the normal arrangement of candlesticks, vases, and pictures on the red marble shelf above the burial slab. The central part of the shelf is used by the Greek Orthodox, the left-hand part and left angle by the Latins, and the right-hand part and right angle by the Armenians: cf. Figs 96 and 100. The main marble ikon is Greek, the silver-covered picture to the left belongs to the Latins, and the painting to the right to the Armenians. The false crack cut into the burial slab is seen in the foreground. Cf. Figs 1 and 102. (Photograph John Crook)

Fig. 102. Photogrammetric wire-frame 3D computer graphics model of a section through the interior of the Tomb Chamber, the passage, and the Chapel of the Angel. Perspective view, partly surfaced, in progress. (Engineering Surveying Research Centre, City University, London)

Angel (Fig. 85). The north and south walls of the Tomb Chamber are up to 1.75 m thick, and the east and west walls up to 1.0 m. The walls of the Chapel of the Angel average about 1.0 m in thickness. There may be some voids in the walls around the Tomb Chamber, but it seems likely that they are for the most part solid. Even allowing for upstanding rock in the north and south walls of the Tomb Chamber (see above, p. 115), there is clearly room for elements of the structure of earlier Edicules to have survived as skins sandwiched between the outer and inner faces. The rough masonry visible behind the ikon of the Virgin in the west wall of the Tomb Chamber (Fig. 96) suggests that early work was left standing here in the reconstruction of 1809–10. There is no reason to suppose that the same is not the case in the other walls of the Tomb Chamber and in the walls of the Chapel of the Angel.

xiv.   Observations made by torch and feel in the gaps (e.g. Fig. 74) which have opened up in many places between the stones forming the exterior surface of the Edicule show (a) that these stones were all cramped together with iron ties set in lead and that everywhere (which could be inspected) the iron has rotted to nothing at the junctions, allowing the stones to move out of position under the weight of the superstructure; and (b) that these stones are normally only about 20 cm thick and form no more than a skin against the inner core of the walls to which they seem not to have been adequately if at all tied back.

xv.   As noted above (p. 108), the stones in the lower part of the east face of the Edicule appear to have moved significantly over the period 1990–3, presumably for the reasons set out in the last paragraph. Surveys by Professor Cooper have shown, however, that the spike on top of the cupola (Figs 6–8, 11) moved, if at all, no more than 2 mm between 1989 and 1992. These observations may suggest that the outer cladding is moving, or has moved, independently of the vault and cupola over the Tomb Chamber. While no certain explanation of this situation can be offered, it is possible that the superstructure of the Tomb Chamber is firmly founded on the rock-cut and masonry walls of the Tomb Chamber, while the lower part of the external cladding is subsiding under the weight of the upper part of the walls, the lower parts being no more than a skin no longer, if ever, securely attached to the earlier wall core behind.

It is clear that the Tomb of Christ conforms to the principle set out above, that structures which have been many times restored and even completely rebuilt around an enduring core usually preserve indications of their structural development in anomalies detectable in their final form (p. 11). Inside the skin of 1809–10 as in an onion lie the remains of earlier Edicules. From a combination of archaeological observation and photogrammetry a series of hypotheses is emerging to guide the investigation and recording of the tomb when the present structure is dismantled as a necessary part of the now urgently needed reconstruction.

THE HOLY FIRE

At the end of this lengthy enquiry into the most sacred shrine of Christianity we should remember the wise words of Mgr M. Andrieu in the introduction to his edition of the *Ordines Romani*:

> On a beaucoup écrit et savamment, sur l'architecture de nos cathédrales et de nos vieilles églises, mais l'on s'est rarement demandé ce qui avait pu se passer à l'intérieur de ces édifices et pourquoi nos ancêtres les avaient bâtis à si grands frais. On n'a considéré que le cadre de pierre, comme si, ayant lui-même sa raison d'être, il était toujours demeuré vide.[1]

The Edicule was designed by Constantine to enclose the place of Jesus' burial and Resurrection and to this end the Tomb Chamber has, as far as the events of history have permitted, been preserved intact. Before the entrance to the Tomb Chamber, since the moment of discovery, a fragment of the stone which plays so important a part in the Gospel accounts has been preserved, now enclosed in a central altar. In the Tomb Chamber, over the place of burial, and in the Chapel of the Angel, over the altar of the Sacred Stone, the Eucharist is still celebrated daily by the three great communities who guard the Holy Sepulchre, as it has been since at the latest the dedication of Constantine's church in 335. Over the centuries, from the later ninth century at least,[2] the annual miracle of the Descent of the Holy Fire has been celebrated in the Rotunda of the Resurrection on the Saturday of Easter.[3] The essentials of the ceremony have remained almost unchanged, but over the years the form of the Edicule has been modified to provide its setting, first, after the destruction of 1009, by the construction of a cupola over the Tomb Chamber, and later by the formation of openings in the walls of the Chapel of the Angel through which the Fire might be passed out to the waiting multitude. The continued annual celebration of the Holy Fire provides as vivid an argument as one could wish against studying such a structure as no more than a 'cadre de pierre' (Fig. 103).

Opposite:
Fig. 103. The ceremony of the Holy Fire, Easter Saturday, 1990. (Photograph Martin Biddle)

ACKNOWLEDGEMENTS

The credit for the initiation of this project belongs entirely to Dr G.S.P. Freeman-Grenville, K.H.S., F.S.A., F.R.A.S., who saw that the opportunity was grasped and with his wife, Lady (Mary) Kinloss, has been the support and encouragement of the work throughout, establishing and maintaining a wide range of diplomatic, ecclesiastical, and professional contacts both in Israel and at home, in addition to carrying out research in libraries in London and Jerusalem.

My gratitude is due first and foremost to the authorities in the Church of the Holy Sepulchre who have been from the beginning a constant source of generous help and support, and in particular to Timothy, Senior Metropolitan of Vostra, Secretary General of the Greek Orthodox Patriarchate of Jerusalem, Father Carlo Cecchitelli, o.f.m., Custos of the Holy Land, and his successor Father Guiseppi Nazzaro, o.f.m., Bishop Guregh Kapikian, Supervisor of the Restoration in the Armenian Section of the Holy Sepulchre, and the late Anba Basileos IV, Coptic Archbishop in Jerusalem. We owe special debts to Metropolitan Daniel, Guardian of the Sanctuary and head of the Greek Orthodox Confraternity in the Church of the Holy Sepulchre, for many personal and scholarly kindnesses; to Professor George Lavas, architect of the Greek Orthodox Patriarchate in the Holy Sepulchre, and his colleague Mr Th. Metropoulos, for much good advice and encouragement; to Fr. Albert Prodomo, o.f.m., architect of the Latin Custody of the Holy Sepulchre, for kindly interest and the gift of copies of plans and drawings; to our friend Brother Fabian Adkins, o.f.m., formerly Latin Sacristan in the Church of the Holy Sepulchre, for constant trust and encouragement, the answers and solutions to innumerable queries, and for arranging a workroom in the church; to Mr Yacoub Zreineh, Chief Dragoman of the Latin Convent, for many kindnesses, not least in translation; to Father Peter Vasco, o.f.m., K.H.S., for welcoming us into the editorial offices of the *Terra Santa* review where some of the writing and research for this book was done in the summer of 1993; to the Library of the Israel Antiquities Authority at the Rockefeller Museum; to the staff of the public search rooms at the Israel State Archives in Jerusalem and the Public Record Office at Kew; to the staff of the Bodleian Library and the Ashmolean Library in the University of Oxford; and to Mr Bernard Nurse and Mr Adrian James of the Library of the Society of Antiquaries of London.

The initial funding for the project in 1989–90 was generously provided by Gresham College, through the good offices of then Gresham Professor of

Divinity, now Bishop of London, the Rt Revd Richard Chartres. In 1992 the work in Jerusalem was partly supported by a crucial grant from Bayerische Rundfunk, through the kind intervention of Dr Carsten Peter Thiede of the Institut für Wissenschaftstheoretische Grundlagenforschung in Paderborn, and in 1993 substantial support from the office of the British Council in East Jerusalem, through the good offices of Mr Chris McConville and Mr Peter Morison, with the kind intervention of the British Council Offices in Oxford (Fiona Fenton) and Tel Aviv (Peter Sandiford), allowed Martin Biddle and Birthe Kølbye-Biddle to spend a long summer season writing in Jerusalem. In all four years British Airways through their Charities Department (Jacky Ive) generously carried large weights of equipment and research papers free of charge. In 1990 the Leverhulme Trust awarded a major research grant to the University of Oxford and City University, London, under the terms of which techniques have been developed for the analysis and presentation of the photogrammetric data recorded in the field seasons of 1989–90 and 1992. I am as always grateful to Mr David Astor and to Hertford College, Oxford, for the continued privilege of being able to work in such a congenial atmosphere under the terms of the Astor Senior Research Fellowship in Medieval Archaeology, and to the College for the provision of research funds which have materially helped in the preparation of this book.

My principal personal debt is to Magister Birthe Kølbye-Biddle who has been my collaborator in this project from the first reconnaissance in 1988. She has taken charge of the archaeological recording of the Edicule through the long days and nights in the Church of the Holy Sepulchre and has prepared the description and analysis of the structure of the Edicule. She has been assisted by Steven Ashley, Joyce and Walter Marsden, and Hamish Roberton. John Crook has taken the archaeological and architectural 'descriptive' photographs throughout the project.

From the start the project has been a collaboration between two approaches, two universities, and two sets of colleagues. It is a particular pleasure to acknowledge and thank Professor M.A.R. (Michael) Cooper, Director of the Engineering Surveying Research Centre at City University, London, for his contribution to all aspects of the work since we first mentioned the word Jerusalem to him in 1988. He has brought to it not only his scholarship and enthusiasm but also the whole-hearted collaboration of his colleagues in the Centre, notably Dr Stuart Robson, our Leverhulme Post-Doctoral Research Fellow, who has worked with us in Jerusalem since 1989, and has not only been responsible for the capture of the photogrammetric data, but is now pioneering new ways of analysing and presenting the results. By far the greater part of the photogrammetric plotting is the work of Roger Littleworth, who set up the stereopairs and digitized the photographs to produce the line string and surfaced models, and in 1992 was able to join the team in Jerusalem. Support in digitization and computer-modelling has been given by David Stirling, City University. In 1990 and 1992 Jennifer Cooper assisted Michael Cooper with the survey of the Edicule and Rotunda.

A large number of colleagues in several countries have earned our gratitude by facilitating work in libraries and museums, by answering questions and by providing books, references and photocopies. Some have been acknowledged in the text, but we repeat their names here and apologize to those who, in the course of a long and complex project, we have failed to recall: Steven Ashley (Norwich), Dr Dan Bahat (Jerusalem), Dr Anna Ballian (Athens), Professor Leonid Beliaev (Moscow), Dr John Blair (Oxford), Professor A.A.M. Bryer (Birmingham), Father Rigobert Buchschachner (Eichstätt), Professor Johan Callmer (Umeå), Father Kenneth Campbell, o.f.m. (London and Jerusalem), Father Luigi Civilini o.f.m. (San Vivaldo), Dr Rupert Chapman (London), Professor Richard Clogg (Oxford), Sigalit Cohen (Israel State Archives, Jerusalem), Professor Robin Connor (Winnipeg), Professor Jaroslav Folda (Chapel Hill), Shimon Gibson (London), Professor Julian Gardner (Warwick), Nicholas Griffiths (Wilton), Richard Harper (Jerusalem), Canon A.E. Harvey (London), Professor F.W. Hodcroft (Oxford), Dr James Howard Johnston (Oxford), Professor Amos Kloner (Jerusalem), Dom Umberto Livi o.s.b. (Bologna), Arthur MacGregor (Oxford), Professor Cyril Mango (Oxford), Sac. Graziano Marini (Aquileia), Professor Ya'akov Meshorer (Jerusalem), Professor Michael Metcalf (Oxford), Professor Robin Milner-Gulland (Sussex), Father Jerome Murphy-O'Connor O.P. (Jerusalem), Professor Donald Nicol (Athens), Dr Alison Pearn (Cambridge), Ruth Peled (Jerusalem), Professor Maurilio Pérez González (León), Father Michele Piccirillo, o.f.m. (Jerusalem), Dr Ronny Reich (Jerusalem), Dr Rainer Riesner (Gomaringen), Dr Richard Sharpe (Oxford), John Simmons (Oxford), Dr Kenneth Stevenson (Guildford), Dr Gerry Stone (Oxford), Dr Vera Stone (Oxford), Carsten Peter Thiede (Paderborn), Dr Edmund Thomas (Oxford), Miss Sophie Thompson (Jerusalem), Dr Helgard Ulmschneider (Heidelberg), Dr Stephanie West (Oxford), Pamela Willis (London), Professor Roger Wright (Liverpool), Professor Sir Christopher Zeeman (Oxford).

I first discussed the history of the Tomb of Christ in an article which appeared as 'The Tomb of Christ: Sources, Methods, and a New Approach', in Kenneth Painter (ed.), 'Churches Built in Ancient Times': Recent Studies in Early Christian Archaeology, Society of Antiquaries of London Occasional Papers 16 (London, 1994), 73–147. I am most grateful to my friend Kenneth Painter for his help throughout the production of the original paper, and to him and to the Society of Antiquaries of London for their ready agreement to its publication in this enlarged and extensively revised form.

NOTES AND REFERENCES

CHAPTER ONE

1. John Wilkinson, the leading modern student of the tomb, advocated this approach as long ago as 1971, but devoted the bulk of his important analysis to the form of the Edicule before 1555 (Wilkinson 1971, 242–52, esp. 243–4; 1972).
2. Harvey 1935.
3. Contemporary correspondence and reports describing this work and the circumstances surrounding it are preserved among the papers of the Mandatory Government of Palestine, Department of Antiquities, now the Israel Antiquities Authority, and kept in the Record Room at the Rockefeller Museum, Files ATQ/199(a), ATQ/199.1–3, ATQ/1–7/113 and ATQ/1650. For access to these papers and for every facility we are indebted to Dr Ronny Reich, Keeper of the Documentation Department, Ruth Peled and their colleagues.
4. A set of 'Plumbing Records' made in February 1947 recording the then verticality (or rather lack of it) of the Edicule is included in the comprehensive illustrated typescript report on the church prepared in May 1947 by C.T. Wolley of Freeman Fox & Partners, Consulting Engineers, of London, see Paras 62 and 102, Drawing 17, and Photograph 38. The foundation pits for the shoring of the Edicule were dug in March 1947 and a record of the depth of the rock encountered in each was made by the Clerk of Works, Mr G. Musallam, of the Public Works Department (Drawing no. B/1771/19). A copy of the Wolley report and an annotated copy of the PWD drawing are kept in the Record Room at the Israel Antiquities Authority. A report on the state of the Edicule before the earthquake of 1927, by A.C. Holliday, Civic Advisor to the Pro-Jerusalem Society, dated 9 June 1926, accompanied by sixteen whole-plate photographs and a drawn section at one-quarter full-size, shows that the walls of the Edicule were already then bulging outwards and that the joints above and below the lower string moulding had opened up by between 1.5 and 2.5 cm: PRO, CO 733/128/8.
5. Steel Corporation of Bengal, nationalized in 1971: pers. comm. R.A.C. Latter, British Steel (letter of 26 February 1991).
6. Lavas and Mitropoulos 1988.
7. Freeman-Grenville 1987.
8. Toynbee and Ward Perkins 1956, 220–4, and cf. Figs 14 (lower) and 23.
9. Biddle 1990; Biddle 1991; Biddle et al. 1992; Biddle 1994; Biddle 1996; Biddle 1998a; Biddle 1998b; Cooper et al. 1992; Cooper and Robson 1994; Robson et al. 1994; Bentkowska 1997; Biddle et al. in preparation.
10. Willis 1849; Clark 1909; Thompson 1996, 159.
11. Willis 1849, 139–60.
12. Wilde 1840; Schulz 1845; Grenville 1845. Willis's notes from Schulz and Grenville (Lord Nugent) are in Cambridge University Library, Add. MS. 5031/17.
13. Vincent and Abel 1914, 93–6.
14. Dalman 1935, 366–75.
15. Avigad 1976; Kloner 1980; Rahmani 1981–2; Kloner 1985a; Stern (ed.) 1993, 747–57; Bieberstein and Bloedhorn 1994, i, 128–41; and bibliography in Purvis 1988, 67–87.
16. For example, Finegan 1978, 181–208; Mare 1987, 193–9; Bahat 1990, 50–1; Millard 1991, 174–5.
17. Willis 1849, 160–97.
18. The evidence for this is contained among Willis's working papers now preserved in the library of the Palestine Exploration Fund. They include, in addition to J.J. Scoles's drawings of tombs

mentioned above, the originals or contemporary copies of Scoles's survey of the Church of the Holy Sepulchre made in 1825 (Willis 1849, 138 n. 1, 285–90; Williams 1849, i, xiv–xv), and a series of Russian engravings and drawings probably obtained by George Williams when chaplain at St Petersburg in 1844–5 (Williams 1845, x; *DNB*). I am very grateful to Shimon Gibson for first drawing these papers to my attention and to Birthe Kjølbye-Biddle for our joint analysis which lead to the realization that they were the working papers behind Willis's 1849 study of the Church of the Holy Sepulchre. The archive also contains the French originals and drafts of some of the illustrations used in 1864 for Pierotti's *Jerusalem Explored*, probably because George Williams arranged for the English translation of Pierotti's apparently never published French original and revised the proof sheets.

19. Willis 1849, Pl. 2, Figs 6–8, cf. p. 293; see here Fig. 14.
20. Source not yet traced.
21. Pierotti 1864, i, 114–19, ii, Pl. XXXIV. This section was based upon Planche 36 of Pierotti's projected French edition, the original drawing for which is among the papers in the Palestine Exploration Fund: see n. 18.
22. Wilson 1865, 49–50, Pl. XX.2, with folded plan at 1:200.
23. Ioannides 1877, 185–90, 230–4.
24. Vincent and Abel 1914, 97–104, 155–8, 176–7, 181–5, 221–4, 249, 253, 263–6, 291–4, 296–300.
25. Vincent and Abel 1914, 107.
26. Vincent and Abel 1914, 291–4, 296–300.
27. Wilkinson 1971 (reprinted 1981); 1972; 1978, 184–94; 1981, 242–52, 332.

CHAPTER TWO

1. Baldi 1955.
2. Wilkinson 1977; 1988.
3. de Sandoli 1978–84.
4. Baldi 1955.
5. Thematic bibliography of pilgrim literature in Schur 1980; see also Purvis 1988, 293–302.
6. Grabar 1972, i, 257–82.
7. Wilkinson 1971, 95–7, Pl. X.
8. Kartsonis 1986.
9. For example, the Trivulzio and Munich ivories, Volbach 1976, reproductions 110–11, Pl. 33; the British Museum plaque, Kötzsche 1994 and Buckton (ed.) 1994, 58–9, no. 45.
10. For example, Conant 1956, 44–8, Pls IX, XV, XVI; cf. Heber-Suffrin 1991, 71–4, esp. p.71, n.58.
11. Guarducci 1978, 77–87, 116–20, 125–8; Biddle 1996a, 327.
12. Lauffray 1962; cf. Wilkinson 1971, 249–52; 1972, 92–7, Fig. 13, Pl. X; Bonnery 1991; Biddle 1996a, 324.
13. Morey 1926; discussed in Barag 1971, 58–9, Fig. 50; Weitzmann 1974, 41–2; Morello 1996; colour plate in Donati (ed.) 1996, 161.
14. Grabar 1958; Wilkinson 1971, 246–9; Wilkinson 1972, 92–3, Figs 10, 11; Barag 1971, 57–63, Fig. 51; Barag and Wilkinson 1974; Biddle 1996a, 328–9; and other examples in Ross 1962, no. 87 (see here Fig. 18); Engemann 1973, Weitzmann 1974, 42, Fig. 24, and Kötzsche-Breitenbruch 1984, 229–41.
15. Kötzsche-Breitenbruch 1984, 241–6, Taf. 27a, b.
16. Barag 1970, 45–6; 1971, 57–63.
17. Corbo 1988, 419–22, Figs 4, 5; and cf. Metzger 1981, 20–1, 48–9, nos 120–2; Vikan 1982, 26–7, Fig. 20a, b.
18. Meshorer 1986; Eisenstadt 1987; Päffgen 1992, 412–16, Abb. 149–50.
19. Piccirillo 1991, 79–82, colour pl. on p. 124; Piccirillo 1993, 238–9, Fig. 344 (colour). Apparently similar structures in the images of Ascalon (Fig. 352), and perhaps Caesarea (Fig. 345), must be taken into account in evaluating this possible representation of the Edicule.
20. Trolle and Pentz 1983; cf. Underwood 1950; colour plate in Donati (ed.) 1996, 163.
21. Bonnery 1991, 26–7, Fig. 17; colour reproduction, Cortesi 1975, 68.
21A. Vikan 1995, no. 34.
22. Meehan (ed.) 1983, 11, 21, 42–3 [Cap. 2.2]; Wilkinson 1977, 193, 195–7, Pls 5, 6. For the present state of Adomnán studies, his purpose in writing *De locis sanctis*, its date, and the role of Arculf, see O'Loughlin 1997, and his previous articles there quoted. Dr Thomas O'Loughlin's forthcoming study of the drawings which accompany the text both of *De locis sanctis* and of Bede's work of the same name will be fundamental to the question of the use of these 'diagrams' as evidence for form of the Edicule and Rotunda in the seventh century.

23. Milan, MS. Ambrosianus 49–50, pp.569, 598, 630: Grabar 1943, Pls. XLIII.1, XLVIII.3, LII.1.
24. Maspero 1908; *L'Art Copte* 1964, no. 129, cf. no. 128; Grabar 1972, 276, Pl. XV.3
25. Hamilton 1974, 65.
26. Huxley 1925, 177–89.
27. Heber-Suffrin 1991, 71–7, Fig. 10; cf., for example, the tomb shown in the late eleventh-century gospels now Oxford, Wadham College MS 2, f.104^v, reproduced in Alexander 1970, 13, Pl. 33.
28. Dalman 1922; Neri 1971; Bresc-Bautier 1974, esp. 337–42; Ousterhout 1990c.
29. Dalman 1922, 56–65, no. 8; Wilkinson 1972, 90, Figs 7, 8.
30. Neri 1971, 94–139, Figs 49–54; Agnoletto *et al.* 1987, 134–9, 179.
31. Amico 1593–7.
32. Dalman 1922, 81–7.
33. See, e.g., Mitchell 1965, 24, 118; and cf. Woodall 1989, 154–5, 156.
34. Woodall 1989, 150–2, 155, Figs 4, 9; Wilkinson 1972, 87, Pl. IX.
35. Brasca 1966, 145; Baxandall 1982, 30–1, Fig. 13.
36. Davies 1911, xxvi no. 18, Reproduction 43; Prescott 1954, 33n., 136–7, 178; Wilkinson 1972, 87, Fig. 4.
37. Karlsruhe, Badische Landesbibliothek, St. Peter pap. 32, f. 45^v; München 1984, no. 120; Stift Pölten 1994, no. 6/6; Budde and Nachama 1995, no. 1/107, Abb. 175. The drawings are said to have been made by Konrad himself partly following Reuwich (cf. Lehmann-Haupt 1929), but Konrad's drawings of the Edicule and the Church of the Holy Sepulchre from the Parvis are better drawn and more detailed than any others known and seem to be quite independent. Another copy of Konrad's manuscript is preserved at Gotha, some of the drawings from different standpoints and larger.
38. Kraus (ed.) 1986, 9, Abb. 12, after Germanisches Nationalmuseum, Nürnberg, Hs 369, Bl. 36^r. Also reproduced in Neri 1971, Fig. 11, and de Sandoli 1984, 55.
39. Nijhoff 1933–6, 22, Pls 114–15; van Regteren Altena 1967, 20–1, Fig. 11.
40. Vatican, Biblioteca Apostolica, Cod. Urb. lat. 1362, f. 1^v; Vincent *et al.* 1949, 67; Neri 1971, Fig. 35.
41. Dalman 1922, 108–12, esp. p. 110, cf. Taf. X, Abb. 34.
42. The Hague, Koninklijke Bibliotheek, MS. 76 F5, f.1 (was MS. 69); edited and reproduced in colour by Levy 1991, 445–9; also in Nebenzahl 1986, Fig. 5.
43. Buchtal 1986, Pl. 131f.
44. Sabine 1979; Meshorer 1986b, 228–9, Pl. 28.8; Meshorer 1991, 392 no. 8, 398.
45. Blanchet 1943, 73–4, nos 1–8, Pls I.8, XX.4.
46. Mayer 1978, Taf. 1, no. 7; Blanchet 1943, 134–5, nos 163–5, Pl. V.9, cf. Pl. XX.3.
47. Blanchet 1943, 135–6, no. 167, Pl. XX.2.
48. Blanchet 1943, 140, no. 178; illustrated in Schlumberger 1894, 177, Pl. I.1, and Sabine 1979, 132, Pl. 17, no. 5.
49. Buschhausen 1980, 60, 68, Taf 32, 38, discussion of the iconography on pp. 97–9; Claussen 1996, with latest bibliography.
50. Loverance 1988, Fig. 71; Kötzsche 1988; Buckton (ed.) 1994, 187–8 (nos 202–3).
51. van Regteren Altena 1967, Figs 1–3. Lauffray 1962, 216, notes 'fleur de lys' in two texts (apparently prior to 1009?), but gives no references.
52. Københavns Universitet Amager, MS. AM 736, I, 4º; Levy 1991, 467–70.
53. Young 1990, 112 (Ills 141) and 81–2 (Ills 101), respectively.
54. Holland Walker 1927; Clapham 1934, 154; Pevsner 1979, 252–4; Zarnecki 1998, 138–9.
55. Dalman 1922, 81–7, esp. 83, 87. I am most grateful to Dr Helgard Ulmschneider, Heidelberg, for the translation of the caption to the woodcut, which presents several difficulties.
56. Dalman 1922, 106–37, Taf. X–XII.
57. Dalman 1922, 108–12, Taf. X, Abb. 34.
58. Pers. comm. Professor A.A.M. Bryer; Milner-Gulland 1994, 99–100; Ousterhout 1997; and cf. Grzybkowski 1997, Olijnik and Chodorkowski 1997, Boberski 1997, and Biertasz 1997.
59. Baart 1991; Caron 1992, 4; de Kroon 1997, 148. Dr Jan Baart kindly provided the photograph published here as Fig. 43.
60. Dalman 1920; Bagatti 1951b.
61. Bagatti 1951, 135–6.
62. Bushuiev 1995, 10–11, 96–8 [Cat. no. 159]; cf. Ousterhout 1997, 143.
63. van Regteren Altena 1967, 21, Fig. 12.
64. Dam-Mikkelsen and Lundbæk 1980, 90, EFa3a, 3b; Gundestrup 1991, ii, 190–2.
65. Willis 1849, 287–8.
66. Biddle 1996, 331.

67. Wren 1942, 134–5; cf. Acts 19.24.
68. Bagatti (ed.) 1953.
69. Willis 1849, 198, n.2, 285–9; Bagatti (ed.) 1953, 34: the translation on p.43 omits in line 3, after 'divided into', the crucial words 'ten palms, and each palm into', cf. Amico 1620, 1.
70. Zupko 1981, 183–4, s.v. 'palm', cf. 62–3, s.v. 'canna'.
71. Willis 1849, 198, n.2.
72. Willis 1849, 198, n.2.
73. Bagatti (ed.) 1953, 106.
74. Amico 1609, 5; Amico 1620, 44; Bagatti 1938, 320; Bagatti (ed.) 1953, 108.
75. For example, Bagatti (ed.) 1953, 24–5.
76. Zuallardo 1587, 184, 189, 207.
77. Bagatti (ed.) 1953, 109, 111.
78. Willis 1849, 285–7.
79. Bruyn 1698, Pls 144, 146, and 147.
80. Best edition Golubovich 1902; see also Bagatti (ed.) 1962.
81. Golubovich 1902, 18–40; Bagatti (ed.) 1962, 15–22, Figs 3–5, Pls. I–VI, XV.1.
82. Oxford, Bodleian Library, MS. Add. D. 27, ff. 210ᵛ–211ʳ, 219ᵛ–220aʳ.
83. Meinardus 1971.
84. Meinardus 1967; cf. Bagatti 1951a.
85. Neri 1971, Fig. 15; Farris and Storme 1991; Montagni 1994, 48–9, 99–101, Figs 91–2. I owe the two latter references to the kindness of Timothy Wilson of the Ashmolean Museum, Oxford.
86. Athens, Benaki Museum, TA 321, 322; Ballian 1992, 65, no. 30. I am most grateful to Dr Anna Ballian for the gift of photographs of these containers; cf. Fig. 56.
87. Schiller 1978, 121–2, 131; Onne 1980, 51–2, 54, 57, 59, 99; Gernsheim 1984, nos 88, 129–30, 144–5; Perez 1988, 157, 159, 171–2, 215, Figs 121, 242; Wahrman *et al.* 1993, 8–35, Pl. 20; Howe 1997, 16–46, plates on pp. 53, 55, 58–9, 75–6, 106.
88. Zangaki nos 1175, 1184–5: Palestine Exploration Fund Photographic Archives.
89. Patrich 1995, Fig. 12, the painting can just be seen on Fig. 21 at an oblique angle in the far corner of the northern narthex.
90. Mandate Government of Palestine (see ch. 1, n. 3), File ATQ/1650: Inspector of Antiquities O.E.T.A. (South) to Military Governor, 29.12.19; Military Governor (Ronald Storrs) to the Latin Patriarch, Ref. 2274 (MG), 28.2.20.
91. Roberts 1842–9, i, Pl. 10.

CHAPTER THREE

1. Architectural description of the successive Edicules is reserved for another occasion: the Constantinian Edicule has been very fully studied by John Wilkinson (1972, 91–7) but both it and the later Edicules require systematic analysis of the evidence of the many pilgrim accounts, and of the varied sources of visual evidence (above, ch. 2). This is still in progress.
2. Riesner 1997, 47–54.
3. Geva 1993a, 747.
4. As was sometimes the case: Geva 1993a, 749.
5. Vincent and Abel 1914, Fig. 53.
6. For the possibility that the Christian community in Jerusalem may have preserved a knowledge of the location of Golgotha down to 135, and that this knowledge survived the construction of Hadrian's temple, see Schlatter 1966, 99–173; Riesner 1985; and Riesner 1988.
7. Several of which are known: Schick 1885; Vincent and Abel 1914, 194, Figs 114–16, Planche XII; Kloner 1980, 145–6; Corbo 1981, i, 29; ii, Tav. 3 (no. 28), 52, 54, 67; iii, Photos 4, 5; Kloner 1985b; Bahat 1986, 30–2; Gibson and Taylor 1994, 51–6, 61–3, Figs 36–7.
8. Jeremias 1925, 149–50.
9. Meshorer 1989, 19–20; Geva 1993b, 759.
10. *V.C.* 3.26.
11. *Ep.* 58.3.
12. Meshorer 1989, 22 n.32, *pace* Kadman 1956. Meshorer's results mean that all statements about the cult of Aphrodite/Venus in Aelia, in so far as these are based on the identifications of Kadman 1956, must be discarded, e.g. Gibson and Taylor 1994, 68–9.
13. Meshorer 1989, 22–4, 31–2, 38–9.
14. I am grateful to Professor Ya'akov Meshorer for discussing this problem, which deserves fuller consideration on another occasion. Dio Cassius, writing before 229, records that a temple of Jupiter was built 'on the site of the temple of God' when Hadrian founded the colony: *Hist.*

LXIX. 12. 1, discussed by Flussin 1992, 26–8. For the identification of the Kapitolion, and thus presumptively of the temple of the Capitoline Triad, with the site of the Temple Mount, now the Haram al-Sharif, see Flussin 1992, Mango 1992, 2–3, and Gibson and Taylor 1994, 69–70. Father Murphy-O'Connor, arguing against this identification, has stated afresh the case in favour of locating the Capitol on the site occupied today by the Church of the Holy Sepulchre (Murphy-O'Connor 1994).

15. Corbo 1981, i, 33–7, 221; ii, Tav. 68; critically reviewed in Bahat 1986, 32–5; and see now usefully Gibson and Taylor 1994, 65–71.

16. See now Geva 1993b, 763, and note the dotted outlines of temple and basilica on the plan on p. 758. Gibson and Taylor (1994, 65) argue from the supposed height of the original rock surface over the Tomb Chamber now marked by the Edicule that the surface of the podium must here have been at an elevation of at least 757 m above sea level, i.e. about 3.5 m above the present floor of the Rotunda. This is the only archaeological (as distinct from literary) evidence that there is for the existence of the podium: no surviving part of the Roman structure at present known actually survives higher than 753.24 m (Gibson and Taylor 1994, Fig. 43), i.e. about 0.25 m below the floor of the Rotunda.

17. Bar 1993 (in Hebrew); Bar 1998 (in English, with additions).

18. There are, for example, thirty-three dedications to Fortuna in one or other of her forms (on her own, or as Augusta, Redux, Conservatrix, or Servatrix) from military establishments (including bath-houses) in the British provinces, but none to Venus. I am grateful to Nicholas Griffiths for establishing this point from a search of Collingwood and Wright 1965 (for the years down to 1954), and the annual surveys in *The Journal of Roman Studies* (for 1954–68) and *Britannia* (for 1969–96). The index to von Domaszewski's study of the religion of the Roman army contains no references to Aphrodite/Venus and only incidental references to Tyche/Fortuna (von Domaszewski 1895).

19. Bar 1998, 11; for plans, see Isaac 1993, Figs 3–5.

20. Debate to 1950, and Second Wall in particular: Simons 1952, 282–343; Vincent 1954, 90–113. More recent work on northern walls: Kenyon 1974, 144–51, 181–7, 191–204, 223–55; Lux 1972; Schein 1981; Avigad 1984, 26–74; Bahat 1990, 24–31, 34–7, 40–3, 55. Third Wall: Shanks 1987. Most recent reviews of the whole question: Stern (ed.) 1993, 704–7, 716–21, 724–9, 736, 744–5; Wightman 1993, 159–91; Bieberstein and Bloedhorn 1994, i, 102–8, 113–16, 119–20, 125–7.

21. For example, Duckworth 1922, 40–2.

22. Parrot 1955, 39.

23. Hall 1979.

24. Harvey 1966.

25. Hall 1979, xvii–xxii, xlv–xlvi.

26. *P.P.* 72, 506.

27. *P.P.* 93, 692; 94, 693–706.

28. *P.P.* 72, 506; 93, 692; 94, 694.

29. *P.P.* 94, 704.

30. Melito's letter concerning this visit (preserved in Eusebius, *H.E.* 4.26.13–14; Hall 1979, 64–7, Frag. 3) contains the clause, 'going back to the east and reaching the place where it was proclaimed and done'. Some writers have taken this to imply that Melito went specifically to see the sites of Jesus' life and passion; but the meaning of the verbs ἐκηρύχθη καὶ ἐπράχθη (Hall 1979, Frag. 3, 1. 15) cannot be so closely defined. They probably refer more generally to the deeds and prophesies recorded in the books of the Old Testament. The point is important, since the narrower interpretation might suggest that Melito had specifically sought out the site of the Crucifixion and thus might give added weight to his statements about its location.

31. Liddell and Scott 1940, s. πλατύς, IIa; Arndt, Gingrich and Danker 1979, s.v.

32. Robert 1937, 532–6; Milik 1961, 152 n.1: 'jamais place'.

33. *V.C.* 3.39; on the text and correct translation of Eusebius at this point, see Milik 1961, 161–2.

34. Jastrow 1903, ii, 1179.

35. I owe these examples to Dr Edmund Thomas, whose forthcoming monograph *Roman Architecture under the Antonines* (Oxford Classical Monographs), Ch. 3, provides further evidence for this change in use of the term from a meaning a 'street, avenue, boulevard', a meaning which it may in some cases have continued to possess, to a meaning as 'square, open space', giving rise to the French *place* and Italian *piazza*, in the context of an apparently increasing number of these piazzas from the Antonine period onwards.

36. Hall 1979, 52.

37. Avigad 1984, 213–29; cf. Bahat 1990, 59–63, 76–7 and Geva 1993b, 758.

38. cf. Bahat 1990, 66.

39. Lux 1972, 190–2, Plans 3–6; Kenyon 1974, 226–35; Schein 1981, 23–4; and for the final

report on the excavations under the Church of the Redeemer, Vriezen 1994, 14–16, 291–5.

40. Vincent 1954, 237–59, esp. 243, pl. LXI.
41. Simons 1952, 300, 453–4, Fig. 56.
42. Avigad 1984, 26–74.
43. Hall 1979, xl; Eusebius, *H.E.*, 4. 26. 13–14 = Hall 1979, 64–7, Frag.3; cf. Blenkinsopp 1989, 38.
44. Barnes 1975; 1981, 110–11. This dating depends on Eusebius's description of Petra as 'a famous city of Palestine'. Petra was incorporated in the Roman province of *Palestina* by 305 and probably by *c.* 293 when the Tenth Legion was moved from Jerusalem to Aila (Aqabah): Tsafrir 1986; Tsafrir *et al.* 1994, 14–18, cf. Figs 3, 4.
45. Eusebius, *Onomastikon*, 74.19–21
46 Hunt 1984, 149.
47. Topeth: *Onomastikon* 102.14–15; the tomb of Helen of Adiabene: *H.E.* 2.12.3.
48. Hunt 1984, 99–100; Groh 1985, 25–9, esp. 27.
49. *Onomastikon* 75.20–2.
50. But see Gibson and Taylor 1994, 65–8, Fig. 43, nos 12–14.
51. Bahat 1990, 66.
52. Taylor 1993, 120.
53. Taylor 1993, 122, 140–1, 317, 336.
54. In a recent article Dr Taylor has maintained her view that the site of the crucifixion lay to the south of the traditional site of Golgotha, insisting on her interpretation of πρὸς τοῖς βορείοις τοῦ Σιὼν ὄρους as meaning 'right beside the northern parts of Mount Zion' (Taylor 1998, 192–3). She now locates Golgotha 200 m away from the tomb, precisely in the middle of the supposed site of the main east–west street of Aelia, the Decumanus, no certain trace of which has yet been located (Taylor 1998, 180, 182–93, Fig. 4).
55. Bar 1998, 9–11, provides a useful summary of the documentary evidence for conditions on the south-west hill in the later third to fifth centuries.
56. Hall 1984, 2.
57. For example, 'Cyril', *Mystagogical Lectures*, 1.ii, ix, xi, 2.ii–iv; Wilkinson 1981, 61–3, 71–6; cf. Wharton 1992, 315, 320, but not her conclusions, 321 ff.
58. Sweet 1990, 46, 182, 184, and esp. 187.
59. Sweet 1990, 187, brings out well the complexity and superimposition of meanings. See also Hughes 1990, 126–8 where the conflict between an original crucifixion outside the city and this apparent reference to a site within the city becomes part of the argument, although by the time Revelation was written the site was certainly within the walls.
60. *P.P.* 105, 792–3; Hall 1979, xli, 99.
61. For example, Willis 1849, 241–56; Vincent and Abel 1914, 154–94; Duckworth 1922, 71–135; Wistrand 1952; Coüasnon 1974, 12–17, 37–53; Corbo 1981, i, 39–137; Hunt 1984, 7–14; Ousterhout 1990a; Gibson and Taylor 1994, 73–85; for full references to previous work, see Bieberstein and Bloedhorn 1994, i, 154–5, 173–4, and ii, 183–216.
62. Drake 1985; Walker 1990, 235–81; Taylor 1992–3 provides a useful review of the position reached.
63. Barnes 1981, 186, 367 n. 176; cf. Walker 1990, 84–6, 273, 274 n. 136.
64. *De sepulchro Christi* = *L.C.* 11–18.
65. *De laudibus Constantini* = *L.C.* 1–10.
66. *Vita Constantini* = *V.C.*, written 337–9.
67. Walker 1990, 276, with references to recent discussion.
68. Eusebius *V.C.* 3.28.
69. For example, Duckworth 1922, 72; Dalman 1935, 350; cf. Hunt 1984, 7–9.
70. Walker 1990, 272 n. 130.
71. *Catech*. 14.9.
72. Geva 1993a, 747–8.
73. *Catech*. 10.19, 13.39, 14.22; for critical comment, Walker 1990, 270–1.
74. *Catech*. 14.5.
75. *V.C.* 3.28.
76. Toynbee and Ward Perkins 1956, 14, 165–6, cf. 171–2, 181–2.
77. *Theoph.* 3.61; translated Lee 1843, 199; cf. Wilkinson 1981, 42, 168 n.1.
78. Vincent and Abel 1914, 97–104, Planches XII, XIII; Corbo 1981, ii, Pl. 67. During research for the present project, twenty-eight further observations of the rock surface made during shoring and other works in the Mandate period and not previously brought into the discussion have been located: Government of Palestine, Public Works Department, Drawings BR/1468/13 (1939 pits for shoring the Rotunda), B/1771/1 (1947 trial pits at Piers 7 and 14), and B/1771/19 (1947 pits for shoring the Edicule), all now preserved in the Record Room of the Israel Antiquities Authority, see above, p. 143, n. 3, 4.

79. *V.C.* 3.34.
80. Wilkinson 1972, 91–7, Pl. X; 1981, 246–52; on the distortions of the Narbonne model, which forms the principal source for Wilkinson's reconstruction, see Lauffray 1962, 204, 208, and cf. here Fig. 64B and C.
81. Coüasnon 1974, Pls VII, VIII, XI, XVII.
82. Mango has recently suggested (1995, 5, n. 18) that the porch was a later addition, constructed after *c.* 350 when Cyril mentioned Constantine's earlier cutting away of the original rock-cut forecourt (*Catech.* 14.9). Lauffray has, however, convincingly argued (1962, 205–8) that the source of the design of the Narbonne model and hence of the Edicule is to be found in the Round Temple at Baalbek (Fig. 64C and D; Krencker *et al.* 1923, 90–109, Taf. 57–68; alternative reconstruction studies in Ward-Perkins 1981, Fig. 206, and Wheeler 1964, Fig. 74), which has a columned pedimented porch in front of a round cella. If this is correct, the Edicule seems more likely to have been built from the first as a two-part structure. Its porch was apparently in existence by the time of Egeria's visit in 381/4, for she makes several references to the screen(s) (*cancellum, cancellos*) in front of the cave (Egeria, *Itinerary*, 24.2, 3, 4, 5, 10; 25.3; 34; 38.2; 47.1).
83. Bahat 1986, 38.
84. Taylor 1993, 141.
85. On this whole question, see now the many case studies in Kedar and Werblowsky 1998, and (with special reference to Jerusalem in the twelfth century), Benjamin Kedar's own contribution to the same volume (Kedar 1998).
86. Wharton 1992, 322; repeated in almost identical words in Wharton 1995, 88–92, at 91.
87. Wharton 1992, 321–2.
88. *V.C.* 3.30.
89. Drake 1985, 8–10; Walker 1990, 128–30, 240, 276–81.
90. *V.C* 3.30.
91. Dr Joan Taylor, who concluded in 1993 that the tomb 'identified as the tomb of Jesus is very unlikely to be authentic' (Taylor 1993, 336, cf. pp. 136–42), revised her opinion following the appearance of my 1994 article and now 'proposes instead that it may well be authentic' (Taylor 1998, 180, 193–203). She maintains her view about the location of Golgotha, however, which she now places 200 m south-east of the tomb: see above, p. 148, n. 54.
92. Vincent and Abel 1914, 219, 221–2, 242–3; Duckworth 1922, 139–40; Wilkinson 1977, 8–9; Mango 1992, 3–5; Howard Johnston in preparation. I am most grateful to Dr James Howard Johnson for letting me see the relevant parts of his forthcoming book, *The Last Great War of Antiquity*, including his critical evaluation of Strategius' *History*, and his account of the events of 614.
93. Vincent and Abel 1914, 220, 228, 245–6, 248; Duckworth 1922, 151–2 [wrongly dated to 969].
94. Vincent and Abel 1914, 220, 244–5; Duckworth 1922, 159–63.
95. Wilkinson 1977; 1981.
96. cf. Vincent and Abel 1914, 249.
97. Hugeburc, *Vita Willibaldi*, ed. Holder Egger, 97.16–18; cf. Bauch (ed.) 1984, 58–9 (with German translation); and Wilkinson 1977, 11, 125–36, 206–8 (English translation with useful discussion).
98. For example, Vincent and Abel 1914, 222: 'carré à sa base et pointu au sommet'; Wilkinson 1977, 129: 'at the bottom it is square, but it is pointed on top'; Bauch (ed.) 1984, 59: 'unten viereckig und oben schmal'.
99. Grabar 1972, i, 271–4; for comment on Grabar's view, see Bonnery 1991, 12–13, 28.
100. Vincent and Abel 1914, 222; Gurlitt 1926, 194–6.
101. Bonnery 1991, 12–13
102. Lauffray 1962, 215: 'la phrase . . . ne doit s'appliquer qu'à la face orientale du monument ou signifier que le plan au sol s'inscrit dans un rectangle, comme nous l'avons observé au reliquaire de Narbonne'.
103. Willis 1849, 176, n.1.
104. Adomnán, *De locis sanctis*, 42–7; Bernhard, *Itinerary*, 314–15.
105. Gil 1992, 51–6.
106. Canard 1965, 16–27; Gil 1992, 370–81; France 1996.
107. Yahya *History*, 491–2; cf. Vincent and Abel 1914, 249; Gil 1992, 373–5.
108. Adémar, *Chronicon*, 3.47 (pp. 169–71), where the date is given as 1010. Canard (1965, 17) shows that the eastern sources indicate that the destruction began on 28 September 1009. Glaber and other western writers knew that this was the correct year (Glaber, *History*, 3.7; cf Lair 1899a, 18–38). The date III Kal. Oct. (i.e. 29 September) 1010 given by Adémar is either the result of using a year which began on the *preceding* 25 March, or 1 or 24 September

(Cheney (ed.) 1948, 3–6), which would place the turn of 1009/10 before 29 September; or, if the year began on the *following* 25 March, may be a deliberate adjustment to suit an apocalyptic interpretation favoured at Limoges, as Landes has suggested (1995, 95–6, 304–5). For Adémar and the compilation of his history, see Wolff 1979 and now Landes 1995.

109. Adémar, *Chronicon*, 3.48 (p. 171, note k). These words are found only in MS. C of the *Chronicon* (Paris, BN, MS lat. 5926, f.131ᵛ; cf. Lair 1899b, 194), Adémar's definitive and final text, for which see now Landes 1995, 217–21. They indicate that Raoul and not the Greek monk St Symeon of Sinai (for whom, see below, ch. 4, n. 8) was Adémar's source at this point. Raoul's death is sometimes given as 1003 (e.g. Gams 1957, 598), but this date and the circumstances are fictitious (Lair 1899b, 194 n. 2), and Adémar's statement that he died at Périgueux *eo anno* after returning from Jerusalem is to be preferred. If he was a witness to the destruction at the end of September, he is unlikely to have reached Périgueux and died there before the spring of 1010.

110. Adémar, *Chronicon*, 3.47 (p. 170).

111. Glaber, *History*, 4.19. Since Ulric brought back gifts from the Byzantine Emperor Constantine VIII (1025–8), his pilgrimage can only have taken place during these years, despite the contrary indication of Glaber in the first words of 4.19: see John France's introduction and notes to the *History*, pp. xxx, lxvi, and 203, n. 4; but cf. France 1996, 9, n. 29. Ulric was perhaps part of the great pilgrimage which spent the Easter of 1027 in Jerusalem, on which see p. 76.

112. *History*, 3.24 (pp. 134–5).

113. Jeffery 1919, 56–65, Fig. 12; the Kufic inscription recorded by Jeffery (1919, 65, position shown on his Fig. 12) was 'at a height of about 15 feet'; cf. Vincent and Abel 1914, 256.

114. Coüasnon 1974, 26–7, 30.

115. Already in Willis 1849, 180–6.

116. Wilkinson 1972, 84.

CHAPTER FOUR

1. Yahya, *History*, 504–5 (with French translation); cf. Canard 1965, 26.

2. Glaber, *History*, 3.25. Glaber's correct identification of al-Hakim's mother as a Christian encourages belief in his information about her work at the Holy Sepulchre. For Orestes and their relationship, see Gil 1992, 463, and cf. Glaber, *History*, p. 133, n. 4.

3. Yahya, *History* (ed. Cheikho), 230; text and French translation of short extracts only in Vincent and Abel 1914, 246–7 (II.1, 2). For Nikephoros and his dates, see Gil 1992, 455, 463–4, and for further comment, below, p. 151, n. 29.

4. Yahya, *History* (ed. Cheikho), 242–4; Bianquis 1989, 403–4; Gil 1992, 380–1.

5. Adémar, *Chronicon*, 3.65 (pp. 189–90), 3.66 (p. 192), cf. p. vi; Southern 1953, 51–4; Micheau 1979, 89 and nn. 80–8; Landes 1995, 154–8.

6. Wolff 1979, 181–9.

7. Wolff 1979, 142–50, cf. 188–9.

8. The only two editions of Eberwin's *Vita* of Symeon were published three centuries ago and urgently need re-editing in the light of new manuscript and other evidence (Henschenius (ed.) 1695; Mabillon (ed.) 1701; cf. Thomsen 1939, 144–5, n. 1; Coens 1950, 181–3; Wolff 1979, 185, n. 28). Although detailed as to Symeon's movements and the length of time he spent at various places, the *Vita* gives no dates, his encounter with the pilgrims at Antioch providing the only obvious fixed point. The *Vita* does not mention al-Hakim's destruction of the Holy Sepulchre in 1009 nor his attack on Mt Sinai in *c.* 1012, probably because Symeon was present on neither occasion (*pace* Wolff 1979, 184, the Arabs 'besieging' the monastery during the famine at which Symeon was present were the local Arabs, servants of the monastery, who lived at its gates, and not al-Hakim's army or the hostile Bedouin: see Thomsen 1939, 152). Since, however, Symeon was probably Adémar's source for al-Hakim's attack on Mt Sinai and presumably for Adémar's comment on the rebuilding of the Holy Sepulchre, he can only have been at these places after 1009 and *c.* 1012, respectively. The famine affecting the monastery towards the end of Symeon's time there is probably to be identified with that which began in Cairo towards the end of 1024 and continued through the whole of the following two years (O'Leary 1923, 190–1; Bianquis 1989, 443–4). Thus the seven years Symeon passed as a pilgrim guide in Jerusalem (*per septem annos ductor peregrinorum*: Eberwin, *Vita Symeonis*, cap. 1, p. 89b) can be dated to *c.* 1012–18, and his time at and near Mt Sinai to *c.* 1021–6.

9. But he was not Adémar's only source: see above, p. 72, and cf. Landes 1995, 161 and n. 43.

10. Adémar, *Chronicon*, 3.47 (p. 170); cf. Landes 1995, 158. Wolff 1979, 188, cf.144, appears to suggest that Symeon told Adémar about the destruction of 1009. He probably did, but

Adémar's eye-witness evidence for the detail of that event appears to be Raoul de Couhé, as we have seen (above, p. 72).

11. Micheau 1979, 87.

12. Micheau 1979, 87–8.

13. Verdon (ed.) 1979, 89; Micheau 1979, 88–9. The story that the Norman settlement of southern Italy began with the arrival in Capua in 1017 of Norman pilgrims returning from Jerusalem cannot be accepted: Joranson 1948; Douglas 1969, 36–9.

14. Hugh of Flavigny, *Chronicon*, 2.21 (p. 396).

15. Glaber, *History*, 3.19. For the date of Ulric's visit and his report to Glaber, see above, pp. 72, 76. The patriarch at the time was Nikephoros I (see John France, p. 203, n. 2, to Glaber, *History*, 3.19; and for his dates, see below, n. 29). Perhaps Jordanus was a lesser official of the Patriarchate?

16. Hugh of Flavigny, *Chronicon*, 2.21 (pp. 395–6): e.g. *tota . . . aecclesia* or *astabant in circuitu altaris.*

17. Adémar, *Chronicon*, 3.55 (p.178); Micheau 1979, 91.

18. Adémar, *Chronicon*, 3.55 (p.178); Glaber, *History*, 3.2; Micheau 1979, 90–1. Coloman must have been intending to take the Hungarian route when he died near Vienna in 1012: see above, n. 11.

19. This table is based on the pilgrimages listed by Micheau 1979 and France 1996. Madame Micheau states how her list was compiled (1979, 94, n. 2). Those contributing to the discussion of her paper urged the extension of her list through the eleventh century. Dr John France provides an extensive base for such an endeavour, but a critical list of *all* recorded pilgrimages from the fourth to the sixteenth century, and their sometimes multiple sources, remains a desideratum. There are assuredly more for the period 940–1099 than the forty-eight used here.

20. Adémar, *Chronicon*, 3.66 (p. 192), 3.68 (p. 194); Glaber, *History*, 4.18; France 1996, 12.

21. Glaber, *History*, 3.25 (p. 137).

22. Glaber, *History*, 1.21. Duke Richard II reigned from 996–1026. The date of this donation appears not to be known, but it seems possible that it was made in connection with the great pilgrimage of 1026–7 (see above, p. 75 and n. 5), which was being prepared at the time of his death in August 1026, and was sponsored by a Norman duke Richard. This can scarcely be other than Richard II, as Southern supposed (1953, 51), especially since Glaber notes in this same passage that he 'aided with rich presents all who wished to go there on holy pilgrimage', but Runciman suggests Richard III, who reigned 1026–7 (1951–4, i, 47). For Duke Robert I's pilgrimage of 1035, see Douglas 1964, 35–7

23. Gil 1992, 380–1.

24. Gil 1992, 402–3, 480–1; see further, p. 78.

25. Bar Hebraeus, *Chronography*, 196; for references to Ibn al-Athir, see Bianquis 1989, 500; see also Gil 1992, 402–3. Dr Greville Freeman-Grenville kindly converted the dates to the Christian calendar, since the conversions are given differently by the various editors.

26. For example, Gil 1992, 480; Ousterhout 1989; and all standard sources.

27. *Chronicon*, 1, 6.

28. *Chronicon*, Prologue, lines 89–91. See Huygens in *Chronicon*, pp. 2–3, and cf. Edbury and Rowe 1988, 44–5, 53.

29. William of Tyre, *Chronicon*, I.6. The manuals all give Nikephoros as reigning until at least 1048, but this date is based in every case on William of Tyre: Le Quien 1740, iii, col. 496 (who stresses that *ignoremus quonam praecise anno sedere incoeperit, vel quonam obierit, vel etiam quot annos fuerit Patriarcha*); Grumel 1958, 452 (who gives 'juillet 1020 – après 1048'); Fedalto 1988, ii, 1003 (who gives only '(1048–)'). The latest list is provided by Gil 1992, 455, who gives 'Nicephorus I, 1020–1036', followed by 'Ioannicos, 1036–58'. Gil describes his sources, emphasizes the difficulties and uncertainties, and notes on p. 464 that for Ioannikios and his successors down to 1099 'we are almost entirely dependent on comparatively late Greek Church sources.'

30. Skylitzes, *Synopsis Historiarum*, Romanos III, cap. 14 (pp. 387–8). I am most grateful to Professor Cyril Mango for this reference and for his advice on the problem, but I am alone responsible for the conclusions reached. Michael Psellos (1018–after 1081?), a contemporary witness, does not mention the rebuilding of the Holy Sepulchre, even in his long sixth book which devotes 203 chapters to Constantine IX and describes in some detail his construction of the church of St George the Martyr known as the Mangana (*Chronographia*, 6.185–7). Émile Renauld's note on Constantine's other works mentions nothing outside the capital (*Chronographia*, ii, pp. 63–4, n. 1).

31. Kazhdan (ed.) 1991, iii, 2213.

32. Yahya, *History* (ed. Cheikho), 270–3; text and French translation of two short extracts only, in

Vincent and Abel 1914, 247 (II.3, 4). The circumstances, participants, and subject matter of the Constantinople conference of 1034 are fully set out in Bianquis 1989, 496–500.

33. Cedrenus (d. later eleventh century), *Synopsis historion* (Bonn edn), ii, 501.

34. Zonaras (d. after 1159?), *Epitome historion* (Bonn edn), iii, 590, mentions the negotiations for the treaty in much the same terms as Skylitzes but says nothing about the church in his chapters on Romanos III, Michael IV, or Constantine IX Monomachos.

35. Bar Hebraeus (d. 1286), *Chronography*, 200–7; Ibn al-Athir (d. 1233), *Consummate History*: see above, p. 151, n. 25.

36. See pp. 92–4.

37. Schefer (ed.) 1881, 107–9; Le Strange (ed.) 1897, 60; Thackston (trans.) 1986, 38; Najmabadi and Weber (trans.) 1993, 75–6; cf. Vincent and Abel 1914, 252–3, 261. According to Gil 1992, 857, Nasir was in Jerusalem in the spring of 1045, but this is a slip.

38. Ousterhout 1989, 75.

39. France 1996, 4.

40. France 1996, 14.

41. France 1996, 12, 13.

42. France 1996, 14.

43. France 1996, 2, n. 3, and the references to recent support for this view there cited.

44. Wilkinson 1972, 84.

45 Daniel 1988, 128, cf. 168.

46. John of Würzburg 1874, 148; Wilkinson 1988, 261.

47. Theoderic 1976, 13.

48. Theoderic 1976, 13; cf. John of Würzburg 1874, 149.

49. Dalman 1922, 56–65, Abb. 15, 16.

50. Wilkinson 1972, 91.

51. Daniel 1988, 128.

52. Dalman 1922, Taf. VII.

53. John of Würzburg 1874, 148; Theoderic 1976, 14.

54. Bresc-Bautier 1984, 73 (no. 19), cf. 294 (no. 150), 298 (no. 151), and 324 (no. 170).

55. Theoderic 1976, 14; cf. Vincent and Abel 1914, 266.

56. Golubovich 1898, 46–7.

57. Golubovich (ed.) 1902, 34–5, 40.

58. Rock 1989, 71, 79.

59. Vincent and Abel 1914, 292.

60. Knauer 1996.

61. It may be possible to place the later limit considerably earlier if the description of the Edicule by the presbiter Jachintus belongs to the eleventh century. García Villada dated this description to between the seventh and tenth centuries (1925, 323) and was followed by Wilkinson (1977, 11, 215 [*c*. 750]), but Jachintus is clearly describing the Edicule as rebuilt after the destruction of 1009. The text, which is incomplete, occurs on f.5^{r-v} of a manuscript otherwise devoted to the *XL Homilies on the Gospels* by Pope Gregory the Great, now León Cathedral Cod. 14, written in Visigothic minuscule dated by García Villada to 's. X' (1919, 42–3), but perhaps rather to be dated to the eleventh century. The text of Jachintus is an addition, on an inserted bifolium near the start of the volume, and is written in a late eleventh-century hand with caroline features (i.e. 's.XI ex.'). It is a copy, not the original, and breaks off in mid-sentence half-way down the right-hand column on f.5^v. Jachintus' language, reflecting the forms and constructions of a common speech more Romance than Latin, is of a kind which emerged in the later tenth century (Campos 1957, 89). It shows features characteristic of the region of León, but these might be due to the copyist rather than to the author. The text was therefore composed perhaps by a Spanish-speaking author not later than the end of the eleventh century, and could be somewhat earlier. Jachintus' description (text in Campos 1957; translation in Wilkinson 1977, 123, 205) is both detailed and precise. If the arguments set out here are correct, he is the most important source available for the form, appearance and decoration of the Edicule as reconstructed in the eleventh century. Professor Maurilio Pérez González of the University of León very kindly arranged for my wife, Birthe Kjølbye-Biddle, and myself to work on the manuscript in the Archivo Catedral by kind permission of the dean, Dom Perez. Professor Pérez, Professor Roger Wright of Liverpool University, and Professor F.W. Hodcroft of Oxford have all contributed generously to this evaluation of the manuscript, but responsibility for the result is mine alone.

62. Daniel 1988, 128.

63. Bagatti 1975, 33, 42–3, Pls 12.2, 13; Piccirillo 1975, 77–82.

64. Beliaev 1996 and 1997. Professor Beliaev, to whom I am indebted for information and for a copy of his book, also provides (1996, 183–210, Pls L–LXI; English summary, pp. 374–83) by far the fullest survey yet available of the appearance of the three 'port-holes' in western art.

65. Metropolitan Museum of Art, New York, Acc. no. 17.190.735, where the three holes appear no fewer than three times in red enamel, on the inside of the left wing, and in the interior to the left and to the right.

66. For example, Cheetham 1984, no. 197.

67. Daniel 1988, 128.

68. See above, n. 61. Lines 95–7 [numbering corrected from Campos 1957, 79–82] of Jachintus' text refer to *fenestre tres abentur/circa murum sepulcri. super quas missas[sic]/ celebrantur*. This sentence comes at the end of Jachintus' description of the Edicule which begins in the Tomb Chamber and ends on the exterior with the cupola. Although therefore apparently out of sequence, it seems that these words can only refer to the burial couch since it was on its surface that masses were celebrated.

69. Piussi 1977, 551, suggests that the 'port-holes' may be shown in three earlier representations of the Women at the Tomb. None of these suggested identifications is acceptable. (1), the Narbonne ivory (best reproductions in Goldschmidt 1969, i, Pl. XV, no. 31, cf. p. 20; and Hubert *et al.* 1968, Fig. 209, cf. p. 354) shows three roundels on the ?threshold of the *tholos*; the sepulchre on which the angel sits is decorated with a floral scroll. (2), in a tenth-century Mozarabic illumination (Florence, Biblioteca Laurenziana, MS Ashburnham 17, f. 57; Grabar 1968, 523–4, Pl. 136b) the elements to which Piussi refers are three quatrefoils, part of a decorative band of eleven surrounding a sarcophagus seen in section, in an illumination which derives from palaeo-christian art of the third century. (3), on a drawing in an English psalter with pictures of *c.* 1050 (BL, Cotton MS, Tiberius C.VI, f. 13^v; Wormald 1984, Ill. 138, cf. p. 133), the features to which Piussi refers are purely decorative and appear on other unrelated representations in the same MS (ff. 10, 12^v, 15^v, 30^v; Wormald 1984, Ills 131, 136, 142, 149).

70. Beliaev 1996, as above, n. 64.)

71. 1323/4: Fitzsimons 1952, 44. 1347: da Poggibonsi 1945a, cap. 20 (p. 18); cf. da Poggibonsi 1945b, 16. da Poggibonsi's account was copied and from 1500 onwards reprinted at least sixty-three times virtually without alteration (cf. B. Bagatti in da Poggibonsi 1945a, xxxiii–xliv; see also da Poggibonsi 1945b, xxx–xl). These later editions have no value as evidence for the actual state of the Edicule after 1347.

72. Faber 1892–3, i, 410–15.

73. Suriano, in the first draft of his *Treatise* written in 1485, states that this was done in 1435 by Friar Tommaso of Montefalco who was still alive in 1485 (1949, 48–9). Later versions of the *Treatise* give the date as 1430. By the early 1480s Suriano was in charge of the distribution of pieces of the rock of the burial couch removed by the Guardian (name not given) at the time of this remodelling. Although some of the details are circumstantial, the confusions suggest that while the remodelling may be a fact, the date is not secure

74. For example, in 1458, Capodilista 1966, 202; repeated with emendations and additions in 1480, Brasca 1966, 97. Both make the point that mass was celebrated on the burial couch, for which they use the word 'murazolo'. Brasca adds that there was 'uno picolino fenestrello facto per forza de scapelli a man dricta sopra el murazolo per tenere li orzoli sive ampolini dal vino et acque per cellebrare la messa'. This sounds very much like the cupboard behind the hinged ikon of the Virgin still in use today for keeping candles and other items (see p. 124; Figs 95–7), but this in not in the position which Brasca indicates.

75. Dalman 1922, 74–106.

76. For example, by Quaresmius in 1639: Quaresmius 1989, 274–81; or by Horn from 1724 onwards: Golubovich (ed.) 1902, 29–30, and Bagatti (ed.) 1962, 46–8. For Horn, see also above, pp. 49–50, no. 6.

77. Dalman 1922, 106–37.

78. Cambridge, Corpus Christi College, MS 370, ff. 85^v–95^v. The text was printed by Golubovich (Anon. 1923), and translated by Hoade (Anon. 1952). Mrs Gill Cannell, Assistant Librarian of the Parker Library, kindly answered a long series of questions relating to MS 370.

79. MS 370, f. 92b; Anon. 1923, 453; Anon. 1952, 68.

80. da Poggibonsi 1945a, cap. 20 (p. 18); da Poggibonsi 1945b, 16.

81. The word 'porphyry' [Latin, *porphirinus*] seems to indicate here a special stone in general rather than red Egyptian porphyry or green *lapis lacedaimonicus* in particular. The word could cover a range of colours from purple through red to tawny, and is perhaps best taken as meaning 'coloured and variegated', as Dr David Howlett kindly informs me. The English pilgrim used the same word to describe the slabs covering the surface of the Rock of Calvary (Anon. 1923, 452). The present burial slab is a streaked honey-coloured marble of a kind found nowhere else in the Edicule; it has a lip around the edge and a diagonal groove cut across the middle (see pp. 87–8, 126, 129), just as the Englishman described it in 1345.

82. Vincent and Abel 1914, 264.

CHAPTER FIVE

1. Vincent and Abel 1914, 263.
2. Corbo 1981, i, 198. Dr Adrian Boas points out to me that these sculptures could not be the work of a Bolognese sculptor unless he were a member of the 'atelier of the Temple Mount Area'.
3. Corbo 1981, i, 199; iii, Foto 178–88.
4. Corbo 1981, ii, Tav. 4, cf. Tav. 6.
5. Folda 1995, 79–82; cf. 508, n. 19, where he explores the circumstances of the event, without doubting 'the redecoration project of 1119'.
6. Folda 1996, 501–2; Borg 1996, 498–9, respectively.
7. Cafarus, *Liberatio orientis*, 121; Anon., *Brevis Historia*, 129, 135. For the text, see Röhricht (ed.) 1893, no. 45; Imperiale (ed.) 1936–42, i, no. 18; de Sandoli 1974, no .32. The copies in the Genoese *Liber Iurium*, one of which is reproduced by Belgrano in Cafarus, *Liberatio orientis*, Tav. VII (opp. p. 114) and by de Sandoli 1974, Fig. 3 (p. 25), are not facsimiles of the original inscription but copies in an epigraphic script of the mid-thirteenth century (Mayer and Favreau 1976, 24–5). The Golden Inscription has been very thoroughly discussed by Mayer and Favreau, who have attempted to show that it never existed. The case against 'the two epigrapheclasts', as he calls them, has been put by Kedar (1986). Marie-Luise Favreau-Lilie (as she now is) has returned to the fray (1989, 99 n. 206, 106 n. 230, 206, 227, 296–7, 327–34, 355–6, 358–9), and Antonella Rovere has responded with an analysis of their attack on Baldwin I's diploma of 1104 (and hence the inscription of 1105) on the basis of which 'sembrano cadere tutti gli elementi che hanno portato i due studiosi ad esprimere il giudizio di falsità' (1996, at p. 131; I owe this reference to the kindness of Prof. Tiziano Mannoni). There is much still to say.
8. First mentioned by Giorgio Stella (1365/70–1420) in his *Annales Genuenses*: Muratori (ed.) 1730, col. 981, cf. Balbi (ed.) 1975, 32; see also Giustiniano 1537, 33; Quaresmius 1880–2, ii, 285; de Sandoli 1974, no. 33. Stella's source has not been identified (cf. Belgrano and Malagola 1890, 303). If it remains elusive, the question must arise whether the motto itself is genuine or an invention, possibly by Stella.
9. Ferrari 1643, 35–6.
10. Belgrano and Malagola 1890. Malagola added the caveat 'meno che – dato il silenzio delle fonti bolognesi anteriori a lui – non la avesse desunta da fonte non bolognese che non conosciamo' (p. 306). There may still be some room for uncertainty: the details are odd and circumstantial enough to suggest Ghirardacci might have had a source for some elements of the story.
11. For texts, see de Sandoli 1974, 6–15.
12. Phocas, *Description*, col. 944
13. Pringle forthcoming; Avni and Seligman 1997.
14. For example, most recently, Borg 1996, 498; Folda 1995, 177–86, 203, and esp. 543, n. 108; Folda 1996, 503; and cf. Vincent and Abel 1914, 280: 'Nous sommes donc pleinement autorisé à tenir le 15 juillet 1149 pour la date du complet achèvement des travaux des Croisés au Saint-Sépulcre' ('We are thus clearly entitled to take the 15 July 1149 as the date by which the Crusaders' works at the Holy Sepulchre were completely finished').
15. As Folda points out: 1995, 177–9, 228, and nn. 9 (p. 532) and 99 (p. 542).
16. Professor Jaroslav Folda, in his fundamental account, *The Art of the Crusaders in the Holy Land, 1098–1187*, although accepting the Calvary inscription as referring to the dedication of the church at large, provides in his Chapter 7 (1995, 175–245) a full discussion of the problems. For particular parts of the church and its decoration for which he and other scholars suggest a date after 1149, or at least a secondary phase in the works, see pp. 186, 214, 225–9 (south façade), 212 (north transept and the Prison of Christ), 213 (dome over crossing), 234, 238–40 (mosaics and painting), 243–5 (bell tower).
17. The position is given by Theoderic (1976, 20): 'super arcum ipsam Golgatham concludentem, id est in latere Calvarie versus occidentem constituto, tabula quedam in pariete depicta' ('above the arch which closes [the chapel of] Golgotha, i.e. on the side of Calvary facing west, there is a panel painted on the wall . . .').
18. Quaresmius 1639, ii, 483; Quaresmius 1989 [ed. de Sandoli from the edition of 1639], 266–7; de Vogüé 1860, 215–18. For John of Würzburg's text of the verses, see Tobler (ed.) 1874, 152, but de Vogüé had used the edition by B. Pez published in 1721. *Pace* Folda 1995, 542 (n. 100), Würzburg *did* attribute the inscription to Calvary.
19. By Titus Tobler; see now the edition by M.L. and W. Bulst, Theoderic 1976, cap. XII (p. 20); cf. de Vogüé 1860, 217, n. 1. The text of the inscription is no. 63 in Thomsen 1921, 33–4, with further references; cf. Thomsen 1922. It is no. 66 in de Sandoli 1974 (pp. 48–50) and the dating is reviewed by Mayer and Favreau 1976, 31, n. 28.
20. Röhricht (1887, n. 9 on p. 8) gives the date of Fulcher's election as 20 February 1146. De Vogüé used 25 January which he thought was the date of his nomination.

21. This partially restored text is clearly not a final version, even supposing that were possible without the discovery of new evidence in, for example, a pilgrim account. The last word recorded by Quaresmius . . . *ivdices* . . ., which would follow Line 10 as reconstructed here, may preserve a garbled reference to the indiction: 1149 would be the twelfth year of the indiction, and fifty-five whole indictions of fifteen years would have passed since 312, the start of the reckoning (12 + (55 x 15) + 312 = 1149). I am most grateful to Dr Edmund Thomas for discussing the problems of these verses and for his helpful suggestions.
22. De Vogüé 1860, 218.
23. De Sandoli 1974, 51–3, Fig. 11; conveniently redrawn in Folda 1995, Fig. 1 (p. 39).
24. Imperiale (ed.) 1936–42, ii, nos 27–8 (pp. 70–3), with a discussion of the dating
25. Thomsen 1921, 34 (no. 63); cf. Thomsen 1922.
26. Edbury and Rowe 1988, 13–15.
27. See now Metcalf 1995, 57–65; on the depiction of the Holy Sepulchre, see further Metcalf in Pesant 1980, 106–9; see also Folda 1995, 334–7.
28. Metcalf 1995, 53–7.
29. Metcalf in Pesant 1980, 108–9.
30. As Dr John Wilkinson has shown in his review of the texts: 1988, 2–23.
31. See, for example, Wilkinson 1988, 17 (on Abbot Nikolás), 18 ('an Icelandic pilgrim'), 19 (Belard of Ascoli). See also below, n. 34, for the influence of '1149' on the dating of the Icelandic 'Variant Description of Jerusalem'.
32. For the part relating to the Holy Sepulchre, Gildemeister 1885 (German translation from a copy collated by De Goeje with MSS in Paris and Oxford) and Le Strange 1888 (translation from Gildemeister, reprinted in Le Strange 1890, 206–7, and in Wilkinson 1988, 223–4) should be used in preference to Jaubert's French translation (1836–40, i, 342), but neither is satisfactory. Le Strange, who stated that his translation was made from 'the Arabic text printed by J. Gildemeister'(!), includes without explanation words and phrases not found in Gildemeister's German. There are now at least eleven MSS known of the whole or parts of Idrisi's work (Hoenerbach 1938, 3–7), and there is an obvious need for a critical edition of the section relating to the Holy Sepulchre. This would serve as the basis for a new translation which deals with the names, technical words, and phrases in the light of knowledge of the building itself and the various possibilities it presents.
33. My translation from the German of Gildemeister 1885, 124.
34. The Icelandic 'Variant Description of Jerusalem', which describes the completed Crusader choir and ambulatory, has been thoroughly discussed by Kedar and Westergård-Nielsen (1978–9, 195–7, 201–3, text and translation on pp. 206–9 with explanatory diagram, Fig. 1; Wilkinson 1988, 220–2, used an earlier translation). Kedar and Westergård-Nielsen show that the 'Variant Description' must date from before 1187 but use the consecration of 15 July 1149 to suggest that 'the writer was in Jerusalem a relatively short time after the completion' of the Crusader church (1978–9, 196). The evidence presented here suggests that the 'Variant Description' was written after the early 1160s.
35. John of Würzburg 1874, 150.
36. Runciman 1951–4, ii, 467–8; Baldwin 1958, 616–20; Maalouf 1984, 196–200; Peters 1985, 351–2.

CHAPTER SIX

1. Itinerarium Regis Richardi 1864, VI.34 (p. 438); reprinted de Sandoli 1978–84, iii, 156–9; translated Peters 1985, 360–1.
2. Runciman 1951–4, iii, 73–4.
3. De Sandoli 1978–84, iii, 264; Laurent 1873, 26.
4. Runciman 1951–4, iii, 188–9.
5. Matthew Paris 1877, 340, giving the full text (pp. 337–44) of a copy of a letter from Robert, patriarch of Jerusalem, the bishops of the kingdom, the vice-master of the Temple, the prior of the Holy Sepulchre, and others to the prelates of France and England, written at Acre, 25 November 1244, the original bearing twelve seals. See Runciman 1951–4, iii, 225; Prawer 1969–70, ii, 309–13. And cf. Vincent and Abel 1914, 291.
6. Wilkinson 1972, 84.
7. Vincent and Abel 1914, 294.
8. Golubovich 1898, 52–3.
9. Da Treviso (ed.) 1875, appendix, 278–84.
10. Da Treviso (ed.) 1875, 279–80.
11. Da Treviso (ed.) 1875, 59, 187–8. The edition of 1573 is very rare: the only copy known to me

in England is St John's College, Cambridge, Adams S 1719 (kindly checked by Dr Alison Pearn). There are copies in the Library of Congress and in Harvard University Library.

12. Da Treviso (ed.) 1875, 188.
13. For text, see Golubovich (ed.). 1902, 78–9.
14. Da Treviso (ed.) 1875, xvii.
15. Golubovich (ed.) 1902, 114.
16. Da Treviso 1875, 187.
17. Golubovich (ed.) 1902, 19–20, 33.
18. Golubovich (ed.) 1902, 27; Bagatti (ed.) 1962, 27.
19. Tzaferis 1985, 71.
20. Williams 1849, ii, 88–9.
21. Bibliography in Schur 1980, 93.
22. Maximos Simaios 1897, 87–122; cf. Golubovich (ed.) 1902, xlv–liv; Dimitriades 1910; Themeles 1910; Vincent and Abel 1914, 299–300; and cf. Lemmens 1933, 167–85, and Arce (ed.). 1973, 325–401.
23. Ioannides 1877, 188, 230–4; Balsamos 1909. Professor Richard Clogg is studying the inscriptions anew as part of the work on the Edicule.
24. I am indebted to Prof. Donald Nicol for Komnenos' first name, recorded in Ioannides 1877, i, 188; see also Balsamos 1909, 218–21.
25. Mango 1995, 1–3.
26. Misn 1937, 183; pers. comm. Prof. Donald Nicol.
27. Kuriazes 1976; pers. comm. Prof. Cyril Mango.
28. Vincent and Abel 1914, 299, cf. 298 n. 1.
29. For example, Ioannides 1877, 230; Vincent and Abel 1914, 299.
30. Maximos Simaios 1897, 103, 107.
31. It is shown on F.W. Sieber's *Karte von Jerusalem und seiner naechsten Umgebungen*, published in Leipzig and Prague in 1823, in the inset 'Plan der Grabeskirche zu Jerusalem nach dem Zustande im Jahre 1818', where it is called 'Capelle der Kophthen'; see Meyer 1971, no. 64.
32. Willis 1849, 161, n. 1, 293.
33. See Wilkinson 1972, 84.
34. Harvey 1935; Marangoni 1937; Vincent *et al.* 1949, 81–130; Coüasnon 1974.

CHAPTER SEVEN

1. Vincent and Abel 1914, Fig. 53.
2. Geva 1993a, 747, and cf. for example the tomb apparently of the high-priestly family of Caiaphas: Greenhut 1992, Flusser 1992.
3. Kloner 1985a.
4. Vincent and Abel 1914, Fig. 53.
5. Kloner 1985b.
6. Lauffray 1962, 203–4, Fig. 1.
7. Adomnán, *De locis sanctis*, 44–5, adapted.
8. Photius, *Amphilochia*, 123.
9. Adomnán, *De locis sanctis*, 45–7, adapted.
10. Photius, *Amphilochia*, 123.
11. Adomnán, *De locis sanctis*, 46–7, adapted.
12. Bede, *De locis sanctis*, 255.
13. Adomnán, *De locis sanctis*, pl. opp. p. 47.
14. Adomnán, *De locis sanctis*, 48–9.
15. Euclid, Book XI, Proposition 25: *Elementa*, 40; Heath (ed.) 1956, iii, 325–7.
16. Euclid, Book XI, Proposition 24: *Elementa*, 38–40; Heath (ed.) 1956, iii, 323–4. I am grateful to Sir Christopher Zeeman, F.R.S., Gresham Professor of Geometry, who kindly advised me on the framing of this definition.
17. Dvornik 1959; 1960, 3–4; Theodoridis 1982.
18. Mathew 1963, 24–8.
19. Lauffray 1962, Fig. 1.
20. Bagatti 1975, Figs 10 and 11.
21. Photius, *Amphilochia*, 124, lines 59–60; cf. 122.
22. Dvornik 1948, *passim*; Mango 1958, 22.
23. Westerink (ed.) 1986, xxi–xxii.)
24. Geva 1993a, 747–9.

25. Dalman 1922, 63, Abb. 15, 16
26. Amico 1609, Fig. 37; Amico 1620, 111, Fig. 33.
27. Dalman 1922, 40–1. Hohenschwert 1985 provides a critical review of the interpretation of Externsteine and a bibliography. Professor Carsten Peter Thiede, Paderborn, kindly provided a set of excellent new photographs of the tomb replica.
28. Faber 1892–3, I, 414–15; Prescott 1954, 137.
29. Faber 1892–3, I, 534, 575
30. For its possible influence on the Externsteine replica, see above, p. 113.
31. Quaresmius 1989, 196.
32. Mariti 1790, ii, 177.
33. Tobler 1853–4, ii, 232.
34. Pierotti 1864, 206, Pl. LVI, Fig. 5.
35. Wilson and Warren 1871, 30–1; Perez 1988, 157; Wahrman *et al.* 1993, 20–7; Gibson and Jacobson 1996, 9–11.
36. Macalister 1901, esp. 147–53; cf. Kloner 1980, 60–6 [Region 10].
37. Maximos Simaios 1897, 113, 117–18.
38. See Kloner 1980, Figs 1–29.
39. Maximos Simaios 1897, 118.
40. Bagatti 1975, 42–3, Pl. 14.
41. Usually as components of more complex, multi-chamber tombs: for an example demonstrated by particularly clear drawings, see Ritmeyer 1994, 29. A tomb on the Ma'ale Adumim/French Hill road discovered in 1982 has a single three-couch burial chamber behind a shallow partly covered forecourt: Mazor and Stark 1983.
42. Schick 1885, esp. Taf. V; but this tomb may be of a much earlier date.
43. In Israeli archaeological parlance, 'arcosolium' can mean either an arched or a flat-roofed niche, but for the latter Professor Kloner has now suggested the term 'quadrosolium': Kloner forthcoming. For examples of arched arcosolia, see Avni and Greenhut 1996, Figs 1.16, 1.18, 1.34, 1.48–50.
44. Kloner forthcoming.
45. Kloner forthcoming; cf. Kloner 1985b. I am very much indebted to Professor Kloner for detailed discussion of the problems and for allowing me to see the summary of his paper in advance of publication.
46. Arculf reported by Adomnán, *De locis sanctis*, 46–9.
47. Cf. the Tomb of Mary, Bagatti 1975, Fig. 11.

CHAPTER EIGHT

1. See further Biddle *et al.* in preparation.
2. Golubovich (ed.) 1902, 29–30. The incisions are shown on Horn's plan on p. 25; Bagatti (ed.) 1962, 47–8, Fig. 3, Pl. IV.
3. Cust 1929, 23.
4. Pers. comm. Brother Fabian Adkins o.f.m., formerly Latin Sacristan; cf. de Saint-Aignan 1864, 134.

EPILOGUE

1. Andrieu 1948, xii.
2. Bernard, *Itinerary*, 315 (*c.* 870). The Life of Theodore the Sabaïte, bishop of Edessa (836–60?), sometimes used as evidence for the ceremony of the Holy Fire as early as the eighth century, is a highly unreliable hagiographical romance written no earlier than 860 (Pomyalovskii (ed.) 1892, 97–8; Peeters 1930, 81–5; Beck 1959, 558–9, 583).
3. Canard 1965, 27–41; many eye-witness accounts in Peters 1985, 261–7, 523–4, 571–8.

BIBLIOGRAPHY

ANCIENT AND EARLY MEDIEVAL SOURCES AND ABBREVIATIONS

(for pilgrim accounts of the 11th century and later, see below, pp. 159–69)

Adémar, *Chronicon* — Chavanon, J. ed. 1897. *Adémar de Chabannes: Chronique*, Collection de textes pour servir à l'étude . . . de l'histoire 20, Paris [see also Lair 1899b]

Adomnán, *De locis sanctis* — Meehan, D. ed. 1983. *Adamnan's De Locis Sanctis*, Scriptores Latini Hiberniae 3, reprint [1st pub. 1958]

Bar Hebraeus, *Chronography* — Budge, E.A.W. ed. 1932. *The Chronography of Gregory abu'l Faraj . . . commonly known as Bar Hebraeus*, 2 vols., Oxford

Brevis Historia — Belgrano, L.T. ed. 1890. 'Brevis Historia Regni Iherosolymitani', *Annali Genovesi di Caffaro e de' suoi continuatori dal MXCIX al MCCXCIII*, Genova, i, 125–49

Bede, *de locis sanctis* — Fraipont, J. ed. 1965. *Itinera at alia geographica*, CCSL 175, Turnhout

Bernard, *Itinerary* — Tobler, T., and Molinier, A. eds. 1879. *Itinera Hierosolymitana et descriptiones Terrae Sanctae bellis sacris anteriora . . .*, Publications de la Société de l'Orient Latin, série géographie 1–2, Geneva, 309–20

Cafarus, *Liberatio orientis* — Belgrano, L.T. ed. 1890. *Annali Genovesi di Caffaro e de' suoi continuatori dal MXCIX al MCCXCIII*, Genova, i, 95–124

CCCM — *Corpus Christianorum Continuatio Mediaeualis*, Turnhout

CCSL — *Corpus Christianorum Series Latina*, Turnhout

Cedrenus, *Synopsis Historion* — Bekker, I. ed. 1839. *Ioannis Scylitzae ope . . . suppletus et emendatus*, Bonn

CSCO — *Corpus Scriptorum Christianorum Orientalium*, Beirut and Paris

CSEL — *Corpus Scriptorum Ecclesiasticorum Latinorum*, Vienna

Cyril, *Catechetical Lectures* — Reischl, W.K., and Rupp, J., eds. 1848, 1860. *Sancti Cyrilli Opera*, 2 vols., Munich

'Cyril', *Mystagogical Lectures* — Piédagnel, A. ed. 1966. *Catéchèses mystagogiques*, Sources Chrétiennes 126, Paris

DA — Turner, J. ed. 1996. *The Dictionary of Art*, Grove, London

DNB — *Dictionary of National Biography*

Eberwin, *Vita Symeonis* — Henschenius, G. ed. 1695. *Acta Sanctorum* Junii i, 87–107, Antwerp; d'Achery, L., Mabillon, J., and Ruinart, Th., eds. 1701. *Acta Sanctorum Ordinis S. Benedicti*, Saec. 6.i, 367–81, Paris

Egeria, *Itinerary* — Franceschini, E., and Weber, R., eds. 1965. *Itinerarium Egeriae*, CCSL 175, Turnhout, 27–103

Euclid, *Elementa* — Stamatis, E.S. ed. 1973. *Euclidis Elementa* 4, Bibliotheca . . . Teubneriana, Leipzig

Eusebius, *H.E.* — Schwartz, E. ed. 1903–9. *GCS, Eusebius* 2.i–iii, Leipzig

Eusebius, *L.C.* — Drake, H.A., *In Praise of Constantine. A Historical Study and New Translation of Eusebius' Tricennial Orations*, Berkeley, Los Angeles and London, 1976

Eusebius, *Onomastikon* — Klosterman, E. ed. 1904. *GCS, Eusebius* 3.i, Leipzig

Eusebius, *Theophany* — Gressmann, H. ed. 1904. *GCS, Eusebius* 3.ii, Leipzig

Eusebius, *V.C.* — Winkelmann, F. ed. 1975. *GCS, Eusebius* 1.ii, Berlin

GCS — *Griechische christliche Schriftsteller der ersten drei Jahrhunderte*, Leipzig 1897–1941; Berlin and Leipzig 1953; Berlin, 1954–

Glaber, *History* — France, J. ed. 1989. *Rodulfus Glaber. The Five Books of the Histories*, Oxford

Hugeburc, *Vita Willibaldi* — Holder-Egger, O. ed. 1887. *MGH SS* xv.i, 80–106; Bauch, A. ed. 1984. *Quellen zur Geschichte der Diözese Eichstätt*, i, *Biographien der Gründungszeit*, 2nd edn., Regensburg [*Vita Willibaldi*, text and German translation, pp.11–122]

Hugh of Flavigny, *Chronicon* — Pertz, G.H. ed. 1848. *MGH SS* viii, 278–503 [see also *PL* cliv (1853), cols. 9–403]

Ibn al-Athir, *Consummate History* — Tornberg, C.J. ed. 1851–76. *Chronicon quod perfectissimum inscribitur*, 12 + 3 vols., Leiden; reprinted as *Al-Kamil fi'l-ta'rikh*, 13 vols., revised, Beirut, 1965–6

Jerome, *Ep.* — Hilberg, I.A. ed. 1910–18. *CSEL* 54–6, Vienna and Leipzig

MGH SS — *Monumenta Germaniae Historica, Scriptores*

Phocas, *Description* — Allacci, L. ed. 1653. *Patrologia Graeca* 133 (1864), cols. 927–62

Photius, *Amphilochia* — Westerink, L.G. ed. 1987. *Photii . . Epistulae et Amphilochia*, 6.i, Bibliotheca . . . Teubneriana, Leipzig

P.P.   Hall, S.G. ed. 1979. *Melito of Sardis: On Pascha and Fragments*, Oxford

Psellos, *Chronographia*   Renauld, É. ed. 1926–8. *Michel Psellos Chronographie*, Paris [with French translation]; Sewter, E.R.A. trans. 1953. *The 'Chronographia' of Michael Psellus*, New Haven

Skylitzes, *Synopsis Historiarum*   Thurn, J. ed. 1973. *Ioannis Scylitzae Synopsis Historiarum*, Berlin and New York

Stella, *Annales Genuenses*   Muratori, L.A., ed. 1730. *Rerum Italicarum Scriptores* 17 (Milan), cols. 951–1318; Petti Balbi, G. ed. 1975. *Annales Genuenses*, Muratori new edn. 17.2 (Bologna)

Yahya, *History*   Kratchkovsky, I., and Vasiliev, A. eds. 1932. *Histoire de Yahya-ibn-Sa'ïd d'Antioche*, Fasc. II, *Patrologia Orientalis* 23.3, Paris [up to 1013: Arabic text with French translation]

Yahya, *History* (ed. Cheikho)   Cheikho, L., Carra de Vaux, B., and Zayyat, H. eds. 1909. *Annales Yahia Ibn Sa'id Antiochensis*, CSCO 51 (= Scriptores arabici, 3rd ser. 7), 207–73, Beirut and Paris [the only available version for 1013–1027/34: Arabic text only]

William of Tyre, *Chronicon*   Huygens, R.B.C., with Mayer, H.E. and Rösch, G. eds. 1986. *Guillaume de Tyr, Chronique*, CCCM 63, 63A, Turnhout

Zonaras, *Epitome historion*   Büttner-Wobst, T., ed. 1897. Bonn

REFERENCES

Agnoletto, A., Battisti, E., Cardini, F., Pacciani, R., Ferri Piccaluga, G., and Vannini, G. 1987.   *Gli Abbitanti Immobili di San Vivaldo, il Monte Sacro della Toscana*, Firenze

Airaldi, G., and Kedar, B.Z., eds. 1986.   *I comuni italiani nel regno crociato di Gerusalemme*, Collana storica di fonti e studi 48, Genova

Alexander, J.J.G. 1970.   *Anglo-Saxon Illumination in Oxford Libraries*, Oxford

Amico, B. 1609.   *Trattato delle piante et imagini de i Sacri Edificii di Terra Santa*, Rome

—— 1620.   *Trattato delle piante et imagini de i Sacri Edificii di Terra Santa*, Florence

Andrieu, M. 1948.   *Les Ordines Romani de Haut Moyen Âge*, ii, *Les Textes*, Louvain

Anon. 1923.   'Itinerarium cuiusdam Anglici (1344–45)', Golubovich, G., ed., *Biblioteca Bio-bibliografica della Terra Santa e dell'Oriente Francescano*, iv, *dal 1333 al 1345*, Florence, 395–7, 427–90

Anon. 1952.   'Itinerary of a Certain Englishman (1344–5),' Hoade, E., ed., *Western Pilgrims*, Publications of the Studium Biblicum Franciscanum 18, Jerusalem, vii, 47–76

Arce, P., ed. 1973.   *Miscelánea de Tierra Santa*, ii, *Estudios críticos y documentos*, Jerusalem

Arndt, W.F., Gingrich, F.W., and Danker, F.W. 1979.   *A Greek–English Lexicon of the New Testament*, 2nd edn., Chicago and London

Avigad, N. 1976.   'The tombs in Jerusalem', in Avi-Yonah ed. 1976, ii, 627–41

—— 1984.   *Discovering Jerusalem*, Oxford

Avni, G., and Greenhut, Z. 1996.   *The Akeldama Tombs. Three Burial Caves in the Kidron Valley, Jerusalem*, Israel Antiquities Authority Reports 1, Jerusalem

Avi-Yonah, M., ed. 1976.   *Encyclopedia of Archaeological Excavations in the Holy Land*, 1st edn, 4 vols., London and Jerusalem

Baart, J. 1991.   'Jerusalem aan de Zeedijk', *Ons Amsterdam* 1991, 256

Bagatti, B. 1938.   'Fra Bernardino Amico disegnatore dei Santuari Palestinesi alla fine del '500', *Studi Francescani* 35, 307–25

—— 1951a.   'Una veduta inedita di Gerusalemme e dintorni del sec. XVII conservata al Cairo', *Liber Annuus* 1, 247–61

—— 1951b.   'L'industria della madreperla a Betlemme', *Custodia di Terra Santa 1342–1942*, Jerusalem, 133–52

—— ed. 1953.   *Plans of the Sacred Edifices of the Holy Land* [edition of Amico 1620], Publications of the Studium Biblicum Franciscanum 10, Jerusalem

—— ed. 1962.   *Ichnographiae monumentorum Terrae Sanctae (1724–1744)* [2nd edn. of the manuscript of Elzear Horn; see Golubovich ed. 1902], Publications of the Studium Biblicum Franciscanum 15, Jerusalem

—— 1975.   'The Necropolis', in Bagatti *et al.* 1975, 19–47

Bagatti, B., Piccirillo, M., and Prodomo, A. 1975.   *New Discoveries at the Tomb of the Virgin Mary in Gethsemane*, Studium Biblicum Franciscanum, Collectio Minor 17, Jerusalem

Bahat, D. 1986.   'Does the Holy Sepulchre church mark the burial of Jesus?', *Biblical Archaeology Review* 12.3 (May/June), 26–45

Bahat, D., with Rubinstein, C.T. 1990.   *The Illustrated Atlas of Jerusalem*, New York

Baldi, D. 1955.   *Enchiridion Locorum Sanctorum: Documenta S. Evangelii Loca Respicientia*, 2nd edn, Jerusalem

Ballian, A. 1992.   *Treasures from the Greek Communities of Asia Minor and Eastern Thrace [from the] Collections of the Benaki Museum*, 20 October 1992 – 10 January 1993, Athens [in Greek]

Balsamos, N. 1909.   'The inscriptions in the Church of the Resurrection', *Nea Sion* 8, 214–21 [in Greek]

Baldwin, M.W. 1958.   'The Decline and Fall of Jerusalem, 1174–89', in Baldwin, M.W. ed., 1958, 590–621
—— ed. 1958.   *A History of the Crusades*, i, *The First Hundred Years*, Philadelphia
Bar, D. 1993.   'The Southern boundary of Aelia Capitolina and the Location of the Tenth Roman Legion
                               Camp', *Cathedra* 69, 37–56 (Hebrew)
—— 1998.   'Aelia Capitolina and the Location of the Camp of the Tenth Legion', *Palestine Exploration
                               Quarterly* 130, 8–19
Barag, D. 1970.   'Glass pilgrim vessels from Jerusalem: Part I', *Journal of Glass Studies* 12, 35–63
—— 1971.   'Glass pilgrim vessels from Jerusalem: Parts II and III', *Journal of Glass Studies* 13, 45–63
Barag, D., and Wilkinson, J. 1974.   'The Monza-Bobbio flasks and the Holy Sepulchre', *Levant* 6, 179–87
Barnes, T.D. 1975.   'The composition of Eusebius' *Onomastikon*', *Journal of Theological Studies* n.s. 26, 412–15
—— 1981.   *Constantine and Eusebius*, Cambridge, Mass. and London
Baumgartner, S. 1986.   *Reise zum Heiligen Grab 1498 mit Herzog Heinrich dem Frommen von Sachsen*, ed.
                               T. Kraus, Göppinger Arbeiten zur Germanistik 445, Göppingen
Baxandall, M. 1988.   *Painting and Experience in Fifteenth-century Italy: a Primer in the Social History of Pictorial
                               Style*, 2nd edn, Oxford
Beck, H.G. 1959.   *Kirche und theologische Literatur im byzantinischen Reich*, Munich
Belaiev, L.A. 1996.   *Russian Medieval Graveslabs*, Institute of Archaeology, Russian Academy of Sciences,
                               Moscow [especially, pp.183–210, 'Romanesque Elements of the XIIth Century in Russian
                               Iconography of the Tomb of the Lord'; in Russian: English summary, pp. 374–83]
—— 1997   '". . . and all the Christians go there to kiss it." Russian Pilgrim Art from the 12th to 15th
                               Century: "Archaeological" Elements and Problems of Romanesque Influence,' seminar paper,
                               School of Historical Studies, Institute for Advanced Study, Princeton
Belgrano, L.T., and Malagola, C. 1890.   'Prepotens Genvensivm Presidivm', *Giornale Ligustico* 17, 302–6
Bentkowska, A. 1997.   'Historyk Sztuki wobec Ikonografii Cyfrowej, Metody Komputerowe w Badaniach nad
                               Grobem Pańskim w Jerozolimie', in Paszkiewicza and Zadroźnego, eds. 1997, 549–60
Bianquis, T. 1989.   *Damas et la Syrie sous la domination fatimide (359–468/969–1076). Essai d'interprétation
                               de chroniques arabes médiévales*, 2 vols., Damascus
Biddle, M. 1990.   'The tomb of Christ', *Illustrated London News*, Christmas 1990, 83–6
—— 1991.   'Jerusalem: the tomb of Christ', *Current Archaeology* 11.3, February/March, 107–12
—— 1994.   'The Tomb of Christ. Sources, Methods and a New Approach', in Painter ed. 1994, 73–147
—— 1996.   'La Tomba di Cristo', in Donati ed. 1996, 143–9, 324–31
—— 1998a.   'The Tomb of Christ: a New Investigation of its Structural Evolution,' *Actes du XIIIe
                               Congres International d'Archéologie Chrétienne (Split-Porec 1994)*, i, 427–45
—— 1998b.   *Das Grab Christi*, Giessen
——, Cooper, M.A.R., and   'The tomb of Christ, Jerusalem: a photogrammetric survey', *Photogrammetric Record* 14 (79),
    Robson, S. 1992.   25–43
——, Cooper, M.A.R.,   *The Tomb of Christ: History, Structural Archaeology, and Photogrammetry*, monograph
    Kjølbye-Biddle, B., and Robson, S.
    in preparation
Bieberstein, K., and Bloedhorn, H.   *Jerusalem. Grundzüge der Baugeschichte vom Chalkolithikum bis zur Frühzeit des osmanischen
    1994.   Herrschaft*, Beihefte zum Tübinger Atlas des vorderen Orients, Reihe B (Geisteswissen-
                               schaften), Nr. 100/1–3, Wiesbaden
Biertasz, A.W. 1997.   'Obraz Jerozolimy w Rosyjskich Klasztorach od XVIII do Początku XX Wieku', in
                               Paszkiewicza and Zadroźnego, eds. 1997, 321–32
Blanchet, A. 1943.   *Sigillographie de l'Orient latin*, Paris
Blenkinsopp, J. 1989.   *Ezra-Nehemiah. A Commentary*, London
Boberski, W. 1997.   'Jerozolima w Architekturze Rosyjskiej Czasów Nowoźytnych', in Paszkiewicza and
                               Zadroźnego, eds. 1997, 297–319
Bockmühl, K., ed. 1988.   *Die Aktualität der Theologie Adolf Schlatters*, Giessen and Basel
Bonnery, A. 1991.   'L'Édicule du Saint-Sépulcre de Narbonne. Recherche sur l'iconographie de l'Anastasis', *Les
                               Cahiers de Saint-Michel de Cuxa*, 22, 7–41
Borg, A. 1996.   'Church of the Holy Sepulchre', *DA* 17, 497–9
Brasca, S. 1966.   'Il "Viaggio" di Brasca', Momigliano Lepschy, A.L., ed., *Viaggio in Terrasanta di Santo
                               Brasca 1480 con l'Itinerario di Gabriele Capodilista 1458*, I Cento Viaggi 4, Milan,
                               43–158
Bresc-Bautier, G. 1974.   'Les Imitations du Saint-Sépulcre de Jérusalem (9e–15e siècles). Archéologie d'une dévotion',
                               Revue d'histoire de la spiritualité 50, 319–42
—— 1984.   *Le cartulaire du chapitre du Saint-Sépulchre de Jérusalem*, Documents relatifs à l'histoire des
                               Croisades 15, Paris
Brooks, N.C. 1921.   *The Sepulchre of Christ in Art and Liturgy*, University of Illinois Studies in Language and
                               Literature 7.2, Urbana
de Bruyn, C. 1698.   *Reizen . . . Door de vermaardste Deelen van Klein Asia . .* , Delft
Buchtal, H. 1986.   *Miniature Painting in the Latin Kingdom of Jerusalem*, London

Buckton, D., ed. 1994.   *Byzantium. Treasures of Byzantine Art and Culture from British Collections*, British Museum, London

—— and Heslop, T.A., eds. 1994.   *Studies in Medieval Art and Architecture Presented to Peter Lasko*, Stroud

Budde, H., and Nachama, A., eds. 1995.   *Die Reise nach Jerusalem. Eine kulturhistorische Exkursion in die Stadt der Städte: 3000 Jahre Davidsstadt*, Exhibition catalogue, Jüdische Gemeinde zu Berlin, Berlin [includes Kötzsche 1995b and (pp.159–75) 30 catalogue entries by various authors describing objects related to, and early representations of the Holy Sepulchre; fine colour illustrations]

Bulst-Thiele, M.L. 1979.   'Die Mosaiken der 'Auferstehungskirche' in Jerusalem und die Bauten der 'Franken' im 12. Jahrhundert', *Frühmittelalterliche Studien* 13, 442–71

Buschhausen, H. 1978.   *Die süditalienische Bauplastik im Königreich Jerusalem von König Wilhelm II. bis Kaiser Friedrich II.*, Vienna

—— 1980.   *Der Verduner Altar*, Vienna

Bushuiev, S. 1995.   *Russian Travellers to the Greek World (12th–first half of the 19th centuries)*, Exhibition catalogue, Moscow [parallel Russian and English]

Busse, H., and Kretschmar, G., 1987.   *Jerusalem Heiligtumstraditionen in altkirchlicher und frühislamischer Zeit*, Wiesbaden

Campos, J. 1957.   'Otro texto de Latin medieval hispano. El presbitero Iachintus', *Helmántica* 8, 77–89

Canard, M. 1965.   'La Destruction de l'église de la Résurrection par le Calife Hakim et l'histoire de la descente du feu sacré', *Byzantion* 35, 16–43

Capodilista, G. 1966.   'L'"Itinerario" di Capodilista', Momigliano Lepschy, A.L., ed., *Viaggio in Terrasanta di Santo Brasca 1480 con l'Itinerario di Gabriele Capodilista 1458*, I Cento Viaggi 4, Milan, 159–241

Carradice, I.A. ed. 1986.   *Proceedings of the 10th International Congress of Numismatics, London, September 1986*, International Association of Professional Numismatists Publication 11, London

Cheetham, F. 1984.   *English Medieval Alabasters*, London and Oxford

Cheney, C.R. 1948.   *Handbook of Dates for Students of English History*, London

Clapham, A.W. 1921.   'The Latin Monastic Buildings of the Church of the Holy Sepulchre, Jerusalem', *Antiquaries Journal* 1, 3–18 [with large-scale coloured plan]

—— 1934.   *Romanesque Architecture After the Conquest*, Oxford

Clark, J.W. 1909.   'Willis, Robert (1800–1875)', *DNB* 21, 492–4

Claussen, P.C. 1996.   'Nicholas of Verdun', *DA* 23, 97–101

Coens, M. 1950.   'Un Document inédit sur le culte de S. Syméon, moine d'Orient et reclus à Trier', *Analecta Bollandiana* 68, *Mélanges Paul Peeters* ii, 181–96

Collingwood, R.G., and Wright, R.P. 1965.   *The Roman Inscriptions of Britain*, i, *Inscriptions on Stone*, Oxford

Conant, K.J. 1956.   'Original Buildings at the Holy Sepulchre in Jerusalem,' *Speculum* 31, 1–48

Cooper, M.A.R., Robson, S., and Littleworth, R.M. 1992.   'The Tomb of Christ, Jerusalem: analytical photogrammetry and 3D computer-modelling for archaeology and restoration', *International Archives of Photogrammetry and Remote Sensing* 29 (5), 778–85 [Washington]

Cooper, M.A.R., and Robson, S. 1994.   'A hierarchy of photogrammetric records for archaeology and architectural history', *ISPRS Journal of Photogrammetry and Remote Sensing* 49 (50), 31–7

Corbo, V.C. 1981.   *Il Santo Sepolcro di Gerusalemme*, 3 vols., Publications of the Studium Biblicum Franciscanum 29, Jerusalem

—— 1988.   'Il Santo Sepolcro di Gerusalemme: *nova et vetera*', *Liber Annuus* 38, 391–422

Cortesi, G. 1975.   *Sant'Apollinare Nuovo in Ravenna*, Ravenna

Coüasnon, C. 1974.   *The Church of the Holy Sepulchre in Jerusalem*, Schweich Lectures of the British Academy 1972, London

Croon, M. 1992.   'Vier Pelgrimstekens en een Natuurstenen Model van de Jeruzalemskapel', *Catharijnebrief* [Newsletter of the Museum for Religious Art, Het Catharijneconvent, Utrecht] 39, 3–4

Cust, L.G.A. 1929.   *The Status Quo in the Holy Places*, His Majesty's Stationery Office, for the Government of Palestine [Jerusalem]

Dalman, G. 1920.   'Die Modelle der Grabeskirche und Grabeskapelle in Jerusalem als Quelle ihrer älteren Gestalt', *Palästinajahrbuch* 16, 23–31

—— 1922.   *Das Grab Christi in Deutschland*, Leipzig

—— 1935.   *Sacred Sites and Ways. Studies in the Topography of the Gospels*, London

Dam-Mikkelsen, B., and Lundbæk, T., eds. 1980.   *Etnografiske genstande i Det kongelige danske Kunstkammer 1650–1800*, Nationalmuseets skrifter, Etnografisk række 17, Copenhagen

Daniel the Abbot. 1988.   'The Life and Journey of Daniel, Abbot of the Russian Land', translated from the Russian and edited by W.F. Ryan in Wilkinson 1988, 120–71

Dauphin, H. 1946.   *Le Bienheureux Richard, Abbé de Saint-Vanne de Verdun*, Louvain and Paris

Davies, H.W. 1911.   *Bernhard von Breydenbach and his Journey to the Holy Land 1483–4. A Bibliography*, London

Demetriades, S. 1910.   'The burning of the Church of the Resurrection in 1808', *Nea Sion* 11, 270–91 [in Greek]

von Domaszewski, A. 1895.   *Die Religion des römischen Heeres*, Trier

Donati, A., ed. 1996   *Dalla Terra alle Genti. La Diffusione del Cristianesimo nei Primi Secoli*, Exhibition catalogue [Rimini], Milan

Douglas, D.C. 1969.   *The Norman Achievement 1050–1100*, London
Drake, H.A. 1985.   'Eusebius on the True Cross', *Journal of Ecclesiastical History* 36, 1–22
Duckworth, H.T.F. 1922.   *The Church of the Holy Sepulchre*, London
Duval, N. 1994.   'Le Rappresentazioni architettoniche', in Piccirillo and Alliata, 165–230
Dvornik, F. 1948.   *The Photian Schism. History and Legend*, Cambridge
—— 1959.   'Patriarch Photius, scholar and statesman [Pt. I]', *Classical Folia* 13, 3–18
—— 1960.   'Patriarch Photius, scholar and statesman [Pt. II]', *Classical Folia* 14, 3–22
Edbury, P.W., and Metcalf, D.M., eds.   *Coinage in the Latin East. The Fourth Oxford Symposium on Coinage and Monetary History*,
1980.   BAR International Series 77, Oxford
Edbury, P.W., and Rowe, J.G. 1988.   *William of Tyre: Historian of the Latin East*, Cambridge
Eisenstadt, S. 1987.   'Jesus' tomb depicted on a Byzantine gold ring from Jerusalem', *Biblical Archaeology
                                            Review*, 13.2 (March/April), 46–9
Eiján, S. 1945–6.   *El Real Patronato de los Santos Lugares en la historia de Tierra Santa*, 2 vols., Madrid
Engemann, J. 1973.   'Palästinensische Pilgerampullen im F.J. Dölger-Institut in Bonn', *Jahrbuch für Antike und
                                            Christentum* 16, 5–27
Enlart, C. 1928.   *Les Monuments des Croisés*, ii, Paris
Faber, F 1892–3.   *The Book of the Wanderings of Brother Felix Fabri* [sic], trans. Aubrey Stewart, Palestine
                                            Pilgrims' Text Society, 2 vols., London
Farris, G., and Storme, A. 1991.   *Ceramica e farmacia di San Salvatore di Gerusalemme*, Genova [repr. of 1982 edn.]
Favreau-Lilie, M.-L. 1989.   *Die Italiener im Heiligen Land vom ersten Kreuzzug bis zum Tode Heinrichs von
                                            Champagne (1098–1197)*, Amsterdam
Fedalto, G. 1988.   *Hierarchia Ecclesiastica Orientalis* ii, Padua
Ferrari, E. 1643.   *Liguria trionfante*, Genova
Finegan, J. 1978.   *The Archaeology of the New Testament*, paperback edn, Princeton
Fitzsimons, S. 1952.   'Itinerary of Friar Simon Fitzsimons (1322–4),' Hoade, E., ed., *Western Pilgrims*, Publications
                                            of the Studium Biblicum Franciscanum 18, Jerusalem, iv–vi, 1–46
von Flemming, V., and Schütze, S.,   *Ars naturam adiuvans. Festschrift für Matthias Winner*, Mainz am Rhein
   eds. 1996
Flood, G.D., ed. 1993.   *Mapping Invisible Worlds*, Edinburgh
Flusser, D. 1992.   'Caiaphas in the New Testament', *'Atiqot* 21, 81–7
Flussin, B. 1992.   'L'Esplanade du Temple à l'arrivée des Arabes, d'après deux récits byzantins', in Raby and
                                            Johns eds. 1992, 17–31
Folda, J. 1995.   *The Art of the Crusaders in the Holy Land 1098–1187*, Cambridge
—— 1996.   'Jerusalem, Latin Kingdom of [Crusader States],' *DA* 17, 499–507
France, J. 1996.   'The Destruction of Jerusalem and the First Crusade,' *Journal of Ecclesiastical History* 47, 1–17
Fraser, D., Hibbard, H., and   *Essays in the History of Architecture Presented to Rudolf Wittkower*, London
   Lewine, M.J. eds. 1967.
Freeman-Grenville, G.S.P. 1987.   'The basilica of the Holy Sepulchre, Jerusalem: history and future', *Journal of the Royal
                                            Asiatic Society* [no vol. number] for 1987, 187–207
—— 1991.   'Travellers to Christ's tomb', *Hakluyt Society Annual Report for 1990*, 14–28
Gams, P.F. 1957.   *Series episcoporum ecclesiae catholicae*, Berlin
García Villada, Z. 1919.   *Catálogo de los Códices y Documentos de la Catedral de León*, Madrid
—— 1925.   'Descripciones desconocidas de Tierra Santa en Códices Españoles. II, Descripcion del
                                            presbítero Jacinto', *Estudios Eclesiasticos* 4, 322–4
Gernsheim, H. 1984.   *Incunabula of British Photographic Literature. A Bibliography . . . 1839–75 and [of] British
                                            Books Illustrated with Original Photographs*, London and Berkeley
Geva, H. 1993a.   'Tombs [of the Second Temple period around Jerusalem]', in Stern ed. 1993, 747–9
—— 1993b.   'The Roman Period [in Jerusalem]', in Stern ed. 1993, 758–66
Gibson, S., and Jacobson, D.M. 1996.   *Below the Temple Mount in Jerusalem. A Sourcebook on the Cisterns, Subterranean
                                            Chambers and Conduits of the Haram al-Sharif*, British Archaeological Reports,
                                            International Series 637, Oxford
—— and Taylor, J. 1994.   *Beneath the Church of the Holy Sepulchre. The Archaeology and Early History of
                                            Traditional Golgotha*, Palestine Exploration Fund Monograph 2, London
Gil, M. 1992.   *A History of Palestine, 634–1099*, Cambridge
Gildemeister, J. 1885.   'Beiträge zur Palästinakunde aus arabischen Quellen. 5. Idrīsī', *Zeitschrift des Deutschen
                                            Palästina-Vereins* 8, 117–45
Giustiniano, A. 1537.   *Castigatissimi Annali . . . della Eccelsa & Illustrissima Republi. di Genoa*, Genova
Goldschmidt, A. 1969.   *Die Elfenbeinskulpturen aus der Zeit der Karolingischen und Sächsischen Kaiser VIII. – XI.
                                            Jahrhundert*, 3 vols., reprinted, Berlin and Oxford
Golubovich, G. 1898.   *Serie cronologica dei Rev.mi Superiori di Terra Santa (1219–1898)*, Jerusalem
—— ed. 1902.   *Ichnographiae locorum et monumentorum veterum Terrae Sanctae, accurate delineatae et
                                            descriptae a P. Elzeario Horn . . . (1725–44)*, Rome [1st edn of the manuscript of Elzear
                                            Horn; see Bagatti ed. 1962]

Grabar, A. 1943.   *Les miniatures du Grégoire de Nazianze de L'Ambrosienne*, i, *Album*, Paris
—— 1958.   *Ampoules de Terre Sainte (Monza-Bobbio)*, Paris
—— 1968.   'La fresque des saintes femmes au tombeau á Doura', in his *L'Art de la fin de l'Antiquité et du Moyen Âge*, i, Paris, 517–28
—— 1972.   *Martyrium. Recherches sur le culte des reliques et l'art chrétien antique*, i, *Architecture*, reprint, London [1st pub., Paris, 2 vols., 1946, album, 1943]
Greenhut, Z. 1992.   'The "Caiaphas" tomb in North Talpiyot, Jerusalem', *'Atiqot* 21, 63–71
Grenville, G.N. 1845.   *Lands, Sacred and Profane*, 2 vols., London
Groh, D.E. 1985.   'The Onomastikon of Eusebius and the rise of Christian Palestine', *Studia Patristica* 18.i, 23–31
Grumel, V. 1958.   *La chronologie*, Traité des études byzantines, Bibliotheque byzantine 1, Paris
von Grünenberg, K. 1912.   *Pilgerfahrt ins Heilige Land 1486*, Leipzig
Grzybowski, A. 1997.   'Kościoły w Gosławicach i Miszewie jako Pośrednie "Kopie" Anastasis', in Paszkiewicza and Zadroźnego, eds. 1997, 155–68
Guarducci, M. 1978.   *La capsella eburnea di Samagher*, Trieste
Gundestrup, B. 1991.   *Det kongelige danske Kunstkammer 1737*, 2 vols., Nationalmuseet, Copenhagen
Gurlitt, C. 1926.   'Das Grab Christi in der Grabeskirche in Jerusalem', *Festschrift zum Sechzigsten Geburtstag von Paul Clemen*, Bonn
Hall, S.G. 1979.   *Melito of Sardis: On Pascha and Fragments*, Oxford [see also Abbreviations, *P.P.*]
Hamilton, R.W. 1974.   'Thuribles: Ancient or modern?', *Iraq* 36 (1974), 53–65
Hansen, E. 1978.   'Traditionel og Fotogrammetrisk Opmaaling,' in Nordbladh and Rosvall eds. 1978, 102–11
Harvey, A.E. 1966.   'Melito and Jerusalem', *Journal of Theological Studies* n.s 17, 402–4
Harvey, W. 1935.   *Church of the Holy Sepulchre, Jerusalem: Structural Survey, Final Report*, Oxford
Heath, T.L. ed. 1956.   *The Thirteen Books of Euclid's Elements*, 2nd edn rev., Cambridge
Heber-Suffrin, F. 1991.   'Copie et création dans l'enluminure carolingienne. L'exemple de l'architecture', *Les Cahiers de Saint-Michel de Cuxa* 22, 57–77
Hoenerbach, W. 1938.   *Deutschland und seine Nachbarländer nach der grossen Geographie des Idrīsī*, Stuttgart
Hohenschwert, F. 1985.   'Externsteine bei Horn', in F. Hohenschwert, ed., *Der Kries Lippe. Teil II: Objektbeschreibungen*, Führer zu archäologischen Denkmälern in Deutschland 11, Stuttgart, 220–30
Howe, K.S. 1997.   *Revealing the Holy Land. The Photographic Exploration of Palestine*, Santa Barbara
Huber, J., Porcher, J., and Volbach, W.F. 1968.   *L'empire carolingien*, L'univers des formes 13, Paris
Hughes, P.E. 1990.   *The Book of the Revelation. A Commentary*, Leicester and Grand Rapids
Hunt, E.D. 1984.   *Holy Land Pilgrimage in the Later Roman Empire AD 312–460*, Oxford
Huxley, A. 1925.   *Along the Road. Notes and Essays of a Tourist*, London
Imperiale, C. ed. 1936–42.   *Codice Diplomatico della Repubblica di Genova*, 3 vols., Rome
Ioannides, B. 1877.   *The Holy City of Jerusalem and its Environs*, Jerusalem [in Greek]
Isaac, B. 1993.   *The Limits of Empire*, rev. edn., paperback, Oxford
Itinerarium Regis Richardi. 1864.   *Chronicles and Memorials of the Reign of Richard I*, i, *Itinerarium Peregrinorum et Gesta Regis Richardi*, ed. W. Stubbs, Rerum Britannicarum Medii Aevi Scriptores [Rolls Series], London
Jachintus. 1957.   Ed. J. Campos, in Campos 1957.
Jastrow, M. 1903.   *A Dictionary of the Targumim, the Talmud Babli and Yerushalmi, and the Midrashic Literature*, London and New York
Jaubert, A. 1836–40.   *Géographie d'Édrisi, traduit de l'arabe en français*, 2 vols., Paris
Jeffery, G. 1919.   *A Brief Description of the Holy Sepulchre, Jerusalem, and Other Christian Churches in the Holy City*, Cambridge
Jeremias, J. 1925.   'Wo lag Golgotha und das Heilige Grab?', *Angelos* 1, 141–73
John of Würzburg. 1874.   [Letter of John of Würzburg to Dietrich], Tobler ed. 1874, 108–92; trans. Wilkinson 1988, 244–73
Joranson, E. 1948.   'The Inception of the Career of the Normans in Italy – Legend and History', *Speculum* 23, 353–96
Kadman, L. 1956.   *The Coins of Aelia Capitolina*, Corpus Nummorum Palestinensium I, Jerusalem
Kartsonis, A.D. 1986.   *Anastasis. The Making of an Image*, Princeton
Kazhdan, A.P. ed. 1991.   *The Oxford Dictionary of Byzantium*, 3 vols., New York and Oxford
Kedar, B.Z. 1986.   'Genoa's Golden Inscription in the Church of the Holy Sepulchre: a Case for the Defence', in Airaldi and Kedar eds. 1986, 317–35
—— 1998   'Intellectual Activities in a Holy City: Jerusalem in the Twelfth Century', in Kedar and Werblowsky eds. 1998, 127–39
—— and Westergård-Nielsen, C. 1978–9.   'Icelanders in the Crusader Kingdom of Jerusalem: a Twelfth-Century Account', *Medieval Scandinavia* 11, 193–211

—— and Werblowsky, R.J.Z. eds. 1998 — *Sacred Space. Shrine, City, Land*, Proceedings of the International Conference in Memory of Joshua Prawer, London and Jerusalem

Kenyon, K.M. 1974. — *Digging up Jerusalem*, London and Tonbridge

Kloner, A. 1980. — 'The Necropolis of Jerusalem in the Second Temple Period', unpublished Ph.D. thesis, Hebrew University of Jerusalem [in Hebrew]

—— 1985a. — 'A monument of the Second Temple period west of the Old City of Jerusalem', *Eretz-Israel* 18, 58–64 [in Hebrew, with English summary, p.67*]

—— 1985b. — 'The Tomb in the Rotunda of the Holy Sepulchre', *Ariel* 42–42, 118–21 [in Hebrew]

—— forthcoming — 'The Reconstruction of the Tomb in the Rotunda of the Holy Sepulchre according to the Archaeological Finds and the Jewish Burial Customs of the first Century C.E.', paper given at a conference at Tel Aviv, 1997

Knauer, E.R. 1996. — '*Oculus* und Mariae Verkündigung – Eine Nachlese', in von Flemming and Schütze eds. 1996, 75–85

Kötzsche, L. 1988. — 'Zwei Jerusalemer Pilgerampullen aus der Kreuzfahrerzeit', *Zeitschrift für Kunstgeschichte* 1988, 13–32

—— 1994. — 'Die trauernden Frauen. Zum Londoner Passionskästchen', in Buckton and Heslop eds. 1994, 80–90

—— 1995a. — 'Das Heilige Grab in Jerusalem und seine Nachfolge', *Akten des XII. Internationalen Kongresses für Christliche Archäologie, Bonn, 1991*, i, 272–90 (= *Jahrbuch für Antike und Christentum*, Ergänzungsband 20.1; also = *Studi di Antichità Cristiana* 52), Münster and Città del Vaticano

—— 1995b. — 'Das Heilige Grab in Jerusalem und seine Nachfolge', in Budde and Nachama eds. 1995, 64–75 [an abbreviated version of Kötzsche 1995a]

Kötzsche-Breitenbruch, L. 1984. — 'Pilgerandenken aus dem heiligen Land', *Vivarium. Festschrift Theodor Klauser zum 90. Geburtstag, Jahrbuch für Antike und Christentum*, Ergänzungsband 11 (1984), 229–46

Krencker, D. 1923. — 'Der Rundtempel', *Baalbek. Ergebnisse der Ausgrabungen und Untersuchungen in den Jahren 1898 bis 1905*, ii, Berlin and Leipzig, 90–109, Taf. 57–68

Kroll, G. 1988. — *Auf den Spuren Jesu*, 10th edn., Stuttgart

de Kroon, M. 1997. — 'Medieval Pilgrim Badges in the Collection of the Museum for Religious Art: Het Catharijneconvent, Utrecht', *Art and Symbolism in Medieval Europe, Papers of the 'Medieval Europe Brugge 1997' Conference* 5, 145–48

Kuriazes, P. ed. 1976. — *The First Greek Technical Professionals of the Time of Liberation*, Greek Technical Board Papers 4, Athens [in Greek]

Kuriazes, T. 1976. — 'Komnenos Kalpha: the Protomartyr of Greek Professionals and the Restorer of the Great Church of the Resurrection in Jerusalem (1770–1821)', in Kuriazes ed. 1976, 213–16 [in Greek]

Lair, J. 1899a. — *Bulle du Pape Sergius IV. . .* , Études critiques i, Paris

—— 1899b. — *Historia d'Adémar de Chabannes*, Études critiques ii, Paris

Landes, R. 1995. — *Relics, Apocalypse, and the Deceits of History: Adémar of Chabannes, 989–1034*, Harvard Historical Studies 117, Cambridge, Mass., and London

L'Art Copte 1964. — *L'Art Copte*, Petit Palais, 17 juin – 15 septembre, Réunion des Musées Nationaux, Paris

Lauffray, J. 1962. — 'La *Memoria Sancti Sepulchri* du Musée de Narbonne et le Temple Rond de Baalbeck: essai de restitution du Saint Sépulcre constantinien', *Mélanges de l'Université Saint Joseph* 38, 199–217

Laurent, J.C.M., ed. 1873. — *Mag. Thietmari Peregrinatio*, Hamburg, 1857, reprinted apparently unaltered and with the original pagination as a supplement to his *Peregrinatores Medii Aevi Quatuor*, Leipzig

Lavas, G., and Metropoulos, Th. 1988. — ῾Ο Φρικτὸς Γολγοθᾶς: the revelation of the sign of the crucifixion of Jesus Christ', *Nea Sion* 83, 315–46 [in Greek]

—— 1995. — 'Golgotha, Jerusalem. Die Aufdeckung der Kreuzigungsstelle Christi', *Akten des XII. Internationalen Kongresses für Christliche Archäologie, Bonn, 1991*, ii, 964–8 (= *Jahrbuch für Antike und Christentum*, Ergänzungsband 20.2; also = *Studi di Antichità Cristiana* 52), Münster and Città del Vaticano

Lee, S. 1843. — *Eusebius . . . on the Theophania*, Cambridge

Lehmann-Haupt, H. 1929. — 'Die holzschnitte der breydenbachschen Pilgerfahrt als Vorbilder gezeichneter Handschriftenillustration', *Gutenberg Jahrbuch* 4, 152–63

Lemmens, L. ed. 1933. — *Collectanea Terrae Sanctae ex archivo Hierosolymitano deprompta*, ed. G. Golubovich, Biblioteca Bio-Bibliografica della Terra Santa, n.s., Documenti 14, Florence

Le Quien, M. 1740. — *Oriens christianus* 3 vols., Paris

Le Strange, G. 1888. — 'Idrîsî's Description of Jerusalem in 1154', *Palestine Exploration Fund Quarterly Statement* 1888, 31–5

—— 1890. — *Palestine under the Moslems*, London

—— ed. 1897. — *Diary of a Journey through Syria and Palestine by Nasir-i-Khusrau in 1047 AD*, Palestine Pilgrims' Text Society 4, London [separately published 1893]

Levy, M. 1991. 'Medieval Maps of Jerusalem', in Prawer and Ben-Shammai, eds. 1991, 418–507 [in Hebrew]

Levy-Rubin, M., and Rubin, R. 1996 'The Image of the Holy City in Maps and Mapping', in Rosovsky, ed. 1996, 352–79

Liddell, H.G., and Scott, R. 1940. *A Greek-English Lexicon*, Oxford

Loverance, R. 1988. *Byzantium*, British Museum, London

Lux, U. 1972. 'Vorläufiger Bericht über die Ausgrabung unter der Erlöserkirche im Muristan in der Altstadt von Jerusalem in den Jahren 1970 und 1971', *Zeitschrift des Deutschen Palästina-Vereins* 88 (1972), 185–201

Maalouf, A. 1984. *The Crusades Through Arab Eyes*, New York

Macalister, R.A.S. 1901. 'The rock-cut tombs in Wady er-Rababi, Jerusalem [Pt. II]', *Palestine Exploration Fund Quarterly Statement* 1901, 145–58

Männchen, J. 1987. *Gustaf Dalmans Leben und Wirken in der Brüdergemeine, für die Judenmission und an der Universität Leipzig 1855–1902*, Abhandlungen des Deutschen Palästinavereins 9.i, Wiesbaden

—— 1993. *Gustaf Dalman als Palästinawissenschaftler in Jerusalem und Greifswald 1902–1941*, Abhandlungen des Deutschen Palästinavereins 9.ii, Wiesbaden

Mango, C. ed. 1958. *The Homilies of Photius, Patriarch of Constantinople*, Cambridge, Mass.

—— 1992. 'The Temple Mount AD 614–638', in Raby and Johns eds. 1992, 1–16

—— 1995. 'The Pilgrim's Motivation', *Akten des XII. Internationalen Kongresses für Christliche Archäologie, Bonn, 1991*, i, 1–9 (= *Jahrbuch für Antike und Christentum*, Ergänzungsband 20.1; also = *Studi di Antichità Cristiana* 52), Münster and Città del Vaticano

Marangoni, L. 1937. *La Chiesa del Santo Sepolcro in Gerusalemme: Problemi della sua conservazione*, Custody of the Holy Land, Venice

Mare, W.H. 1987. *The Archaeology of the Jerusalem Area*, Grand Rapids

Mariti, G. 1790. *Istoria dello stato presente della città di Gerusalemme*, 2 vols., Livorno

Maspero, G. 1908. 'Un encensoir copte', *Annales du Service des Antiquités de l'Égypte* 9, 148–9

Mathew, G. 1963. *Byzantine Aesthetics*, London

Matthew Paris. 1877. *Chronica Majora*, ed. H.R. Luard, iv, *AD 1240–AD 1247*, Rerum Britannicarum Medii Aevi Scriptores [Rolls Series], London

Mayer, H.E. 1978. *Das Siegelwesen in den Kreuzfahrerstaaten*, Munich

—— and Favreau, M.-L. 1976. 'Das Diplom Balduins I. für Genua und Genuas goldene Inschrift in der Grabeskirche', *Quellen und Forschungen aus italienischen Archiven und Bibliotheken* 55/56, 22–95

Maximos Simaios. 1897. A. Papadopoulos-Kerameus, ed., *Analecta Gleaned of Jerusalem*, St. Petersburg, iii, 87–122 [in Greek]

Mazor, G., and Stark, H. 1983 'Mt. Scopus', *Excavations and Surveys in Israel 1983* 2, 57

Meinardus, O. 1967. 'Greek proskynitaria of Jerusalem in Coptic churches of Egypt', *Studia Orientalia Christiana: Collectanea* 12, 309–34

—— 1971. 'An Armenian Jerusalem proskynitarion in New Julfa', *Liber Annuus* 21, 180–93

Meshorer, Y. 1986a. 'Ancient gold ring depicts the Holy Sepulchre', *Biblical Archaeology Review* 12.3 (May/June), 46–8

—— 1986b. 'Siege coins of Judaea', in Carradice ed. 1986, 223–9

—— 1989. *The Coinage of Aelia Capitolina*, Jerusalem

—— 1991. 'Coins of the Crusader kingdom of Jerusalem' in Prawer and Ben-Shammai, eds. 1991, 388–98 [in Hebrew]

Metcalf, D.M. 1995. *Coinage of the Crusades in the Latin East in the Ashmolean Museum Oxford*, 2nd edn., Royal Numismatic Society Special Publication 28, London

Metzger, C. 1981. *Les ampoules à eulogie du Musée du Louvre*, Notes et documents des musées de France 3, Paris

Meyer, H.M.Z. 1971. *Jerusalem. Maps and Views. Surveying the Surveyers [sic] Work*, Jerusalem

Micheau, F. 1979. 'Les itinéraires maritimes et continentaux des pèlerinages vers Jérusalem,' in *Occident et Orient au Xᵉ siècle*, Publications de l'Université de Dijon 57, Paris

Milik, J.T. 1961. 'La Topographie de Jérusalem vers la fin de l'époque byzantine', *Mélanges de l'Université Saint-Joseph* 37, 127–89

Millard, A. 1991. *Treasures from Bible Times*, Oxford [paperback edn]

Milner-Gulland, R. 1994. 'Symbolic landscapes in Muscovite Russia', in Reid *et al.* eds. 1994

Misn [*alias* M. Is. Nomides]. 1937. [The Church of] *The Zoodochos Pege*, Istanbul [in Greek]

Mitchell, R.J. 1965. *The Spring Voyage. The Jerusalem Pilgrimage in 1458*, Readers Union edn., London

Montagni, L.P. 1994. *Giacomo Boselli: cultura e genio di un ceramista del Settecento*, Genova

Morello, G. 1996. 'Coperchio di reliquiario con dipinti cristologici [dal *Sancta Sanctorum* lateranense]', in Donati ed. 1996, 325–6

Morey, C.R. 1926. 'The painted panel from the Sancta Sanctorum', *Festschrift zum 60en Geburtstag von Paul Clemen*, Bonn, 150–67

München 1984. *Wallfahrt kennt keine Grenzen*, Exhibition catalogue, Bayerisches Nationalmuseum and Adalbert Stifter Verein, München

Murphy-O'Connor, J. 1994. 'The Location of the Capitol in Aelia Capitolina', *Revue Biblique* 101, 407–15

Musée du Louvre 1982. *Félix de Saulcy (1807–1880) et la Terre Sainte: Archives et monuments d'une mission archéologique*, Exhibition catalogue, Notes et documents des musées de France 5, Paris

Najmabadi, S., and Weber, S., trans. 1993.   *Naser-e-Khosrou, Safarname. Ein Reisebericht aus dem Orient des 11. Jahrhunderts*, München

Nebenzahl, K. 1986.   *Maps of Bible Lands. Images of Terra Santa Through Two Millennia*, London

Neri, D. 1971.   *Il S. Sepolcro riprodotto in occidente*, Quaderni de 'La Terra Santa', Jerusalem

Nijhoff, W. 1931–9.   *Nederlandsche Houtsneden, 1500–1550*, 2 vols. and 2 vols. plates, The Hague

Nordbladh, J., and Rosvall, J. 1978.   *Mått och Mål*, Göteborg

Nugent, Lord 1845   See Grenville, G.N.

O'Leary, de L. 1923.   *A Short History of the Fatimid Khalifate*, London and New York

Olijnik, O., and Chodorkowski, J. 1997.   'Jerozolima w Architekturze i Urbanistyce Dawnej Rusi i na Ukrainie. Refleksje Architektów', in Paszkiewicza and Zadroźnego, eds. 1997, 263–76

O'Loughlin, T. 1997.   'Adomnán and Arculf: the case of an Expert Witness', *Journal of Medieval Latin* 7, 127–46

Onne, E. 1980.   *Photographic Heritage of the Holy Land 1839–1914*, Manchester

Ousterhout, R. 1981.   'The Church of S. Stefano: a 'Jerusalem' in Bologna', *Gesta* 20, 311–21

—— 1989.   'Rebuilding the Temple: Constantine Monomachus and the Holy Sepulchre', *Journal of the Society of Architectural Historians* 48, 66–78

—— 1990a.   'The Temple, the Sepulchre, and the *Martyrion* of the Savior', *Gesta* 29, 44–53

—— ed. 1990b.   *The Blessings of Pilgrimage*, Illinois Byzantine Studies 1, Urbana and Chicago

—— 1990c.   'Loca Sancta and the Architectural Response to Pilgrimage', in Ousterhout ed. 1990b, 108–24

—— 1997   'Building the New Jerusalem', in Paszkiewicza and Zadroźnego, eds. 1997, 143–53

Päffgen, B. 1992.   *Die Ausgrabungen in St. Severin zu Köln*, i, Kölner Forschungen 5.1, Mainz

Painter, K., ed. 1994.   *'Churches Built in Ancient Times'. Recent Studies in Early Christian Archaeology*, Society of Antiquaries of London Occasional Papers 16, London

Parrot, A. 1955.   *Golgotha et Saint-Sépulcre*, Cahiers d'archéologie biblique 6, Neuchatel and Paris

Paszkiewicza, P., and Zadroźnego, T., eds. 1997.   *Jerozolima w Kulturze Europejskiej*, Instyt Sztuki Polskiej Akademii Nauk, Warszawa

Patrich, J. 1995.   *Sabas, Leader of Palestinian Monasticism*, Dumbarton Oaks Studies 32, Washington, DC

Peeters, P. 1930.   'La Passion de Saint Michel le Sabaïte', *Analecta Bollandiana* 48, 65–98

Perez, N.N. 1988.   *Focus East. Early Photography in the Near East (1839–1885)*, New York and Jerusalem

Pesant, R. 1980.   'The *Amalricus* coins of the Kingdom of Jerusalem', in Edbury and Metcalf, eds., 1980, 105–21

Peters, F.E. 1985.   *Jerusalem. The Holy City in the Eyes of Chroniclers, Visitors, Pilgrims, and Prophets from the Days of Abraham to the Beginnings of Modern Times*, Princeton

Pevsner, N. 1979.   *Nottinghamshire*, The Buildings of England, revised by E. Williamson, Harmondsworth

Piccirillo, M. 1975.   'The chamber-tomb of Mary in the Crusader Period', in Bagatti *et al.* 1975, 59–82

—— 1991.   *I Mosaici di Giordania*, Bergamo and Jerusalem

—— 1993.   *The Mosaics of Jordan*, American Center of Oriental Research Publications 1, Amman

—— and Alliata, E. 1994.   *Umm al-Rasas Mayfa'ah*, i, *Gli Scavi del Complesso di Santo Stefano*, Studium Biblicum Francisanum, Collectio Maior 28, Jerusalem

Pierotti, E. 1864.   *Jerusalem Explored*, 2 vols., London and Cambridge

Piussi, S. 1977.   'Il Santo Sepolcro di Aquileia', *Aquileia e l'oriente mediterraneo: Antichitá altoadriatiche* 12.i, 511–59; 12.ii, Figs. 2–9, 11, 12, 14–20

da Poggibonsi, N. 1945a.   Bacchi della Lega, A., and Bagatti, B., eds., *Libro d'Oltramare (1346–1350)*, Publications of the Studium Biblicum Francisanum 2, Jerusalem

da Poggibonsi, N. 1945b.   Bellorini, T., and Hoade, E., eds., *A Voyage Beyond the Seas (1346–1350)*, Studium Biblicum Francisanum, Collectio Maior 2, reprinted 1993, Jerusalem

Pomyalovskii, I.V., ed. 1892.   *Life . . . of Theodore, Archbishop of Edessa*, St Petersburg

Prawer, J. 1969–70.   *Histoire du royaume latin de Jérusalem*, 2 vols., Paris

Prawer, J., and Ben-Shammai, H., eds. 1991.   *The History of Jerusalem: Crusaders and Ayyubids (1099–1250)*, Jerusalem [in Hebrew]

Prescott, H.F.M. 1954.   *Jerusalem Journey. Pilgrimage to the Holy Land in the Fifteenth Century*, London

Pringle, D. forthcoming.   *The Churches of the Crusader Kingdoms of Jerusalem. A Corpus*, iii, *Jerusalem, Acre and Tyre*, Cambridge

Pullan, W. 1993.   'Mapping Time and Salvation: Early Christian Pilgrimage to Jerusalem', in Flood ed. 1993, 23–40

Purvis, J.D. 1988.   *Jerusalem, The Holy City. A Bibliography*, Metuchen and London

Quaresmius, F. 1639.   *Historica Theologica et Moralis Terrae Sanctae Elucidatio*, 2 vols., Antwerp

—— 1880–2.   *Historica . . . Terrae Sanctae Elucidatio*, ed. C. de Tarvisio, Venice

—— 1989.   *Elucidatio Terrae Sanctae*, ed. S. de Sandoli, Publications of the Studium Biblicum Francisanum 32, Jerusalem

Raby, J., and Johns, J., eds. 1992.   *Bayt al-Maqdis. 'Abd al-Malik's Jerusalem*, i, Oxford Studies in Islamic Art 9, Oxford

Rahmani, L.Y. 1981–2.   'Ancient Jerusalem's Funerary Customs and Tombs', *Biblical Archaeologist* 44 (1981), 171–7, 229–35; 45 (1982), 43–53, 109–19 van Regteren Altena, I.Q. 1967. 'Hidden records of the Holy Sepulchre', in Fraser *et al.* eds. 1967, 17–21

Reid, R., Andrew, J., and Polukhina, V., eds. 1994. *Structure and Tradition in Russian Society*, = Vol. 3 of *Papers from an International Conference on the Occasion of the Seventieth Birthday of Yury Mikhailovich Lotman, 'Russian Culture: Structure and Tradition'*, 2–6 July 1992, Keele University, United Kingdom, Slavica Helsingiensia 14, Helsinki, 96–104

Riesner, R. 1985. 'Golgota und die Archäologie', *Bibel und Kirche* 40, 21–6

—— 1988. 'Juda Kyriakos und Golgotha,' in Bockmühl ed. 1988, 61–5

—— 1997. *Paul's Early Period. Chronology, Mission, Strategy, Theology*, Michigan and Cambridge, UK

Ritmeyer, L. and K. 1994. 'Akeldama: Potter's Field or High Priest's Tomb?', *Biblical Archaeology Review* 20.6 (November/December), 22–35, 76, 78

Robert, L. 1937. *Études anatoliennes. Recherches sur les inscriptions grecques de l'Asie Mineure*, Paris

Roberts, D. 1842–9. *The Holy Land, Syria, Idumea, Arabia, Egypt and Nubia. From Drawings Made on the Spot*, London

Robson, S., Littleworth, R.M., and Cooper, M.A.R. 1994. 'Construction of accurate 3D computer models for archaeology, exemplified by a photogram-grammetric survey of the Tomb of Christ in Jerusalem', *International Archives of Photogrammetry and Remote Sensing* 30 (5), 338–44 [Melbourne]

Rock, A. 1989. *The Status Quo in the Holy Places*, Holy Land Publications, Jerusalem

Röhricht, R. 1887. 'Syria Sacra', *Zeitschrift des Deutschen Palästina-Vereins* 10, 7–48

—— ed. 1893. *Regesta Regni Hierosolymitani (MXCVII–MCCXCI)*, Innsbruck

Rosovsky, N. ed. 1996. *City of the Great King. Jerusalem from David to the Present*, Cambridge, Mass., and London

Ross, M.C. 1962. *Catalogue of the Byzantine and Early Medieval Antiquities in the Dumbarton Oaks Collection* i, *Metalwork, Ceramics, Glass, Glyptics, Painting*, Washington, DC

Rovere, A. 1996. '"Rex Balduinus Ianuensibus privilegia firmavit et fecit". Sulla presunta falsità del diploma di Baldovino in favore dei Genovesi', *Studi Medievali*, 3rd ser., 37.1 (1996), 95–133

Rubin, R. 1990. 'The Map of Jerusalem (1538) by Hermanus Borculus and its Copies – a Carto-genealogical Study,' *Cartographical Journal* 27.1, June, 31–9

Runciman, S. 1951–4. *A History of the Crusades*, 3 vols., Cambridge [the Pelican edn., Harmondsworth, 1971, has the same pagination]

Sabine, C.J. 1979. 'Numismatic iconography of the Tower of David and the Holy Sepulchre: an emergency coinage struck during the siege of Jerusalem, 1187', *Numismatic Chronicle* 139, 122–32

de Saint-Aignan, L. 1864. *La Terre Sainte. Description topographique, historique et archéologique de tous les lieux célèbres de la Palestine*, Paris and Orléans

de Sandoli, S. 1974. *Corpus Inscriptionum Crucesignatorum Terrae Sanctae (1099–1291)*, Publications of the Studium Biblicum Franciscanum 21, Jerusalem

—— 1978–84. *Itinera Hierosolymitana Crucesignatorum (saec. XII–XIII)*, 4 vols., Publications of the Studium Biblicum Franciscanum 24, Jerusalem

—— 1984. *Calvary and the Holy Sepulchre (Historical Outline)*, The Holy Places of Palestine, Jerusalem

Schefer, C., ed. 1881. *Sefer nameh: Relation du voyage de Nassiri Khosrau*, Paris

Schein, B.E. 1981. 'The Second Wall of Jerusalem', *Biblical Archaeologist* 44, 21–6

Schick, C. 1885. 'Neu aufgedeckte Felsengräber bei der Grabeskirche in Jerusalem', *Zeitschrift des Deutschen Palästina-Vereins* 8, 171–3

Schlatter, A. 1895. 'Der Chronograph aus dem zehnten Jahre Antonius,' *Texte und Untersuchungen zur Geschichte der altchristlichen Literatur* 12.1

—— 1955. *The Church in New Testament Times*, trans. P. Leventoff, London

Schiller, E., ed. 1978. *The Old City. The First Photographs of Jerusalem*, Jerusalem

Schlumberger, G. 1894. 'Neuf sceaux de l'Orient latin', *Revue de l'Orient latin* 2, 177–82

Schnitzler, H. 1965. 'Die Elfenbeinskulpturen der Hofschule', in *Karl der Grosse. Werk und Wirkung*, Exhibition catalogue, Aachen, 309–59

Schürer, E. 1973–87. *The History of the Jewish People in the Age of Jesus Christ (175 B.C.–A.D. 135)*, new English edn., revised and ed. by G. Vermes and F. Millar, 3 vols in 4, Edinburgh

Schulz, E.G. 1845. *Jerusalem. Eine Vorlesung . . . mit einem Plane von H. Kiepert*, Berlin

Schur, N. 1980. *Jerusalem in Pilgrims' and Travellers' Accounts. A Thematic Bibliography of Western Christian Itineraries, 1300–1917*, Jerusalem

Seligman, J., and Avni, G. 1997. *Jerusalem: the Coptic Patriarchate in the Holy Sepulchre. Preliminary Report*, Israel Antiquities Authority, illustrated typescript

Shanks, H. 1987. 'The Jerusalem wall that shouldn't be there', *Biblical Archaeology Review* 13.3 (May/June), 46–57

Simons, J. 1952. *Jerusalem in the Old Testament. Researches and Theories*, Leiden

Southern, R.W. 1953. *The Making of the Middle Ages*, London

Stern, E., ed. 1993. *The New Encyclopedia of Archaeological Excavations in the Holy Land*, Jerusalem

Stift Pölten 1994 *Wallfahrt. Wege zur Kraft*, Exhibition catalogue, Pölten

Suriano, F. 1949. Bellorini, T., Hoade, E., and Bagatti, B., eds., *Treatise on the Holy Land*, Studium Biblicum Franciscanum, Collectio Maior 8, reprinted 1983, Jerusalem

Sweet, J. 1990.   *Revelation*, TPI New Testament Commentaries, London and Philadelphia
Taylor, J.E. 1992–3.   'Review article: Helena and the Finding of the Cross', *Bulletin of the Anglo-Israel Archaeological Society* 12, 52–60
—— 1993.   *Christians and Holy Places. The Myth of Jewish-Christian Origins*, Oxford
—— 1998.   'Golgotha: a Reconsideration of the Evidence for the Sites of Jesus' Crucifixion and Burial', *New Testament Studies* 44, 180–203
Thackston, W.M. trans. 1986   *Naser-e Khosraw's Book of Travels (Safarnama)*, Persian Heritage Series 36, New York
Themeles, T.P. 1910.   'The latest rebuilding of the Church of the Resurrection', *Nea Sion* 11, 292–319 [in Greek]
Theoderic. 1976.   *Libellus de locis sanctis*, ed. M.L. and W. Bulst, Editiones Heidelbergenses 18, Heidelberg; translated in Wilkinson 1988, 274–314
Theodoridis, C. 1982.   *Photii Patriarchae Lexicon*, 1, Berlin and New York
Thompson, M.W. 1996.   'Robert Willis and the Study of Medieval Architecture', in *The Archaeology of Cathedrals*, Oxford University Committee for Archaeology Monograph 42, 153–64
Thomsen, P. 1921.   'Die lateinischen und griechischen Inschriften der Stadt Jerusalem und ihrer nächsten Umgebung', *Zeitschrift des Deutschen Palästina-Vereins* 44 (1921), 1–168
—— 1922.   *Die lateinischen und griechischen Inschriften der Stadt Jerusalem und ihrer nächsten Umgebung*, Leipzig
—— 1939.   'Der heilige Symeon von Trier,' *Zeitschrift des Deutschen Palästina-Vereins* 62, 144–61
Tobler, T. 1853–4.   *Topographie von Jerusalem und seiner Umgebungen*, 2 vols., Berlin
—— ed. 1874.   *Descriptiones Terrae Sanctae ex Saeculo VIII. IX. XII. et XV.*, Leipzig
Toynbee, J.M.C., and Ward-Perkins, J.B. 1956. *The Shrine of St Peter and the Vatican Excavations*, London
da Treviso, C., ed. 1875.   Bonifazio Stefani [Boniface of Ragusa], *Liber de perenni cultu Terrae Sanctae et de fructuosa eius peregrinatione*, Venice
Trolle, S., and Pentz, P. 1983.   'Den hellige Grav i Jerusalem', *Nationalmuseets Arbejdsmark 1983*, 97–112
Tsafrir, Y. 1986.   'The Transfer of the Negev, Sinai and Southern Transjordan from *Arabia* to *Palestina*,' *Israel Exploration Journal* 36, 77–86
——, Di Segni, L., and Green, J. 1994.   *Iudaea Palestina. Eretz Israel in the Hellenistic, Roman and Byzantine Periods*, Tabula Imperii Romani, Jerusalem
Tzaferis, V. 1985.   *Museum of the Greek-Orthodox Patriarchate in Jerusalem*, Jerusalem
Underwood, P. A. 1950.   'The Fountain of Life in Manuscripts of the Gospels', *Dumbarton Oaks Papers* 5, 41–138
Verdon, J., ed. 1979   *La chronique de Saint-Maixent 751–1140*, Les Classiques de l'Histoire de France au Moyen Âge 33, Paris
Vikan, G. 1982.   *Byzantine Pilgrimage Art*, Dumbarton Oaks Byzantine Collection Publications 5, Washington
—— 1995.   *Catalogue of the Sculpture in the Dumbarton Oaks Collection from the Ptolemaic Period to the Renaissance*, Washington, DC
Vincent, L.-H., and Abel, F.-M. 1914.   *Jérusalem: Recherches de topographie, d'archéologie et d'histoire*, ii, *Jérusalem nouvelle*, fasc. I and II, Paris
——, Baldi, E., Marangoni, L., and Barluzzi, A. 1949. *Il Santo Sepolcro di Gerusalemme. Splendori. Miserie. Speranze*, Bergamo
—— and Steve, M.-A. 1954.   *Jérusalem de l'Ancien Testament. Recherches d'archéologie et d'histoire*, Paris
de Vogüé, M. 1860.   *Les Églises de la Terre Sainte*, Paris [reprinted with a preface and bibliographical supplement by J. Prawer, Toronto, 1973]
Volbach, W.F. 1976.   *Elfenbeinarbeiten der Spätantike und des frühen Mittelalters*, 3rd edn., Mainz
Vriezen, K.J.H. 1994.   *Die Ausgrabungen unter der Erlöserkirche in Muristan, Jerusalem (1970–1974)*, Abhandlungen des Deutschen Palästinavereins 19, Wiesbaden
Wahrman, D., Gavin, C., and Rosovsky, N. 1993. *Capturing the Holy Land. M.J. Diness and the Beginnings of Photography in Jerusalem*, Exhibition catalogue, Cambridge, Mass.
Walker, J.H. 1927.   'Notes on a Font in the Church of the Holy Trinity, Lenton, Notts.', *Journal of the British Archaeological Association* 33, 191–7
Walker, P.W.L. 1990.   *Holy City, Holy Places? Christian Attitudes to Jerusalem and the Holy Land in the Fourth Century*, Oxford
Ward-Perkins, J.B. 1981.   *Roman Imperial Architecture*, Harmondsworth [new impression, Harvard and London, 1994]
Waugh, E. 1953.   *The Holy Places*, London and New York [see also Gallagher, D., ed., *The Essays, Articles and Reviews of Evelyn Waugh*, London, 1983, 410–20]
Weitzmann, K. 1974.   '*Loca Sancta* and the representational arts of Palestine', *Dumbarton Oaks Papers* 28, 31–55
Westerink, L.G., ed. 1986.   *Photii Patriarchae Constantinopolitani Epistulae et Amphilochia* iv, *Amphilochiorum Pars Prima*, Leipzig [see also Abbreviations, Photius, *Amphilochia*]
Wharton, A.J. 1992.   'The Baptistery of the Holy Sepulcher in Jerusalem and the politics of Sacred Landscape', *Dumbarton Oaks Papers* 46, 313–25
—— 1995.   *Refiguring the Post Classical City: Dura Europos, Jerash, Jerusalem and Ravenna*, Cambridge

Wheeler, R.E.M. 1964.   *Roman Art and Architecture*, London

Wightman, G.J. 1993.   *The Walls of Jerusalem. From the Canaanites to the Mamluks*, Mediterranean Archaeology Supplement 4, Sydney

Wilde, W.R. 1840.   *Narrative of a Voyage to Madeira, Teneriffe and along the Shores of the Mediterranean, including a Visit to . . . Palestine*, 2 vols., Dublin

Wilkinson, J. 1971.   *Egeria's Travels to the Holy Land*, London [reprinted as 1981]

—— 1972.   'The tomb of Christ: an outline of its structural history', *Levant* 4, 83–97

—— 1977.   *Jerusalem Pilgrims before the Crusades*, Jerusalem

—— 1978.   *Jerusalem as Jesus Knew It: Archaeology as Evidence*, London

—— 1981.   *Egeria's Travels to the Holy Land*, Jerusalem and Warminster [corrected reprint of 1971]

——, with J. Hill and W.F. Ryan, 1988.   *Jerusalem Pilgrimage 1099–1185*, Hakluyt Society, 2nd ser. 167, London

Williams, G. 1845.   *The Holy City; or Historical and Topographical Notices of Jerusalem*, 1st edn, London

—— 1849.   *The Holy City. Historical, Topographical, and Antiquarian Notices of Jerusalem*, 2nd edn, 2 vols., London

Willis, R. 1849.   *The Architectural History of the Church of the Holy Sepulchre at Jerusalem*, London [published simultaneously from the same type in Williams 1849, ii, 129–294; the page references used here are those of Williams' edition as the separate publication is rare]

Wilson, C.W. 1865.   *Ordnance Survey of Jerusalem*, 3 parts, London; facsimile reproduction, 2 vols., Jerusalem, 1980

Wilson, C.W., and Warren, C. 1871.   *The Recovery of Jerusalem*, London

Wistrand, E. 1952.   'Konstantins Kirche am Heiligen Grab in Jerusalem nach den ältesten literarischen Zeugnissen', *Acta Universitatis Gotoburgensis, Göteborgs Högskolas Årsskrift* 58:1

Wolff, R.L. 1979.   'How the News Was Brought from Byzantium to Angoulême; or, The Pursuit of a Hare in an Ox Cart,' *Byzantine and Modern Greek Studies* 4, 139–89

Woodall, J. 1989.   'Painted immortality: portraits of Jerusalem pilgrims by Antonis Mor and Jan van Scorel', *Jahrbuch des Berliner Museums* 31, 149–63

Wormald, F. 1984.   'An English Eleventh-Century Psalter with Pictures', *Collected Writings*, i, *Studies in Medieval Art from the Sixth to the Twelfth Centuries*, London and Oxford, 123–37 [originally published in the *Walpole Society* 38 (1962), 1–13]

Wren, C. 1942.   'Tracts on Architecture by Sir Chr. Wren', *Wren Society* 19, 121–45

Young, B. 1990.   *The Villein's Bible. Stories in Romanesque Carving*, London

Zarnecki, G. 1998   'The Romanesque Font at Lenton,' *Southwell and Nottinghamshire: Medieval Art, Architecture and Industry*, British Archaeological Association Conference Transactions 21, 136–42

Zuallardo, G. 1587.   *Devotissimo viaggio di Gerusalemme*, Rome

Zupko, R.E. 1981.   *Italian Weights and Measures from the Middle Ages to the Nineteenth Century*, American Philosophical Society Memoirs 145, Philadelphia

INDEX

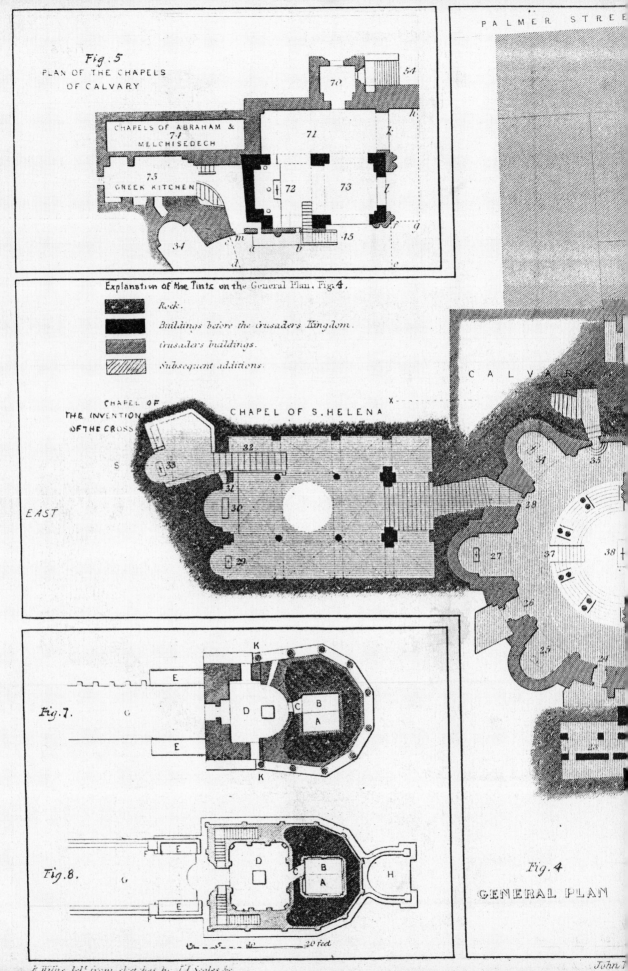

Fig. 5
PLAN OF THE CHAPELS
OF CALVARY

70

54

CHAPELS OF ABRAHAM &
74
MELCHISEDECH

71

75
GREEK KITCHEN

72   *73*

34

15

Explanation of the Tints on the General Plan. Fig. 4.

Rock.

Buildings before the Crusaders Kingdom.

Crusaders buildings.

Subsequent additions.

CHAPEL OF
THE INVENTION
OF THE CROSS

CHAPEL OF S. HELENA

32

33

31

30

29

EAST

34   *35*

28

27

37   *38*

26

25   *24*

23

PALMER STREET

CALVARY

Fig. 7.

E

K

D   C   B

A

E

K

G

Fig. 8.

E

D   C   B

A

H

E

G

Fig. 4.
GENERAL PLAN

0   5   10   20 feet

R. Willis del.t from sketches by J. J. Scoles &c.

John T

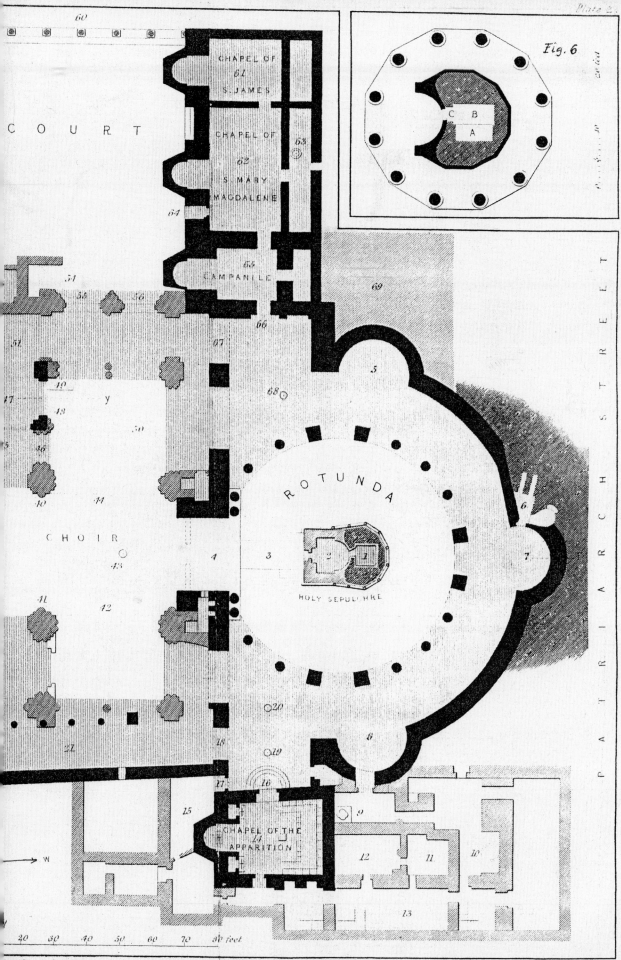

Plate 2.

Fig. 6

P A T R I A R C H   S T R E E T

C O U R T

CHAPEL OF
61
S. JAMES

CHAPEL OF
62
S. MARY
MAGDALENE

64   63

65
CAMPANILE

66   69

67

54

55   56

51

49
47   48   y

50
45
46

40   44

CHOIR   5

41   43   4   3

42

ROTUNDA

68

HOLY SEPULCHRE

6

7

20   8

19   9

27   16
15   12   11   10

CHAPEL OF THE
14
APPARITION

W

13

C   B
A

20 30 40 50 60 70 80 feet